I0127764

"Health psychologists operate in a variety of settings and can take a number of diverse training pathways. Finally, there is a book that answers the most asked question I get in teaching Health Psychology for over 20 years, cleanly unpacking and illuminating how one becomes a health psychologist. I look forward to sharing this with my students, widely and often. The book not only shows students how to get in but what to expect in graduate school. That's not all, walking the health psychology walk, the book also discusses stress and coping in training—this is the complete package."

—Regan A. R. Gurung, Ph.D., Professor of
Psychological Science, Oregon State University

"As a 'senior' member of the health psychology community, I am frequently invited to offer my perspectives on my career choice and path. Finally, in addition to sharing my personal story, I can highly recommend *Becoming a Health Psychologist* as a definitive source for information about the field and educational and career opportunities, and advice for graduate students and early career psychologists. Four distinguished colleagues provide reliable and actionable guidance and resources, including pearls of wisdom from others, as a toolkit for anyone contemplating a career in health psychology."

—Robert D. Kerns, Ph.D., Professor of Psychiatry,
Neurology and Psychology, Yale University

"As a reflection of the maturity of the field of health psychology, this book provides an outstanding practical guide for those students considering a career in this vibrant field, and for graduate students already on the journey. It takes students through everything from applying to graduate school and getting through graduate school, to starting a career, and it highlights all the choices, opportunities, and challenges along the way. Will certainly become the go-to guide for a health psychology career."

—Norman B. Anderson, Ph.D., Assistant Vice President for
Research and Academic Affairs, Florida State University

BECOMING A HEALTH PSYCHOLOGIST

Becoming a Health Psychologist provides an overview of the different training paths students can take to prepare themselves for graduate school and careers in the field of health psychology.

You'll find tips on how to choose and apply for graduate programs as well as numerous practical examples such as emails to potential advisors and questions to ask during interviews. Throughout, the authors provide examples of different health psychology careers, along with references, resources, and first-hand experiences. It details what is involved in becoming a health psychologist, what a health psychology career entails, and how to reach that goal.

The inclusion of tips from a diverse group of successful students, early career, and senior health psychologists makes this book an invaluable resource for anyone looking to start their career or for advisors who are counselling students about career choices. For many readers, this book may serve as "the mentor they never had".

Tracey A. Revenson, Ph.D., is Professor of Psychology at Hunter College and the Graduate Center of the City University of New York, and Director of Research Training for Health Psychology & Clinical Science at the Graduate Center of the City University. She received a B.A. from Yale University, a Ph.D. in psychology from New York University, and postdoctoral training in social ecology at the University of California, Irvine. Trained as one of the first generation of health psychologists, Dr. Revenson brings a social-ecological perspective to the study of how stress and coping processes affect psychological adjustment to chronic physical illness, and how these processes are influenced by the social context. Her research focuses on coping processes among individuals, couples, and families facing serious physical illnesses such as rheumatoid arthritis and cancer as well as the influence of gender and race/ethnicity on psychosocial adaptation. In addition to numerous chapters and articles, Dr. Revenson is the co-author or co-editor of 12 volumes, including the *Handbook of Health Psychology*, *The Cambridge Handbook of Psychology, Health & Medicine*, *Caregiving in the Illness Context*, and *Couples Coping with Stress*. Dr. Revenson is Editor-in-Chief of the *Annals of Behavioral Medicine* and serves on the editorial board of the journal *Health Psychology*. She is the former Co-Editor-in-Chief of *International Journal of Behavioral Medicine* and a past-president of the Society for Health Psychology of the American Psychological Association. She is a fellow of the American Psychological Association, the Society for Behavioral Medicine, and the European Health Psychology Society. In 2013, she was awarded the Nathan Perry Award for Career Contributions to Health Psychology from the Division of Health Psychology, APA and in 2019 she won the Society's Excellence in Health Psychology Mentoring Award.

Patrice G. Saab, Ph.D., is Professor in the University of Miami's Department of Psychology, College of Arts and Sciences. She completed her doctoral training in clinical psychology with a health concentration at Ohio University and her postdoctoral research training in cardiovascular behavioral medicine at the University of Pittsburgh. Dr. Saab has a longstanding interest in education and training in health psychology. She is the clinical track coordinator for the University of Miami's Department of Psychology Health Division and a past Chair of the Society for Health Psychology's Education and Training Council. Dr. Saab is actively involved in mentoring and providing research training to health psychology doctoral students. Her basic research examines blood pressure regulation, cardiovascular responsivity to stress, and cardiovascular risk. Her applied research has addressed primary prevention in youth at risk for cardiovascular disease and secondary and tertiary prevention in patients with heart disease. Dr. Saab's current research is directed at health education and promotion efforts to address cardiometabolic risk. Together with her graduate students and colleagues, she uses innovative and novel strategies (such as health-oriented summer camp programs for youth, K-12 outreach, and interactive science museum health exhibitions) to promote healthy lifestyle and behavior change.

Peggy M. Zoccola, Ph.D., is an experimental health psychologist and Associate Professor of Psychology at Ohio University. Dr. Zoccola conducts laboratory and field research on psychosocial stress, physiology, and health. Her program of research contributes to the field of health psychology by establishing a connection between ruminative thought and prolonged exposure to cortisol in the laboratory and in everyday life, and by revealing individual differences and environmental and social factors that predict altered cortisol responding. Dr. Zoccola is a passionate teacher and mentor who enjoys teaching health psychology and research methods courses, including those on the topics of psychoneuroimmunology and the science of stress. Dr. Zoccola has served as an academic advisor and research supervisor to hundreds of undergraduate students and more than a dozen graduate students, and she is the recipient of multiple teaching and mentoring awards. Dr. Zoccola currently serves as the Chair of the Education and Training Council for the Society for Health Psychology.

Lara Traeger, Ph.D., is a clinical-health psychologist at the Massachusetts General Hospital (MGH) Cancer Center and Behavioral Medicine Service and Assistant Professor in Psychiatry at Harvard Medical School. She serves as the Associate Director of the MGH Qualitative Research Unit and is an active member of the MGH Cancer Outcomes Research Program. Dr. Traeger conducts behavioral research in cancer, with a focus on strategies to help patients enhance their quality of life and quality of cancer care. She is actively involved in research mentoring and clinical supervision. She has served as a therapist and investigator on numerous funded trials of cognitive-behavioral therapy for patients with cancer and other chronic conditions. In 2018, she served as the Scientific Program Chair for the International Congress of Behavioral Medicine.

BECOMING A HEALTH PSYCHOLOGIST

Tracey A. Revenson, Ph.D.
Patrice G. Saab, Ph.D.
Peggy M. Zoccola, Ph.D.
Lara Traeger, Ph.D.

Routledge
Taylor & Francis Group

NEW YORK AND LONDON

First published 2020
by Routledge
52 Vanderbilt Avenue, New York, NY 10017

and by Routledge
2 Park Square, Milton Park, Abingdon, Oxon OX14 4RN

Routledge is an imprint of the Taylor & Francis Group, an informa business

© 2020 Tracey A. Revenson, Patrice G. Saab, Peggy M. Zoccola and Lara Traeger

The right of Tracey A. Revenson, Patrice G. Saab, Peggy M. Zoccola and Lara Traeger to be identified as authors of this work has been asserted by them in accordance with sections 77 and 78 of the Copyright, Designs and Patents Act 1988.

All rights reserved. No part of this book may be reprinted or reproduced or utilised in any form or by any electronic, mechanical, or other means, now known or hereafter invented, including photocopying and recording, or in any information storage or retrieval system, without permission in writing from the publishers.

Trademark notice: Product or corporate names may be trademarks or registered trademarks, and are used only for identification and explanation without intent to infringe.

British Library Cataloguing-in-Publication Data
A catalogue record for this book is available from the British Library

Library of Congress Cataloging-in-Publication Data
A catalog record for this book has been requested

ISBN: 978-0-8153-8550-9 (hbk)
ISBN: 978-0-8153-8554-7 (pbk)
ISBN: 978-1-351-20127-8 (ebk)

Typeset in Joanna
by Apex CoVantage, LLC

We dedicate this book to our students, fellows, and mentees—past, present, and future—who keep us inspired and excited about what the future of health psychology may hold. As Oscar Hammerstein II said, "If you become a teacher, by your pupils you'll be taught".

We also dedicate this to our loved ones who supported us on our journey to becoming health psychologists.

CONTENTS

ILLUSTRATIONS

Figure

Tables

FOREWORD

We need more health psychologists. That is why I expect *Becoming A Health Psychologist* to be an important guide for students and for the professors who advise them. The authors of this book did not start their careers with the objective of becoming health psychologists. They didn't have that option because health psychology was just gaining a foothold at the time they were trained. But over the last couple of decades interest in health psychology has exploded and now health psychology training is offered in many excellent doctoral programs.

A bit of history and context: Health Psychology was not recognized or discussed when the American Psychological Association (APA) was founded. This did not happen until 1978: 86 years later. The Division of Health Psychology was not one of the original divisions of the organization. In fact, it was the 38th. But today, the division (renamed in 2015 as the Society for Health Psychology) has among the largest membership of any APA division. The division's journal, *Health Psychology*, can be found in more libraries than any of APA's other 37 divisional journals. In addition to the divisional journals, APA publishes 29 general journals. With the exception of the *American Psychologist*, which goes to all APA members, more people subscribe to *Health Psychology* than any of the other 28 general journals. The time has come.

Perhaps the reason interest in health psychology is growing is that psychological and behavioral principles are now recognized as crucial, not only in psychology but also by the fields of medicine, nursing, and public health. Health psychologists work on problems ranging from the initial steps in disease prevention through coping with chronic illness in the terminal stages of life.

A few examples illustrate how healthcare and public health have turned their focus toward health psychology. The American Heart Association, arguably the most influential healthcare organization in the world, recently revised its mission statement. Their new goal is to be a "relentless force for a world of longer, healthier lives". Notice that this statement does not mention heart disease and instead focuses on activities that will improve both the length of life and quality of life. In 2019, the American Heart Association, in collaboration with the American College of Cardiology, released their new guidelines on the primary prevention of cardiovascular disease. The first take-home message: "The most important way to prevent atherosclerotic vascular disease, heart failure, and atrial fibrillation is to promote a healthy lifestyle throughout life". Similarly, the American Cancer Society, the American Diabetes Association, and several other major medical organizations have re-crafted their missions to place a stronger emphasis on healthy lifestyle as the most fundamental ingredient in preventing the most serious diseases. In 2017, each of the top ten causes of death in the United States was associated with behavioral risk factors. Most of these killers were chronic diseases brought about by cigarette smoking, physical inactivity, poor nutrition, alcohol and drug abuse, self-destructive activity, and failure to comply with medical treatment. The Oxford Health Alliance argues that just a few behaviors, including physical inactivity, smoking, and poor diet, increase the risks for four chronic diseases, diabetes, heart disease, lung diseases, and some cancers. These four diseases account for 50% of all premature deaths in the world today (www.oxha.org).

When patients enter the healthcare system, assistance from health psychologists is becoming increasingly important. Some treatment decisions might be completely driven by the biology of the disease; a heart attack or an episode of appendicitis requires quick action. But for many healthcare problems, the treatment decision depends upon a patient's willingness to accept risk, to balance potential benefits vs. side effects of treatments, and to consider what their lives would be like after a potentially helpful treatment alters their appearance or their ability to function. These choices require shared medical decision-making, now a widely recognized component of high-quality medical care. With shared decision-making, patients and their providers work together to find the best treatment pathway.

Physical health and mental health problems are often "co-morbid". That means that psychological conditions like anxiety and depression are common companions of diabetes, heart failure, cancer, and many other chronic medical conditions. We now know that patients with chronic illnesses are more costly and have poorer health outcomes if their mental health challenges are left unattended. Major healthcare systems, including the Veterans Administration and Kaiser Permanente, have begun redesigning their treatment facilities to better integrate physicians and mental healthcare providers. So if those of you reading this book do become health psychologist, you will likely be working seamlessly alongside other medical providers.

Health psychology has come a remarkable distance in a relatively short period of time. But we are still at the beginning, and the demand for intelligent, well-trained, and empathetic health psychologists is likely to accelerate. Whether you decide to become a health psychologist who provides care within a medical setting, a health psychologist who conducts research on how stress affects health, or a health psychologist who sets health policy—or a combination of all three—you will be entering an exciting field. The authors of this book have provided information, advice, and "behind the scenes" tips to start you on that career path.

Robert M. Kaplan, Ph.D.
Stanford, California
April 2019

PREFACE

For many of you, this book can be the mentor you never had. From cover to cover, we hope to provide the advice that a "live" mentor would give you about the path to becoming a health psychologist, along with the straight talk that you might need to hear. We also hope to inspire you with first-hand accounts of how health psychologists are advancing our understanding of health and wellness every day. The four authors are all Ph.D.-level health psychologists with many years of experience advising students and career changers. We vary in our specialties, experiences, and interests, and together, show how there is not just one path that you might take to become a health psychologist.

Our Stories

Tracey A. Revenson started out with aspirations to become an actress when a number of serendipitous events led to her leaving that career path for psychology. Not accepted to any programs in clinical psychology as a college senior, she was accepted into New York University's Ph.D. program in community psychology. There was no field of health psychology at the time, but working with a mentor, Barbara J. Felton, who had just received a grant to study *Coping with Illness in Late Life*, she began conducting research into stress and coping processes at the time that health psychology was becoming a field. After graduate school, she accepted a post-doctoral fellowship in Environment, Development, and Health in the Social Ecology program at the University of California, Irvine, where she thought she would be *learning* about health psychology and ended up *teaching* it. Currently, she is Professor of Psychology at Hunter College and the Graduate Center, City University of New York, where she is Director of Research Training in the Ph.D. program in Health Psychology & Clinical Science.

When **Patrice G. Saab** decided to major in psychology as an undergraduate, she didn't know what was involved in becoming a psychologist or what kind of path she would take. Research in physiological psychology (what we refer to today as behavioral neuroscience) initially hooked her. But when it came time to apply to graduate school, her advisor, Hans Schmidt, Jr. (a physiological psychologist), encouraged her to apply to clinical psychology programs where she could be involved in more physiologically based research. She first completed a master's degree in clinical psychology, where she did sleep research monitoring participants' brain activity while they slept. In 1979, as graduate training in the field of health psychology was just beginning to emerge, Patrice entered the doctoral program in clinical psychology at Ohio University to work with Kenneth Holroyd on research addressing stress and coping and cardiovascular processes. That training cemented her interests in cardiovascular psychophysiology and in cardiometabolic disorders. After a postdoctoral fellowship at the University of Pittsburgh in Cardiovascular Behavioral Medicine, she joined the faculty of the University of Miami, Department of Psychology, Health Division where she is a Professor of Psychology.

Starting at a young age, **Peggy M. Zoccola** was interested in science and math. During high school she became enamored with every new science course she took and became interested in understanding human behavior and mental health. She thought that the logical way to merge her interests in biological sciences and human behavior was to become a psychiatrist. Starting out as a pre-med student, Peggy took courses in neuroscience, biology, psychology, and sociology. She became more interested in the individual and interpersonal processes that she was learning about in her psychology courses than the cellular and chemical processes of her pre-med work, so she switched her major to psychology during her sophomore year. It wasn't until the final semester of her senior year that she took an advanced biology seminar on the topic of behavioral medicine that she became remotely aware of the work done by health psychologists. Upon graduating from college, Peggy opted for a two-year research assistant position at a nonprofit institute focused on substance use disorder prevention, treatment, and policy so she could get more experience under her belt before applying to graduate school. She knew she wanted to take an experimental and basic science approach to study mind-body phenomenon, so she applied to a handful of experimental psychology Ph.D. programs that had faculty who specialized in stress and health. Within weeks of beginning graduate school, Peggy began a programmatic line of research on perseverative thought (i.e., ruminative thinking) and its physiological and health correlates and consequences.

She continues this line of work today as Associate Professor of Experimental Health Psychology at Ohio University.

Lara Traeger started telling her parents that she wanted to be a clinical psychologist as early as grade school. But her college years opened doors to new interests and left her head spinning. She took a few years after college to work at a consulting firm in New York, among other professional adventures. From there, she began clarifying her psychology interests in earnest by taking classes, gaining clinical experience, and serving as a research assistant at an academic medical center. These chaotic but useful years helped her to thread her disparate experiences together, and her interest in studying individual health and resilience emerged. She was accepted into the health track of the clinical psychology doctoral program at the University of Miami, working with Frank Penedo on research addressing psychosocial factors in cancer, and she has never looked back. After completing her clinical internship and a postdoctoral fellowship at the Massachusetts General Hospital, she is now on their faculty and an assistant professor at Harvard Medical School, where she conducts psycho-oncology research and provides psychotherapy to patients with chronic medical conditions.

As you can see, none of our career paths was linear; some parts were planned and others serendipitous. That's the mindset we'd like you to adopt while reading this book. We will try to give you as much help as possible in deciding whether you want a career in health psychology and how to attain your goals, but we also want you to remember that you never know everything that will happen along the yellow brick road.

Who Is This Book Written for?

We assume that the majority of readers of this book will be undergraduate students or recent graduates who are planning the first phase of their career. In some ways, the middle of your undergraduate years is an ideal time to start preparing, even if you're not sure that becoming a health psychologist is the path you want to take. If you're a current graduate student or recent graduate of a doctoral program in psychology, the latter part of this book is for you.

Many people change careers more than once in their adult lifetime. Recent data from the National Longitudinal Survey of Youth show that Americans born in the early 1980s held an average of 7.8 jobs between the ages of 18 and 30 (U.S. Bureau of Labor Statistics, 2018). So if you are someone who is looking to change careers but don't know how to start, this book will help you take the first steps. We also envision this book serving as an invaluable resource for advisors and faculty in psychology departments, especially for faculty who are not familiar with the field of health psychology.

Just as there is no single path to becoming a health psychologist, there are different opinions about the best way to prepare for graduate training. In this book we provide both a broad overview of the different options and issues pertaining to training while focusing on specific guidelines and examples that are tailored to the field of health psychology.

How to Read This Book

We wrote this book from two specific vantage points. First, this is a book about becoming a *health psychologist*, not becoming any kind of psychologist. Although there are a lot of aspects of say, applying to graduate school that are the same across any type of psychology graduate school, much of our advice is very specific to the field of health psychology. We are trying to tell you what faculty expect from you—both in applications and in graduate school—and how you can think outside of the box to get the best health psychology training possible.

Second, a career can unfold over many years, with each phase preparing you for the next one. We have written this volume to take you through the many early stages of a career. The first two chapters will help you to think carefully about your own desires, abilities, and future possible selves (Markus & Nurius, 1986) and most importantly, whether health psychology is really the right career choice for you, *at this time*. Even if you think you have made up your mind, please read those chapters anyway because there are a lot of different health psychology careers and programs that are more or less suited to helping you achieve your career goals.

Once your decision to enter the field of health psychology is an unequivocal "yes", it's time to choose and apply to doctoral programs. Chapters 3 and 4 provide lots of tips on how to do that successfully. The second half of the book guides you in preparing for your future career while in graduate school and in the post-graduate years. Don't toss this book aside once you make a decision to apply to graduate school in health psychology or once you are accepted! In Chapters 5 and 6, we explain what is expected of you in graduate school and how to navigate personal and professional issues to keep your career on track. Chapter 7 provides information about what you can do during graduate school to prepare you for research postdoctoral fellowships and internships. For those pursuing a career in clinical health psychology, Chapter 8 provides insider tips on how to handle the internship application and match processes. The last chapter talks you through to how to choose and make the most of your first position after graduate school—whether a postdoctoral fellowship, faculty position, or research career. So keep the book handy for its helpful suggestions to strengthen your skills throughout the early career years and keep you on the road to becoming a health psychologist.

Throughout the book, we provide many examples of different types of health psychologists and different health psychology careers. We also provide a ton of references and resources in the Appendix—one can never be prepared enough! We also don't want you to depend only on our experience. Throughout the book our health psychology colleagues and students "pop in" with their own stories, experiences, and advice.

Acknowledgments

Many people have helped make *Becoming a Health Psychologist* happen and deserve our heartfelt thanks. First and foremost is our original editor at Taylor & Francis/Routledge, Christina Chronister. After attending a panel on career paths at the American Psychological Association's annual convention in 2016, she approached the first three authors individually with the idea for this volume. We all turned her down. But over drinks later that day, we realized that such a book was needed and that we were the ones to write it. (Lara joined us a few months later after Christina's suggestion to add more clinical expertise.) Lucy Kennedy took over as editor during the last months and Molly Selby, our editorial assistant, kept the frenzy of detail to a minimum. We thank them both for their support and knowledge.

We also thank Emily Walsh, our intrepid research assistant, who combed through many drafts and is responsible for compiling the Appendix and finding many of the resources. As an added plus, Emily was applying to doctoral programs while working on the book and is now a doctoral student in health psychology. A number of colleagues provided useful information on topics we were not as well versed on: Ana Fins, Catherine Grus, and Don Nicholas. We appreciate their taking the time to mentor us. We also are grateful to our students and colleagues who reviewed sections of the book: Evelyn Behar, Ana Abraído-Lanza, Ana Fins, Jennifer Ford, Elana Gloger, Michael Hoyt, Jennifer Kowalsky, Simona Lysakova, Lily McFarland, Emilia Mikrut, Patricia O'Brien, Carolyn Peterson, Megan Renna, Katy Roberts, Ashley Tudder, Dominic Ysidron, and Mariah Xu.

Tracey A. Revenson would also like to thank Hunter College, City University of New York for supporting her sabbatical in 2017–2018 to write the book and, several years earlier, for reintroducing her to the joys of undergraduate teaching and launching undergraduates on their career paths. She would also like to thank her mentors on her own path to becoming a health psychologist: Lou Heifetz, J. Lawrence Aber, Barry Farber, Dorothy Singer, Barbara Felton, Beth Shinn, Phil Shaver, Beth Meyerowitz, David Altman, Dan Stokols, Karen Rook, Howard Friedman, Bob Kaplan, Christina Williams, and Kay Deaux. Patrice G. Saab would like to thank the University of Miami for her 2018 sabbatical leave to work on the book as well as the many undergraduate and graduate students that sought her advice and those she has mentored over the years. Patrice continues to be grateful to her mentors, Kenneth A. Holroyd, J. Richard Jennings, Karen Matthews, Thomas Roth, and Hans Schmidt, Jr., for their guidance and support. Peggy M. Zoccola would like to thank Ohio University for supporting her faculty fellowship leave to write the book as well as her own mentors, including Sally Dickerson, Ilona Yim, and Julie Suhr. Lara Traeger would like to thank Frank Penedo, Elyse Park, Steve Safren, and Jennifer Temel for modeling true mentorship, which is a guiding force in this book.

Most importantly, this book wouldn't have its voice without the health psychologists whose words pepper the volume. They took the time to share their stories publicly and to provide helpful advice that we might otherwise have forgotten. Many are our current and former students, and we are so proud of them.

References

Markus, H., & Nurius, P. (1986). Possible selves. *American Psychologist*, 41(9), 954–969.

U.S. Bureau of Labor Statistics. (2018). *National longitudinal surveys*. Retrieved from www.bls.gov/nls/nlsfaqs.htm

1

WHAT IS A HEALTH PSYCHOLOGIST?

Introduction

When asked at age five what they wanted to be when they grew up, none of the four authors of this book chimed, "I want to be a health psychologist!" To be fair, for half of us, the field of health psychology didn't exist at that time, but even if it had, we wouldn't have known what it was, and our parents and teachers wouldn't have guided us to it.

The field of health psychology does exist now—in fact, it is a thriving area of psychology—and it presents an exciting career choice for those interested in the connections between health and psychology, for those in the helping professions, or for those who want to conduct scientific research (or all three). We presume that is why you have taken this book off the shelf or have pulled it up on your tablet.

Health psychology is an evolving field, boasting many potential job opportunities and predicted growth in the future. In the next ten years, the job outlook for psychologists is expected to grow by 14% (U.S. Bureau of Labor Statistics, 2018). Specifically for health psychologists, evolving healthcare reform is expected to enhance the role of psychologists within the healthcare system in treating behavioral components of health and chronic illness (Norcross, Pfund, & Prochaska, 2013). Additionally, health psychologists can be found in a variety of different professional settings and roles, from clinics and research to teaching, consulting, and government roles. So, pursuing a career in the field of health psychology is not a path to a single destination but a way of gaining skills and knowledge useful for several opportunities and ever-changing environments.

Today nearly 70% of U.S. psychology departments offer an undergraduate course in health psychology (Norcross et al., 2016), compared to only 26% in the 1990s (Panjwani, Gurung, & Revenson, 2017). Health psychology features prominently in many recent introductory psychology textbooks (Griggs, 2014) and is rated as one of the most important topics covered in introductory psychology (McCann, Immel, Kadah-Ammeter, & Adelson, 2016), a course taken by approximately 1.5 million students a year (Gurung et al., 2016). There are now numerous graduate programs that offer doctoral-level training in health psychology (Byrne, Gethin, & Swanson, 2017).

Some of you may have taken an undergraduate course in health psychology or read a chapter on health psychology in a textbook or encyclopedia. For others, a classmate, colleague, or mentor may have suggested that health psychology is the field for you. At the moment, you may think that you want a career in health psychology. But do you really? In this book, we will describe what it means to be a health psychologist and offer information and advice on how to prepare yourself for a career in health psychology regardless of what stage you are in your training or career. We will give you advice on deciding which type of graduate program is best for you, how to apply to health psychology programs and choose among them, and how to prepare for the career ahead while you are in graduate school and beyond.

What Is Health Psychology?

Health psychology is a relatively young field within psychology. In the late 1970s, interest in the contributions of psychological, social, and behavioral factors to physical health led to the emergence of health psychology as an area within the field of psychology. In 1978, this contributed to the founding of the division of Health Psychology (Division 38) within the American Psychological Association (APA), the major membership organization for psychologists in the United States. That division changed its name in 2015 to the Society for Health Psychology (SfHP) and currently boasts 3,237 members, of whom 719 are students in training. Those who would like to read a more detailed history of the field will find it in the writings of Taylor (1990), Pickren and Degni (2011), and Friedman and Adler (2011).

Although many descriptions of the field have been offered over the past 40 years, the SfHP description captures the breadth of and diversity of activities in which health psychologists engage:

> Health psychology is "[t]he field of psychology that addresses the interactions of psychological, social, cultural, and biological influences, mechanisms, and consequences as they relate to the development, prevention, treatment and management of illness and disability and the promotion of health and wellbeing. The field of health psychology produces and evaluates rigorous health research, products, and services, and translates the research for the purpose of enriching empirical knowledge, public understanding, clinical practice, program design, and policy across diverse populations and settings".
>
> (Block, 2015)

There is a lot to unpack in that definition. First, it states that the field of health psychology is based on the *biopsychosocial model*, first developed by a psychiatrist, George Engel, in 1977 and adopted in psychology soon after (Schwartz, 1982). In the biopsychosocial model (see Figure 1.1), health and disease outcomes are

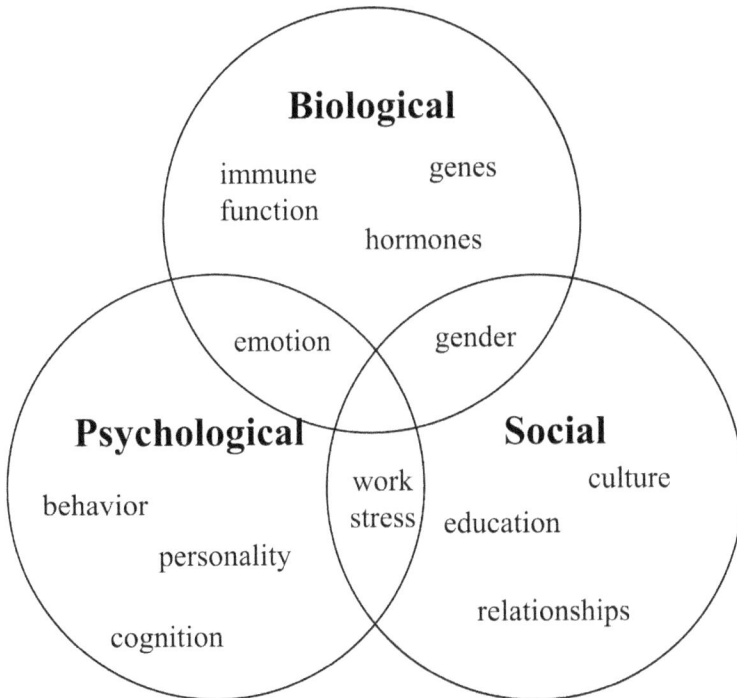

Figure 1.1 *Biopsychosocial Model*

not the result of some single cause-single effect pathway, but the results of multiple interacting influences, some biological, some psychological, and some from individuals' social environments. Second, health psychology is relevant along the entire continuum of health to illness—from promoting health and wellness to the prevention of disease (e.g., cancer screening, smoking cessation programs) to making difficult medical decisions and adhering to medical treatment and to living with chronic illness. Third, health psychology is research-based. This involves conducting original research to determine the causes and consequences of health conditions and using evidence-based treatment approaches (that is, those based on research evidence) in clinical practice. Fourth, health psychology is a field that serves the public interest by producing research findings that can improve health and quality of life for all people (not just those who have easy access to healthcare).

During the past four decades, health psychologists have worked to understand the biological, psychological, and social factors that affect health, health behavior, and illness. They have worked to turn those answers into help for people faced with illness or for those who might benefit from changing their health behavior. Recently, the first author of this book suggested that we move toward a biopsychosociocultural model in order to address important questions of health disparities and inequities (Revenson & Gurung, 2019). As you read the following research examples, consider the breadth of topics that health psychology comprises, from the study of biobehavioral mechanisms of stress and illness, to the study of social justice concerns such as the impact of economic and social disparities on health. Researchers continue to grapple with probing questions that examine the bidirectional nature of mind and body, such as:

> How does depression contribute to the pathophysiology of cardiovascular disease?
> How do inflammatory processes influence depressive symptoms?
> How can we convince more people to engage in regular cancer screening?
> How can we increase uptake and adherence rates for pre-exposure prophylaxis, or PrEP, the first biomedical prevention strategy for HIV?
> How do perceived racism and daily microaggressions lead to greater cardiovascular risk for African-Americans?
> How can we use the research evidence in health psychology to develop more effective and cost-effective behavioral interventions for those living with chronic illness?

These questions (among many others) are the terra firma of health psychology. Addressing such questions offers the potential for research evidence to be translated into clinical practice and health policy.

"Growing up, I always envisioned that I would become a physician since I liked science, I did well in school, and I wanted to help people. I completed all the pre-med requisite courses as an undergraduate, studied for the medical school entrance exams, and volunteered in the local emergency department to prepare for my future. Through my undergraduate coursework and experience as a research assistant in psychology, as well as personal experiences, I came to realize that my true interest was in resilience, particularly how people manage illness and injury. My journey to becoming a health psychologist began when I recognized that my passion was in the intersection of the biological, psychological, and social factors that affect health".

—Laura Forsythe, Ph.D., M.P.H., Director of Evaluation and Analysis, Patient-Centered Outcomes Research Institute

The Difference Between Health Psychology and Behavioral Medicine

Interest in the contributions of biological, psychological, social, cultural, and behavioral factors to physical health and well-being is a hallmark of health psychology, but it is not unique to health psychology. This emphasis also characterizes the broader field of behavioral medicine, which coincidently came on the scene at the same time as health psychology in the late 1970s. And, if you browse through research journals in the two fields, you won't see much of a difference in the content. Health psychology can be viewed as a sub-discipline of behavioral medicine, which is part of the broader public health, healthcare, and medical domains (Freedland, 2017).

Although health psychologists play a central role in behavioral medicine as valued members of interdisciplinary research and clinical teams, behavioral medicine careers are not limited to health psychologists. Rather, behavioral medicine careers include any profession that "promote[s] healthy behaviors to improve health and well-being" (Society of Behavioral Medicine, n.d.). As such, other fields like medicine, nursing, public health, pharmacy, social work, nutrition, exercise, dentistry, physical therapy, and health education offer many excellent options for those interested in health and behavior.

"There are many positives of interdisciplinary collaboration, including a broader perspective and a deeper understanding of the biological, psychological, and social forces that combine to shape health-related behavior. For example, my work on the development of chronic low back pain is informed by both basic learning principles (e.g., after an acute back injury, restriction of spinal motion is negatively reinforced by avoidance of pain) and physiological processes (e.g., over time, continued restriction of spinal motion promotes muscle tissue changes that increase risk for re-injury). In my experience, the challenges of interdisciplinary collaboration, which include differences in knowledge bases, settings, job descriptions, and reward structures, are overcome by mutual respect and a commitment to good communication".

—Chris France, Ph.D., Distinguished Professor
of Psychology, Ohio University

"As a physician, I would not be able to do the meaningful research work I am currently doing if it wasn't for my close collaborations with psychologists who share the common interests and goals of improving the quality of life and reducing distress of patients living with cancer and their caregivers. Our research projects are built on our interdisciplinary strength and require close collaboration. For example, I have worked closely with several of my psychology colleagues to develop and test a psychological intervention to promote effective coping for caregivers of patients undergoing hematopoietic stem cell transplantation. My clinical expertise in this population coupled with the psychological training that my colleagues bring has allowed us to build innovative models of healthcare delivery for patients with cancer and their families. Importantly, throughout these experiences, my psychology colleagues have helped me become a better clinician, capable of recognizing patients' various coping strategies and helping them think about how to strengthen their resilience and ability to deal with the challenges of a life-threatening illness. I often say that by working with psychologists, I wish I had chosen their career path given their immense contribution to my thinking and perspective on illness and medicine".

—Areej El-Jawahri, M.D., Assistant Professor of Medicine,
Massachusetts General Hospital

What Is a Health Psychologist?

The multiple facets of health psychology hint at the diverse opportunities for specialization. Although there are many types of health psychologists, the two most common types are clinical health psychologists (who are trained both to provide health services and conduct research) and health psychologists (who are trained to conduct research but are *not* trained to be health service providers).

While all health psychologists address some aspect of health, well-being, or illness in their work, clinical health psychologists are distinct in that they receive specialized training to engage in the clinical practice of health psychology. Clinical health psychologists might be part of a multidisciplinary team working with doctors, nurses, dieticians, and other healthcare providers treating patients in a medical setting or they might work to promote well-being in otherwise healthy clients.

Health psychologists who do not have clinical expertise are a broad group with diverse training. For example, there are health psychologists with expertise in statistics, psychophysiological methods, brain imaging, neuroendocrine and immunological assessment, social relationships, developmental processes, or population health. Many health psychologists "work the hyphen" within psychology and call themselves social-health psychologists, developmental-health psychologists, or health neuroscientists. For example, social-health psychologists address the influence of social processes and the social environment on health-related processes. As such, they might work to understand how attitudes contribute to health behavior change or how the social environment contributes to health and illness by affecting immune processes (Taylor & Broffman, 2011). Health psychologists also may refer to themselves by the methods they use: experimental health psychologists or, for those who use qualitative methods, critical health psychologists.

"A social-health psychologist can do many different things, from studying how people adapt to stressful situations (e.g., serious illness), to examining factors that contribute to more effective medical care (e.g., good patient-provider communication), to understanding what social factors contribute to a longer lifespan (e.g., having high quality close relationships). Depending on the specific research questions, a social-health psychologist might listen to people's social interactions [using electronically activated recorders], like I do in my work, conduct a longitudinal study where they repeatedly monitor participants' health and ask them questions about psychological and social aspects of their lives, or conduct an experiment in the lab".

—Megan Robbins, Ph.D., Assistant Professor of
Psychology, University of California, Riverside

Independent of specialization (e.g., clinical health, experimental health, or social health), health psychologists are often interested in similar research questions and are trained in many of the same research methods. For example, many clinical health psychologists also ask the same research questions and address the same issues as social health psychologists. To illustrate, although author Peggy Zoccola is an experimental health psychologist and author Patrice Saab is a clinical health psychologist, both use psychophysiological and neuroendocrine methods in their research. In fact, despite their different training backgrounds both have conducted research directed at understanding biobehavioral mechanisms underlying disease. As a clinical health psychologist, Pat might also want to understand whether stress management interventions for heart patients affect the cardiovascular system, whereas an experimental social health psychologist like Peggy might want to identify the factors underlying the relationship between stress and progression of heart disease. Health psychologists with different training backgrounds often collaborate with each other, and with other health professionals, bringing important complementary expertise and team science perspectives to clinical and community endeavors, and to research projects.

> "A neuroscientist/health psychologist is a scientist that seeks to understand the neurobiological bases of behavior as it relates to health outcomes in both clinical and non-clinical populations. Well versed in neuroimaging design and analysis, these scientists explore topics such as the neural representation of pain, neurocognitive changes associated with chemotherapy in breast cancer, and neural correlates of stress reactivity in persons with elevated risk for cardiovascular disease. Clinically trained neuroscientists may even use fMRI to explore the functional brain changes associated with varying measures of health following mindfulness or cognitive stress management interventions".
> —Roger McIntosh, Ph.D., Assistant Professor of
> Psychology, University of Miami

Health psychologists, whether trained as clinical, experimental, or social psychologists, may also be involved in teaching. In fact, as suggested earlier, many students first learn about health psychology by taking an undergraduate course. In addition to teaching in colleges and schools of arts and science, health psychologists also teach in medical schools and public health programs. Moreover, clinical health psychologists often teach patients health behavior skills in medical and community settings.

A Day in the Life of a Health Psychologist

"My days as a clinical health psychologist are typically dynamic, dimensional, and certainly meaningful. One day this week, the day started with a 30-minute phone conversation on the way to work with a friend in a new healthcare consulting position. I then spoke with an APA staff member and several colleagues about the possibility of our collaborating on a new Association policy related to perinatal mental health. After another conversation with a family member in the hospital, I arrived at the University of Colorado School of Medicine where I serve as Clinical Director for the Department of Psychiatry's Women's Behavioral Health and Wellness Service Line. During the morning clinical session, I saw several women across the life span coping with survivorship issues after acute treatment for breast cancer, caregiver stress, and chronic pain affecting sexual health. The consultations were followed by the necessary documentation in EPIC (the hospital's medical information system) and emails with collaborating physicians and staff regarding patient care.

The afternoon started with an interview by a magazine writer preparing a piece on self-care in women. I then focused on program development for our department's new initiative in women's behavioral health and wellness. After writing position announcements to recruit psychologists and psychiatrists, I drafted an executive summary on integrating health psychologists into the women's health service line. After that, I met with a medical student interested in reproductive psychiatry, completed a credentialing document for hospital privileges, started to lay out an EPIC template for clinical services in women's behavioral health outpatient and integrated services, and began to think about strategies to document patient, provider and health system outcomes for the entire new initiative. I left work around 5:30 pm to play 90 minutes of singles tennis and drove home at 8:00 pm to enjoy dinner with my partner, Larry. My typical days as a clinical health psychologist include collaborating with colleagues, clinical care to women of all ages, leadership responsibilities, professional service, vital and fun exercise most days, and connection with family and friends. No matter how busy the day, I find it a privilege to translate health psychology science into practice to improve the well-being of patients and families".

—Helen L. Coons, Ph.D., A.B.P.P., Associate Professor, Department
of Psychiatry, University of Colorado School of Medicine

"I wanted a career that combined my interests in biology, psychology, and making a positive difference in people's lives and the healthcare system. As a first-generation college student, it perplexed me that these fields were so fragmented and in different silos. As a junior at Indiana University, I took a health psychology class and learned that there was a field that combined these approaches, and I knew my career path was set—a health psychologist".
—Misty Hawkins, Ph.D., Assistant Professor
of Psychology, Oklahoma State University

What Does a Health Psychologist Do?

A Day in the Life of a Health Psychologist

"I can't describe my day without starting with my night—I go to bed embarrassingly early at 8:30 pm and read escapist fiction. I sleep for eight hours (non-negotiable) and wake up at 5:00 am. The first hour of my day is writing, defined as anything that moves a manuscript or grant forward—data analyses, drafting a paper, brainstorming new grant ideas, etc. What does not count as writing: email, peer-reviewing papers, class prep, and other "workcrastination". Hour 2 is exercise (also non-negotiable), which I keep efficient by doing at home (currently: Peloton). Hour 3 is getting my toddler, Clark, up and fed. Unfortunately, Hour 4 is spent in the car battling Los Angeles traffic, but podcasts help (currently: "Armchair Expert"). After daycare drop-off, my day begins in earnest at 9:30 am, typically with nonstop meetings—undergrads, grad students, postdocs, research staff, committees, and colleagues. There's also teaching and seminars, office hours and, when I can, a quick Clark visit—luckily, his daycare is on campus. My days can get so overrun that I'm always grateful for that hour spent at the beginning of the day when my mind was freshest, conducting the most important work for moving my career forward. And I'm not quite complaining about meetings—I'm a health psychologist who studies eating behavior, and everyone eats, so I love that I can have meaningful conversations on the science of food and eating with everyone who crosses my path. Daycare closes at 5:30 pm, and it's back in traffic to end up at home, eating the meal I'd cooked the night before. After Clark's gone to sleep, I cook tomorrow's meal . . . and am back in bed at the embarrassingly early hour of 8:30 pm".
—A. Janet Tomiyama, Ph.D., Associate Professor of
Psychology, University of California, Los Angeles

A Day in the Life of a Health Psychologist

"I divide my time between research, administration, and teaching/mentoring. In addition to conducting my own research with colleagues across the U.S. and abroad, I mentor graduate students who are in the University of Miami Clinical Health Psychology Ph.D. program and those who have moved on to postdoctoral positions. I am involved with the cancer control program at the Sylvester Cancer Center through assorted academic and administrative roles and serve as Associate Editor for the peer-reviewed journal *Psychology & Health*. A typical day opens with me returning emails to colleagues overseas, with whom I consult/collaborate on studies of stress, stress management, and biobehavioral processes in medical populations. Then I might spend some editorial time assigning reviewers and making decisions on manuscripts submitted to *Psychology & Health*. Next, I might work on a presentation for an upcoming conference or on a contract for a consultant. After that I often meet with colleagues at the medical school to plan studies, review progress, or plan the writing of articles or grant proposals before attending lunchtime cancer center meetings for scientific steering, protocol review and monitoring, or education and training. Then I head back to the main campus for meetings. These might be with faculty, clinical supervisees, or students, especially as concerns a thesis or dissertation defense. Occasionally I will present in a webinar or teach a graduate or undergraduate lecture. But the day is not done! Later I might have meetings with grants management administrators to deal with pressing budgetary or regulatory issues or attend a late afternoon colloquium or campus event. Each day ends at the campus wellness center for exercise—cardio and weights. After dinner, my evenings often involve returning emails that have accumulated over the day, catching up on reading recent articles, writing or editing manuscripts and, if I'm lucky, rehearsing new arrangements with my jazz band or R & B band and planning the set lists for the next gig".

—Michael Antoni, Ph.D., Professor of Psychology, University of Miami

As illustrated previously, health psychologists do a lot of different things. This can be hard to describe in a single neat package because health psychologists can be involved in many activities depending on their specific jobs and their training. Many health psychologists—both those with and without clinical training—conduct their own original scientific research, present their research at scientific conferences, and publish their research in peer-reviewed scientific journals. They also evaluate others' research as part of committees that award research grants and help make decisions about which research merits presentation at conferences and which deserves to be published in journals. Health psychologists educate and train professionals not only in health psychology but also in other allied fields such as nursing, medicine, exercise physiology, and public health.

"After earning my Ph.D., I worked in a V.A. hospital and a major medical center for five years, and I assumed that I would spend my career in an academic medical setting. However, when an unexpected faculty position became available at a teaching university, I surprised myself by applying. I am now in my fourth year of teaching undergraduate students, inspiring them to discover health psychology. In addition to teaching, I am able to do much more research, supervise students, and run a part-time private practice in which I provide evidence-based treatment to healthcare providers and people coping with cancer. I miss working in a hospital and being part of a medical team, but I enjoy the tasks of my current job, greater personal autonomy and flexibility, and several months off in the summer. As a psychologist, I am appreciative of the numerous career options that are available to me".

—Amanda Kracen, Ph.D., Associate Professor
of Psychology, Webster University

"I was working toward a doctorate in personality/social psychology, in a basic social science program at Lehigh University. The program provided strong conceptual and methodological training in social cognition and experimental psychology, but I had applied, health-related interests as well and wasn't sure how I would pursue those. As luck would have it, in my third year of the program a faculty member approached me about a research assistantship that entailed spending one day a week at a local hospital. My responsibilities were two-fold: (1) to support the medical residents in their research endeavors, and (2) to deliver monthly lectures on research design and statistical issues. I'll never forget my first day at the hospital. It was that feeling of being in one's element! While I was only 25 years old at the time and intimidated about working with the physicians, it soon became clear that they lacked formal research training and could benefit from my knowledge. After that, I sought out and secured a postdoctoral fellowship in behavioral medicine and have been working in interdisciplinary settings ever since".

—Shelby Langer, Ph.D., Associate Professor, College of
Nursing and Health Innovation, Arizona State University

Health psychologists are involved in activities at all points on the health-illness spectrum. They engage in primary prevention (i.e., strategies to promote wellness or to lower chances of developing illness), secondary prevention (e.g., lipid screening, early detection of disease), and treatment/intervention (i.e., strategies to promote wellness in the context of a medical illness or to lower the chances of worsening illness). A health psychologist may be involved in clinical and education activities that influence policy to improve the health of individuals and communities (Society for Health Psychology, 2018). Throughout this book, we highlight the interesting and diverse activities of health psychologists to illustrate the options available to those interested in becoming a health psychologist.

A Day in the Life of a Health Psychologist

"A 'typical' day as a pediatric psycho-oncologist is dynamic, fast-paced, and constantly interactive. I start my day at 6:00 am with a run, which helps to clear my body and mind. During an hour commute on the NYC subway, I read research articles, respond to emails, or listen to podcasts. When I arrive at work, I hit the ground running with an 'outline' for the day. Patients are scheduled in our outpatient oncology clinic either the day before or that day as their schedule and treatment goals constantly change during treatment—which means I need to be flexible. I often have sessions with children and families in the waiting area, IV room, or at bedside. It is important to meet them where they are both physically and mentally that day. My psychological evaluations and interventions are developmentally focused, family-systems oriented, and follow a consultation-liaison model. Each session is often followed by discussions with the oncology (cancer) and psychosocial teams. Throughout the day, I am contacted about patient updates, new consultations, or a patient crisis. In the afternoons, I transition to the inpatient floor. Constantly on the move, it is crucial to wear comfy shoes and have pockets for notes and snacks! Add to this: meetings on program development, research, and interdisciplinary clinical supervision; collaboration; and treatment planning. The end of the day and evenings are filled with writing patient notes, corresponding to e-mails, and following up with patient phone calls. I am constantly exploring ways to process this clinical work and set boundaries to the day's work. I do this by seeing friends (not all psychologists!), creating art, and going to the theatre. Yes, it's stressful, but what I love about this work is the incredible the depth of human life I bear witness to. It is inspiring, deeply moving, and grounding. I am constantly learning".

—Marie Barnett, Ph.D., Assistant Attending Psychologist,
Memorial Sloan Kettering Cancer Center

What Academic Degree(s) and Skills Does a Health Psychologist Need to Have?

Health psychologists have doctoral degrees. Training to become a health psychologist happens in graduate school (often referred to as predoctoral training) and/or after one has received a doctoral degree (known as postdoctoral training). Most often the degree received is the Ph.D. (i.e., Doctor of Philosophy degree), but sometimes it is the Psy.D. (i.e., Doctor of Psychology degree). Graduate training for a Psy.D. is often intended for those seeking careers devoted to the direct delivery of clinical psychological services. As such, Psy.D. programs provide a more general education in clinical psychology, more emphasis on practice and stress understanding, and more weight on applying research methods and findings to practice. (The other types of training are discussed in more detail later on.)

Much has been discussed about the skills or competencies that a beginning health psychologist should have (see Table 1.1). We believe that *all* health psychologists need to demonstrate competencies in four areas: in-depth knowledge of psychological science; empirical research skills; professional skills; and knowledge of cultural diversity and ethical practice.

Table 1.1 Competencies in Health Psychology

For all health psychologists
- In-depth knowledge of psychological science
- Empirical research skills
- Professional skills
- Cultural diversity and ethical practice

Additional competencies for clinical health psychologists
- Assessment skills
- Intervention skills

In-Depth Knowledge of Psychological Science

During graduate training you will develop expertise in health psychology, specifically the biological, psychological, social, and cultural determinants of health and illness. You also will develop a broad knowledge of many of the basic areas of psychology, including social psychology, cognitive psychology, developmental psychology, the biological bases of behavior, and possibly neuroscience. You will develop the ability to conceptualize research problems in terms of broader theory as a means to understand relevant physical and mental health phenomena in more meaningful ways.

Empirical Research Skills

On the most basic level, health psychologists need to be astute consumers of research findings published in the scientific literature. They must master research skills that involve expertly applying scientific methods to design, conduct, analyze, and disseminate empirical research. Empirical health psychology research is defined broadly to include studies conducted in a laboratory and in the field (community), with medical populations or with healthy people. For example, research might focus on trying to change a health behavior, such as increasing exercise, or examine biopsychosocial factors that contribute to health, such as negative mood.

It is important that health psychologists learn appropriate data analysis skills to examine if and why their research ideas are (or are not) supported by their data. Such skills involve quantitative methods (experimental research design, statistics) as well as qualitative methods and even program evaluation skills. This is why almost every doctoral program requires undergraduate methods and statistics courses for admission and has more advanced methods and statistics courses as part of the required curriculum.

In addition to conducting research and collecting data, health psychologists must be able to accurately present and explain their research results to others—experts in the field, novices, policymakers, and the lay public. As a result, both written and verbal communication skills are essential to becoming a health psychologist. This is achieved through writing up one's research for publication in scientific journals, giving talks or poster presentations at scientific conferences (more about this in later chapters), writing blogs or tweeting about research, and speaking with reporters. Most often these skills are "learned by doing". As a graduate student, training might occur in courses, in your research laboratory, or in professional workshops in your department or at scientific conferences.

Most doctoral students are expected to maintain an active research program in collaboration with faculty members throughout their training to enhance the breadth and sophistication of their research skills. Even if you don't go on to have a major research career (or don't plan to), empirical research skills are important for teachers and clinical practitioners to keep up to date and understand "what's new" in the field. For practitioners, it is essential to know the research evidence for a particular type of therapy and what types of people might benefit most from a particular type of therapy.

Professional Skills

Health psychologists need to be proficient in a variety of professional skills: communication skills (for teaching and dissemination of their work to others, including journalists), writing (for publishing their work in scientific and professional journals), working on a team (e.g., a multidisciplinary medical team or a trans-disciplinary research team), and management skills (for running a research lab and administering a research grant). Doctoral students will learn many of these skills through hands-on experiences and training rather than through traditional coursework.

"My career began at an academic medical center teaching, providing patient care, and conducting clinical research. Battling for reimbursement and working with individuals or small groups seemed very limiting. Given the role that behavior has in the development of disease and the value of behavior change in the management of chronic disease, I believe strongly that behavioral science could be employed to significantly enhance population health and control healthcare costs. Utilizing an entrepreneurial approach, my colleagues and I decided to sell behavior change services to self-funded employers who would directly benefit from the improved health status of plan members and lower healthcare costs. Diabetes was an obvious target because it typically represents about 20% of a health plans' losses, has serious health consequences, and patient compliance with evidence-based standards of care is very low. Our approach was to recruit diabetic plan members to participate in a health behavior change program and realign their incentives. Participants were provided health improvement plans, monitored, messaged, and rewarded for completion of all evidence-based standards of care. This behavioral intervention is very effective, significantly improving patients' clinical measures and lowering employer healthcare costs through the reduction of unnecessary hospitalization.

Most health psychologists have a number of the requisite skills to be successful as entrepreneurs including data analytic skills, intervention management, and the ability to write and communicate effectively. However, to be a successful entrepreneur, additional skills are required, such as knowledge of healthcare financing, the ability to write and execute a business plan, and understanding profit and loss statements. If a health psychologist does not possess all of these characteristics, they can collaborate with others who have complementary skill sets. I firmly believe that health psychologists can make, either directly, or through strategic collaboration, significant contributions to our healthcare delivery system, but it will require an 'out of the box' approach".

—Michael Follick, Ph.D., CEO, Abacus Health Solutions LLC

Knowledge of Cultural Diversity and Ethical Practice

Health psychologists must be able to study and interact with individuals from a variety of cultural backgrounds and to conduct research that takes cultural factors into account. They need to develop skills to work collaboratively, particularly on teams that include members from different backgrounds, disciplines, and fields. It is imperative that health psychologists understand ethical principles and apply them to their research and clinical work. Early in your graduate career you will receive basic training in ethics and the responsible conduct of research.

What Additional Skills Does a Clinical Health Psychologist Need to Have?

In addition to the skills discussed earlier, clinical health psychologists need to develop an additional set of competencies, including assessment techniques, intervention skills, consultation skills, and supervision skills. We cover each briefly here. For more detail we encourage you to review France et al.'s (2008) description of the desired competencies for entry-level clinical health psychologists.

Assessment Techniques

Clinical health psychologists must understand and be able to select and implement measures to assess biological, psychological, social, cultural, and environmental aspects of health. For example, if you want to assess whether a novel behavioral treatment for pain is working, what outcomes would you measure before and after the treatment? You might include self-reports of pain, family members' reports of pain, days off from work due to pain, or pain medication use. How would you measure each of these? And how do you know if the measures you choose are valid and reliable in your population of interest?

Intervention Skills

Clinical health psychologists need to be familiar with a broad range of evidence-based therapies to treat patients' conditions in order to choose the best one(s) for a particular patient in a particular circumstance. They may deliver therapies that focus on improving health behaviors, psychological adjustment to illness, daily functioning, quality of life, or a combination of these outcomes. On one hand, you will need to learn how to deliver manualized interventions (i.e., those using a "manual", that is, a structured format that can easily be replicated by others) with high fidelity (that is, as the creators designed them) to obtain optimal results. On the other hand, you will need flexibility to adapt evidence-based treatments that have been established in the general population (e.g., treatment for major depressive disorder) for use with patients with health conditions (e.g., addressing depressive symptoms such as sleep problems that overlap with the symptoms of many chronic medical conditions).

Consultation Skills

Consultation involves interacting with professions in other health disciplines to best address the needs of a medical patient. Recently, clinical health psychologists have become involved in *integrated care*, in which psychologists, physicians, nurses, and other allied health professionals work as a team to diagnose physical and psychological health problems, plan and provide treatment, and evaluate whether that treatment is effective. (See Novotny, 2010, for some examples.) This will require you to be able to explain your clinical perspectives and treatment recommendations effectively to other health professionals and to highlight the importance of mental health factors to overall patient health.

Supervision Skills

Clinical health psychologists oversee the health service delivery activities of psychology graduate students, interns and postdoctoral fellows, and sometimes psychologist colleagues or colleagues from other disciplines, as they assess and treat medical patients. This supervision is essential in training supervisees to competently address the needs of health-related patients. According to Belar (2008), there are many unique supervisory issues associated with medical settings. To address the needs of medical patients and the trainees working with them, supervisors need to be readily available and on-site at the health setting. Supervisors initially work closely with supervisees until they are ready to do more on their own. With this model, supervisees learn therapeutic and assessment strategies by actually observing the clinical activities of their supervisors.

Health Psychology Intersects With Many Areas of Psychology

As you can see from the descriptions provided, health psychology intersects with many areas of psychology. And although they overlap in many ways, health psychology students are uniquely trained to understand the link between health and behavior from multiple vantage points.

Let's illustrate this in terms of clinical practice first and then in terms of research. Both clinical health psychologists and pediatric psychologists are trained to clinically address health-related issues. A clinical health psychologist might work with an adult with Type 2 diabetes to help make the necessary lifestyle changes to manage the illness. In contrast, a pediatric psychologist might work with the parents of a young child with Type 1 diabetes to maximize the child's adherence to the treatment regimen. Likewise, a depressed individual would be treated well by a clinical psychologist using an evidence-based therapy. However, a patient who had a heart attack and comorbid major depression would be best treated by a clinical health psychologist, with expertise in both cardiovascular disorders and depression and who understands the connection between the two.

Let's move to research examples. Social health psychologists may apply theoretical models of stress and coping developed by traditionally trained social or personality psychologists to understand how coping behaviors may contribute to adjustment among women with early-stage breast cancer. Or they might examine how the family helps a patient adapt to their illness. Social neuroscientists may study brain activation during interpersonal interactions in the laboratory (for example, what happens to the brain when a friend rejects you?), while health neuroscientists may study brain activation during actual interactions. A general psychophysiologist might examine the physiological characteristics of patients with certain kinds psychopathology (e.g., high frequency heart rate variability in patients with self-regulation and cognitive control deficits). In contrast, a health psychologist would use psychophysiological methods to examine factors associated with cardiovascular or other health risks (e.g., stress-induced blood pressure responses in individuals at risk for hypertension).

Alternative Career Options That Focus on Health and Behavior

The psychological aspects of health and illness clearly impact most healthcare fields. Notably, medical training has increasingly included some training on behavioral science topics such as how to help patients adhere to medication regimens or how to deliver "bad news" to patients with serious illness. Physicians and registered nurses may work with patients to adopt healthy lifestyle behaviors. Given the multidisciplinary nature of health psychology research topics, health psychologists often collaborate with healthcare professionals that are interested in psychological aspects of health and illness. For example, at the academic hospital where Lara Traeger works, nurses have helped health psychology researchers to deliver a brief behavioral intervention at the bedside to reduce anxiety and breathlessness in patients with lung disease and to develop a workshop to reduce emotional fatigue in healthcare professionals who work with acutely ill patients.

A Day in the Life of a Health Psychologist

"Life will never be dull if you choose a career as a clinical health psychologist working in a medical school. My job depends on close collaborations with other psychologists, with physicians, with patients, and with leadership of the school and the hospital. So, a typical day involves meetings with some groups of these stakeholders to update them on progress, ask for their input on funded projects, or to continue progress on system-wide initiatives. I get the opportunity to teach, and my focus recently has been on teaching junior faculty how to be future leaders of medical school and hospitals. This executive physician academy is co-run with our business school faculty, so I get to learn about executive business courses and skills from the best, while ensuring it is useful for my own faculty. I also get to work with a number of multidisciplinary colleagues on submitting grant and contract applications. These junior colleagues bring passion and determination to improve a patient-focused problem, and it is a delight to work with them as they think about what scientific problem and approach they are going to take to tackle their area of investigation. Finally, my day is never complete without hearing from 'graduated' mentees who stay in touch. I hear frequently of their recent challenges and achievements, and I love discussing with them the new directions they are launching in their patient care, science, and teaching missions. My daily inspiration is drawn from the ways we as clinical health psychologists can uniquely aid our students, patients, colleagues, and systems. The methodological rigor and thinking that was provided to me in my training has been a great gift and will stand you in good stead should you choose to work in a medical school".

—Karina W. Davidson, Ph.D., M.A.Sc., Vice President of
Research & Dean of Academic Affairs, Northwell Health

A number of helping professions are closely related to health psychology in terms of their focus on health and behavior. Preparation for many of these careers can be achieved with a bachelor's degree or a master's degree. Different degrees offer different career options, so you will need to weigh the time needed to complete the degree. In general, the more intense the training, the more skills you develop, and the more career options you have. This "weighing" will be different for each person.

Consider the following professionals and how their work is different or similar to the work of health psychologists:

Some social workers provide care to medical populations—for example, oncological (cancer) social work. The day-to-day work of oncological social workers may focus largely on delivering clinical care, helping patients cope with their diagnosis, or linking people to community and home-based social services (e.g., transportation to medical appointments).

Health educators (often with Certified Health Education Specialist, or CHES, credentials) may conduct research or provide services that focus on helping communities, and sometimes individuals, to embrace health promotion and illness prevention behaviors through legislation (e.g., seatbelt laws, tobacco laws), digital health (e.g., activity tracking devices), or patient education (e.g., condom use, adherence to medication).

Those trained in public health aim to affect entire populations by applying interventions to a whole community. (In many cases, these interventions are based on psychological theory.) For example, a mass media campaign targeting high school students to prevent smoking may be based on social cognitive theory. Public health focuses more on structural or environmental interventions to shape health, which is less common in health psychology (e.g., changing cafeteria food options to promote healthy eating, putting a wide inviting staircase in a lobby to promote stair usage over elevators, or installing bike lanes). But many health psychologists also engage in these types of activities, so the line is blurred a bit. People with a master's degree in public health may be researchers or community health workers that work in local community or global settings to develop or evaluate programs and policies, as well as conduct research or practice on large-scale interventions.

How do these different fields differ from health psychology? First, the training—what one learns and the practical experiences that one has in graduate school—is different. Second, the time to degree is different—in social work, health education, and public health, a master's degree often lets you practice in the field, although a few people go on to receive a doctoral degree after a few years of experience. Third, and most important, is the focus of the profession: health psychologists focus more on the "why" questions—Why do people take health risks? What motivates people to embrace health promotion and illness prevention? What personality and social relationship factors help ill individuals and their families adjust to living with a chronic physical illness? Although there are some exceptions, health psychologists focus their research and practice at the individual- or interpersonal-level more so than public health workers or health educators, who focus their efforts more at the community, population, or policy levels.

Obtaining a Master's Degree

If you are thinking about pursuing training in health psychology, it is important to know that there are only a few master's degree programs in the United States that specialize in health psychology. Furthermore, in the United States, a master's degree currently is not sufficient to qualify you as a health psychologist. A doctorate is required. This is because the APA currently considers a doctorate to be "the minimal educational requirement for entry into professional practice as a psychologist (www. apa.org/about/policy/chapter-4b.aspx#doctorate-minimum). However, the APA appointed a task force in July 2018 to study whether master's programs in clinical, counseling, and school psychology should be accredited or recognized with a status that qualifies program graduates to perform specific psychology-related activities.

If this were to occur, it would ensure that master's level practitioners with psychology degrees have access to the same kinds of opportunities and credentialing as other master's degrees in psychology-related fields such as social work or mental health counseling (APA, 2016). It would also help ensure that clinical therapy and assessment training at the master's level is based on scientific evidence. We do not know what recommendations the task force will make in the next few years. Stay tuned!

Completing what is called a "terminal" master's degree in psychology is not out of the question, however. There are several job opportunities for individuals with a master's degree who are interested in health psychology. For instance, someone with a master's degree might work on a health psychology research project as a research assistant or project director or have a role in delivering behavioral interventions or conducting assessments as part of a research project. We should note that in some states, individuals with a master's degree are required to conduct clinical work only under the supervision of a licensed supervisor. So, if you plan to complete a terminal master's degree with the primary aim of practicing therapy independently in a health context, you may be better served by completing a master's degree in social work or mental health counseling.

You also might be wondering about whether to complete a master's program in psychology before pursuing a doctoral degree in health psychology to strengthen your application. We are asked by a lot of potential applicants whether it "helps" to have a master's degree or if they "must" have a master's degree. In the United States, a master's degree is not required for admission to most doctoral programs. (It is more common in Europe.) It is possible and quite common to be admitted to a doctoral program with a bachelor's degree in psychology. However, if your bachelor's degree is in a field other than psychology, a master's degree in psychology can provide you with the basic required coursework in psychology, research methods, and statistics that is required for entry into a doctoral program. A master's degree may also help you if your undergraduate grades are not competitive for a doctoral program. Certainly, good grades in master's level courses show that you can handle graduate level coursework.

But we will always tell potential applicants who majored in psychology that your application will be much stronger if you gain research experience in the field than if you have a master's degree. Why? Master's programs vary in the degree to which they provide opportunities for gaining hands-on research experience. If you are considering applying to a master's program in psychology, be sure to check this out in advance. Working in a lab while completing your degree can give you an opportunity to demonstrate your potential for doctoral work, especially if you conduct a research-based master's thesis. However most master's degree programs in psychology are large and, to be honest, students go searching for an advisor for their thesis. Again, we recommend to students that research training is what they need to strengthen their application, and it's even better if you can obtain specific research training on a health psychology or behavioral medicine project in a university or medical setting (and get paid while you are getting the experience!)

So, if you have a bachelor's degree in psychology and you have a strong undergraduate record but want more experience before applying to a doctoral program then we would recommend that get real-world research experience working on a funded research study instead of getting a master's degree. The kind of research experience you will obtain as a research assistant or project director or clinical research coordinator in a medical setting is invaluable. It will demonstrate to the doctoral programs that you are seriously interested in research and that you truly know what day-to-day research activities entail. Working on a research project may even give you practice in presenting research at conferences and writing publications, two of the essential skills of being a health psychologist.

Are you still struggling over the decision whether to obtain a master's degree in psychology before moving on to a doctoral program? A master's program can seem appealing because it takes a relatively short time to complete your degree. At the same time, the tuition can be significant. Classes can be large and are sometimes taught by adjunct professors instead of tenured or tenure-track faculty. Many doctoral programs will accept a limited number of master's level transfer credits and sometimes only for elective, not required, courses. Unfortunately, this may only be decided after you have been matriculated. Similarly, you cannot count on your master's thesis being accepted by the doctoral program. The bottom line is not to assume that you will knock two years off your time to the Ph.D. with a master's degree.

If you have any hesitations about pursuing a doctorate, a master's degree is a good way to test the waters before committing to a doctoral program, but be sure to get research experience while obtaining your master's degree!

"I first developed a passion for health psychology during my time as an undergraduate health psychology research assistant. During that time, I worked with patients that had a variety of health conditions. Interestingly, most of these conditions were preventable (e.g., obesity, diabetes, renal failure) and caused in part by lifestyle factors. This highlighted the importance of health promotion efforts in patient outcomes and led me to pursue my graduate training in clinical psychology with a health concentration. I was drawn to the field of health psychology as it synthesized the complex interplay of biological, social, and psychological contributions to an individual's physical and mental health. I am privileged to have spent my graduate career researching and implementing effective health promotion methods and I find the field of health psychology to be both intellectually stimulating and rewarding on a personal level".

—Mary Kate Clennan, M.S., Doctoral Student, University of Miami

"My decision to go into health psychology was heavily influenced by my interest in understanding how psychological and social factors 'get under the skin' to influence biological process that are important for physical health. As an honors undergraduate student, I also had the opportunity to take courses such as the psychobiology of stress and health psychology with really great professors. Despite being at a large research university, my professors were very involved in undergraduate education and encouraged me to pursue research opportunities and graduate work in health psychology".

—Matthew R. Cribbet, Ph.D., Assistant Professor, University of Alabama

"I stumbled into the field of health psychology quite by accident. I had just begun work in a psychophysiology/health lab trying to get research experience when I saw the Oklahoma City Bombing on a TV in the student union. Within days we were on-site collecting data, which led to my first publication documenting associations between event-related stress and biomarkers. I was hooked!"

—John M. Ruiz, Ph.D., Associate Professor
of Psychology, University of Arizona

Moving Ahead . . .

Health psychology is a vibrant and growing field, but it may not be for everyone. And even if you do think it is the right one for you, there are still more decisions to be made: What type of health psychology is right for you? Let's ponder that in the next chapter.

References

American Psychological Association. (2016). *Proceedings of the summit on master's training in psychological practice.* Washington, DC: American Psychological Association. Retrieved from www. apa.org/pi/mfp/masters-summit/training-proceedings.pdf

Belar, C. (2008). Supervisory issues in clinical health psychology. In C. A. Falender & E. P. Shafranske (Eds.), *Casebook for clinical supervision: A competency-based approach* (pp. 197–209). Washington, DC: American Psychological Association.

Block, C. (2015). Division 38: Health psychology. *APA division sponsors.* Retrieved September 1, 2018 from www.wihpt.com/apa-division-sponsors.html

Byrne, M., Gethin, N., & Swanson, V. (2017). Health psychology practice in Europe: Taking stock and moving forward together. *The European Health Psychologist, 19*(2), 314–320.

Engel, G. (1977). The need for a new medical model: A challenge for biomedicine. *Science, 196*(4286), 129–136. https://doi.org/10.1126/science.847460

France, C. R., Masters, K. S., Belar, C. D., Kerns, R. D., Klonoff, E. A., Larkin, K. T., . . . & Thorn, B. E. (2008). Application of the competency model to clinical health psychology. *Professional Psychology: Research and Practice, 39*(6), 573–580. https://doi.org/10.1037/0735-7028.39.6.573

Freedland, K. E. (2017). A new era for health psychology. *Health Psychology, 36,* 1–4. https:// doi.org/10.1037/hea0000463

Friedman, H. S., & Adler, N. E. (2011). The intellectual roots of health psychology. In H. S. Friedman (Ed.), *Oxford handbook of health psychology* (pp. 3–14). New York, NY: Oxford University Press.

Griggs, R. A. (2014). Topical coverage in introductory textbooks from the 1980s through the 2000s. *Teaching of Psychology, 41,* 5–10. https://doi.org/10.1177/0098628313514171

Gurung, R. A. R., Hackathorn, J., Enns, C., Frantz, S., Cacioppo, J. T., Loop, T., & Freeman, J. E. (2016). Strengthening introductory psychology: A new model for teaching the introductory course. *American Psychologist, 71,* 112–124. https://doi.org/10.1037/a0040012

McCann, L. I., Immel, K. R., Kadah-Ammeter, T. L., & Adelson, S. K. (2016). The importance and interest of introductory psychology textbook topics: Student opinions at technical college, 2-, and 4-year institutions. *Teaching of Psychology, 43,* 215–220. https://doi. org/10.1177/0098628316649477

Norcross, J. C., Hailstorks, R., Aiken, L. S., Pfund, R. A., Stamm, K. E., & Christidis, P. (2016). Undergraduate study in psychology: Curriculum and assessment. *American Psychologist, 71*(2), 89–101. https://doi.org/10.1037/a0040095

Norcross, J. C., Pfund, R. A., & Prochaska, J. O. (2013). Psychotherapy in 2022: A Delphi poll on its future. *Professional Psychology: Research and Practice, 44*(5), 363–370. https://doi.org/ 10.1037/a0034633

Novotny, A. (2010). Integrated care is nothing new for these psychologists. *Monitor on Psychology*, 41, 40–45. Retrieved from www.apa.org/monitor/2010/01/integrated-care.aspx

Panjwani, A. A., Gurung, R. A. R., & Revenson, T. A. (2017). The teaching of undergraduate health psychology: A national survey. *Teaching of Psychology*, 44, 268–273. https://doi.org/10.1177/0098628317712786

Pickren, W. E., & Degni, S. (2011). A history of the development of health psychology. In H. S. Friedman (Ed.), *Oxford handbook of health psychology* (pp. 15–41). New York, NY: Oxford University Press.

Revenson, T. A., & Gurung, R. A. R. (2019). Health psychology rising: The current status and future direction of health psychology. In T. A. Revenson & R. A. R. Gurung (Eds.), *Handbook of health psychology* (pp. 3–14). New York, NY: Routledge.

Schwartz, G. E. (1982). Testing the biopsychosocial model: The ultimate challenge facing behavioral medicine? *Journal of Consulting and Clinical Psychology*, 50(6), 1040–1053. https://doi.org/10.1037/0022-006X.50.6.1040

Society of Behavioral Medicine. (n.d.). *Behavioral medicine?* Retrieved from www.sbm.org/about/behavioral-medicine

Society for Health Psychology. (2018). *Definition of health psychology.* Retrieved from www.societyforhealthpsychology.org/

Taylor, S. E. (1990). Health psychology: The science and the field. *American Psychologist*, 45(1), 40–50. https://doi.org/10.1037/0003-066X.45.1.40

Taylor, S. E., & Broffman, J. I. (2011). Psychosocial resources: Functions, origins, and links to mental and physical health. In J. M. Olson & M. P. Zanna (Eds.), *Advances in experimental social psychology* (pp. 1–57). New York, NY: Academic Press.

U.S. Bureau of Labor Statistics. (2018). *Occupational outlook handbook: Psychologists.* Retrieved from www.bls.gov/ooh/life-physical-and-social-science/psychologists.htm#tab-2

2

TRAINING OPTIONS FOR HEALTH PSYCHOLOGISTS

Introduction

As we explained in Chapter 1, there is no single way to become a health psychologist. Nor is there a "right time" when one should make that decision. Many students begin the work toward becoming a health psychologist during college, often after they have been introduced to the area through a health psychology course or being part of a professor's health psychology lab. Others complete an undergraduate degree in a field outside of psychology such as English, history, or anthropology, but after working as a research assistant or while pursuing a master's degree in general psychology, decide that health psychology is the right path for them. Still others change careers; we have mentored health psychology doctoral students who previously worked as nurses, social workers, business professionals, lawyers, and even a funeral home director before deciding that what they desired was a more direct focus on health psychology.

Health psychologists can receive their training in a number of different ways. Clearly, one can find training in doctoral psychology programs specifically named "Health Psychology" or "Behavioral Medicine". But one can also gain training in health psychology within other types of doctoral programs, including clinical psychology, social psychology, experimental psychology, community psychology, counseling psychology, and neuroscience. The type of graduate program that you choose is important because it will impact the training you receive in graduate school and the career options you will have.

The amount and intensity of health psychology training available in doctoral programs varies by program and institution. One psychology department might have a single health psychologist whereas others may have a large number of health psychology faculty members. Some programs offer extensive health psychology coursework and health research training opportunities; other programs may only have one of these two components. Although some health psychology programs have a curriculum that is tailored specifically to health psychology, others may offer coursework together with clinical psychology or social psychology programs. This is what you will learn from researching specific doctoral programs *before* you apply.

This chapter focuses on doctoral programs only, as a doctoral degree is currently necessary for most health psychology careers. Before we move on, there are two important things you need to know about pursuing doctoral education: (1) in many programs, a relatively small number of students are admitted each year; (2) doctoral study is typically full-time; and (3) financial costs vary widely across programs.

How to Start Thinking About Choosing Programs

If you are deciding to pursue a doctoral degree in health psychology, the first questions you need to ask yourself are:

> *What do I want to do?*
> *What kind of career do I want to have?*
> *What type of doctoral program do I want to apply to?*

At first, you may feel that you do not have answers to these questions and may want to put this book away. These questions can be intimidating, particularly if you're interested in many aspects of health psychology. But we encourage you to continue thinking about those questions during long showers and walks, after talks with family, friends and faculty advisors who know you well, and after exploring many doctoral programs' websites. (We'll give you clear instructions on how to do this in the next chapter.) This is all part of the process of reaching a clearer sense of your preferences.

As you think about your interests and the options, one of the initial issues that you'll need to consider is whether or not you want to apply to programs that provide clinical training. This is an important decision because it will determine the kinds of training opportunities that will be available to you in graduate school. For want of a better term, we will refer to the programs that do not offer clinical training as *research-only health psychology programs* and those that do as *clinical health psychology programs*. Note, however, that all clinical health psychology programs involve research training.

Research-Only Programs

There are few "freestanding" health psychology programs in North America. Some health psychology programs have both research-only and clinical tracks, although they may not be labeled as such. To decide if you want to be a research-only health psychologist, another important question to ask yourself is:

Do my interests intersect more with social psychology, developmental psychology, or neuroscience, or some other subspecialty?

Answering this question will direct you to identify programs and mentors that can provide the training you desire. Your answer is important since many research-only doctoral programs are not "general" programs. Instead, they typically use a "mentor model" and accept students whose interests best "fit" with the mentor's research interests and the program's training goals. A further discussion of fit with a mentor and a program can be found in Chapter 3.

On average, research-only health psychology doctoral programs last four to five years. Coursework emphasizes the theoretical frameworks underlying health-behavior relationships and provides sophisticated training, advanced statistical courses and, occasionally, policy-based research courses. Both in-classroom and hands-on training in conducting research is a hallmark of research-only health psychology.

> "I am particularly interested in the functional brain changes associated with Human Immunodeficiency Virus (HIV) infections. We have known for some time that HIV accelerates brain aging and leads to early neurocognitive impairment. However, I am specifically interested in early cardiovascular disease risk within this population and whether HIV alters the function of brain regions supporting cardio-autonomic regulation. We also use functional magnetic resonance imaging (fMRI) to explore whether activity in limbic networks corresponds with peripheral inflammation and levels of mood disturbance in persons living with HIV/AIDS".
>
> —Roger McIntosh, Ph.D., Assistant Professor
> of Psychology, University of Miami

"I have always loved biology. I went to college wanting to be pre-med excited to take my biology interests to a new level. Of course, medicine is not all biology. When I took chemistry my pre-med dreams changed. I morphed into a biology major and was loving that until I took some psychology and became a double major. Carleton College had students do a comprehensive project in their major, and if you have two majors you do two comprehensive projects. Sure I liked biology, but not that much, so I focused on psychology instead and did a senior project on the stress of performance that focused on individual differences but included biological measures. This use of biology led me to apply to both biological psychology and social psychology programs for graduate school. I chose social psychology and loved my program at the University of Washington. I was fascinated by looking at how the situation and personality both influence behavior and I was intrigued by behaviors that had biological consequences. The perfect follow-up to that was health psychology, and so I applied for postdoctoral fellowships in health psychology and ended up at UCLA working with Shelley Taylor and Chris Dunkel-Schetter. That wonderful (and not totally planned) experience shaped me into a health psychologist".
—Regan Gurung, Ph.D., Professor of Psychological Science,
Oregon State University

"As someone who was deeply interested in both social and health psychology, as well as the connections between the two, attending a combined program [at Stony Brook University] provided a great opportunity for training in different methods, frameworks, and perspectives. I completed a graduate certificate in women's studies simultaneously. The combined training in all three of those areas helped me to formulate innovative, interdisciplinary ideas that have been the foundation of my work".
—Lisa Rosenthal, Ph.D., Associate Professor
of Psychology, Pace University

A research-only health psychology program is perfect for students who are interested in health psychology and do not want to engage in clinical practice (e.g., conduct therapy). Students in research-only health psychology programs will not receive any training in the clinical practice of health psychology and will not be qualified to treat people. Let us just add here, that research-only does not mean, "I don't like people". Health psychology researchers conduct interviews with people living with chronic illness, conduct focus group research with people about changing health behaviors, design and implement community-based interventions, administer neuroimaging scans, and lead research teams. They often teach in colleges or medical schools as part of their job. So if you don't like to interact with people, consider carefully whether health psychology is the right career path for you.

We have known individuals who graduated from research-only programs (e.g., neuroscience, developmental, or social programs) and decided later that they wanted to be able to practice as a clinical health psychologist. They had to complete additional graduate coursework and clinical practica, which added years to their training. Although these "clinical retraining" opportunities are an option, they are not widely available and delay you from settling into a career. This is yet another reason we encourage you to think carefully about the type of career you want before applying to graduate school.

Health Psychology Programs Offering Clinical Training

If you are interested in receiving training in the clinical practice of health psychology, three options are available to you: (1) a Ph.D. in clinical psychology; (2) a Ph.D. in counseling psychology; or (3) a Psy.D. in clinical psychology. (In this book, for ease of presentation, we use clinical health psychology to refer to clinical health psychology as well as counseling health psychology programs.) The American Psychological Association's (APA) Commission for the Recognition of Specialties and Proficiencies in Professional Psychology has recognized clinical health psychology as a specialty since 1997. Clinical health psychology is firmly rooted in research-driven, evidence-based practice; this means that there is research evidence for the different types of therapies and assessment strategies taught.

There are three major training models in clinical psychology: (1) scientist-practitioner, (2) clinical scientist, and (3) scholar-practitioner (Routh, 2015). Although both scientist-practitioner programs and clinical scientist programs provide training in research and practice, clinical scientist programs place an even greater emphasis on research. Most clinical Ph.D. and counseling Ph.D. programs use the scientist-practitioner model. Fewer programs adopt the clinical scientist model, although the number is growing. Scholar-practitioner programs emphasize practice and focus their training toward that goal. Most Psy.D. programs and some counseling programs adopt this scholar-practitioner model. And, given the differences in clinical assessment and intervention approaches for children vs. adults, many doctoral programs in clinical psychology offer separate child and adult program tracks, and they require that you select whether you want to train in the care of children or adults at the time you apply to graduate school.

Clinical health psychology training involves coursework in assessment, intervention techniques, consultation and supervision, as well as supervised clinical practica and externships. Students also are required to complete a year-long supervised clinical internship before receiving their doctoral degree. The clinical internship is usually done at an institution that is *not* where you received your graduate training. (You will learn more about internships in Chapter 8.)

Although opportunities for clinical health psychology training are most likely to be found in clinical Ph.D. programs, a handful of counseling programs also offer this training (Nicholas & Stern, 2011). The Society for Counseling Psychology (Division 18 of the APA) has its own health psychology webpage (see Appendix). You will also find a few Psy.D. programs that provide some clinical health psychology training opportunities.

Clinical and counseling Ph.D. programs share more similarities than differences. Although every program is unique, an analysis of differences between general clinical and counseling programs revealed that psychopathology training was emphasized in clinical programs while multicultural training was emphasized in counseling programs (Morgan & Cohen, 2008). The major training difference between Psy.D. vs. Ph.D. programs is that students in Psy.D. programs spend more time in clinical training pursuits and comparatively less time involved in research during their graduate training.

Frequently Asked Questions

By this point, we have provided a lot of information for you to make a crucial decision and you may be feeling a little anxious. Take a breath. Maybe take a break and come back to the chapter. Uncertainty is a good thing at this point in the process as you mull on all the factors that may affect your decision. Here's more input for your decision.

How Long Will It Take Me to Finish My Degree?

Including the internship year, Ph.D. programs in clinical psychology and clinical health psychology and Ph.D. programs in counseling psychology typically take five to six years to complete. Research-only health psychology programs usually take a year less, as they don't require a year of internship. Psy.D. programs typically take four to five years to complete.

How Difficult Is It to Gain Admission to a Doctoral Program in Health Psychology?

Admission to doctoral programs in health psychology is highly competitive. Unlike law school or medical school, Ph.D. programs tend to be small, taking between three to 12 students a year. Why? There are a number of reasons. First, the training is intensive. Faculty act as mentors and it is key that faculty have sufficient time to guide, advise, and instruct the students that they have committed to train. Since there is frequent and direct supervision of both research training and clinical training, it would be difficult for any single faculty member to mentor large numbers of students and do it well. (As faculty members, we have heard that a good rule of thumb is to mentor no more than five students at a time; this corresponds to one student at each year of training.) Recently a Ph.D. student whose mentor was leaving for another university talked with author Tracey Revenson about becoming her new advisor and the first (and very smart) question was "Do you have enough time to mentor me?"

Second, many programs provide Ph.D. students with research and/or teaching assistantships or fellowships, which often come with stipends (salaries) and waivers of tuition costs that are paid by the university. As a result, the availability of these financial resources limits the number of students that can be admitted to a program in any one year. (We'll discuss more how finances might affect your graduate school decision in Chapter 4.) Third, admitting a limited number of students helps build cohesiveness and community among the students and faculty. It ensures that the program can meet all its students' needs. On the positive side, each year brings a small cohort of students that train together, get plenty of faculty attention, and often bond in a way during training that lasts through their entire careers.

In contrast, Psy.D. programs typically admit larger numbers of graduate students, making admission to a Psy.D. program less competitive. In Psy.D. programs there is greater emphasis on clinical training, which is often done at external sites by outside supervisors, and a lesser emphasis on mentored research training. This enables Psy.D. programs to train more students. Psy.D. programs typically do not provide stipends and tuition waivers to their students. Instead Psy.D. students are encouraged to obtain their own funding whether in the form of loans, other sources of financial aid, or outside jobs.

Doctoral training is almost always full-time training, at least during the first several years of most programs. This makes sense, in light of the intensity of taking classes, conducting research and, for students in a clinical psychology or clinical health psychology graduate program, practicing clinical skills under supervision. As you will learn, doctoral training is much more than coursework. This contrasts with master's degree programs, which focus primarily on coursework and may or may not have a required master's thesis.

Some types of doctoral stipends, scholarships, and fellowships offered by universities or outside sources (such as the National Institutes of Health) require full-time status. As a result, most Ph.D. programs do not admit part-time students, and many do not allow students to hold an outside job that is not part of their graduate training.

How Do You Prepare for Clinical Health Psychology Practice?

In the United States, clinical psychology is a regulated profession. This means that after training is completed (doctoral degree plus internship), you have to take a licensing exam. If you want to be able to practice independently as a clinical or counseling psychologist (regardless of whether you focus on health psychology or not), you will need to complete a number of requirements for professional licensure. Each state varies in the specific requirements but generally you will need to complete these steps: (1) obtain your doctoral degree in clinical or counseling psychology from an accredited program (more on accreditation later in this chapter), (2) complete supervised clinical hours including clinical placements during graduate school, (3) complete an approved year-long clinical internship (described in detail in Chapter 8), (4) complete additional postdoctoral hours of supervised clinical practice (in most states), and (5) pass a comprehensive examination called the Examination for Professional Practice in Psychology (EPPP), administered by the Association of State and Provincial Psychology Boards (ASPPB). Many states have additional requirements, such as passing a licensing examination that focuses on state mental health laws. After you obtain your license, your state may require that you complete continuing education hours each year to maintain your licensure.

"After I completed a master's in health communication, I was working with the Mind-Body Medical Institute at Harvard Medical School as part of my job in community health promotion. I began working with patients with medical illness exacerbated by their experience of stress. I came upon the first edition of the *Handbook of Health Psychology* and was reading the chapter on Adjustment to Chronic Illness. I had an ah-ha moment! I was meant to be a health psychologist. I had questions I wanted to answer—How does stress get under the skin and affect medical symptoms in chronic illness patients? What can we do to interrupt the negative impact of stress? How are the ways in which we cope with life circumstances conferring risk or benefit to patients? I wanted the training and knowledge to lead research to answer these questions and to sit across from a patient and apply that knowledge. My doctoral training at Arizona State University and my postdoctoral training at UCLA taught me how to integrate the science and practice of health psychology. Nothing was more satisfying than co-authoring the chapter on 'Adjustment to Chronic Illness' in the current edition of the *Handbook of Health Psychology*!"

—Michael Hoyt, Ph.D., Associate Professor, Public Health, University of California, Irvine

"Prior to attending graduate school, I knew I had an unwavering interest in health psychology, but I was unsure of the 'right' program for me. Given this uncertainty, I chose to attend a scientist-practitioner program focused on health psychology in order to keep all of my professional options open. I knew that I had a strong interest in research but also wanted the ability to directly help people through clinical work. After I graduated, I sought a career in an applied research setting. I worked at Memorial Sloan-Kettering Cancer Center (MSKCC) for 17 years, prior to moving to a more traditional academic position at a university, while maintaining a small private practice. During my time at MSKCC, I was fortunate enough to become a successful researcher and clinician. I found that the balance of working on research grants and manuscripts that contributed to the field of health psychology (and more specifically, psycho-oncology) was intellectually rewarding. At the same time, seeing patients in the clinical practice at the hospital fulfilled a different type of professional satisfaction, especially in the short-term, as I was able to help patients and their families cope with cancer. I am incredibly grateful to have had a career that has been so diversified and rewarding".

—Jennifer S. Ford, Ph.D., Professor, Hunter College & the Graduate Center, City University of New York

If I Want to Be a Researcher, Do I Need Clinical Training?

If you are interested in a health psychology research career, you may wonder whether you want or need to obtain clinical training and be eligible for licensure. Clinical training and licensure may help you to lead research projects in which you develop, test and implement individual or group initiatives with a clinical component. Examples of such research would be: adapting cognitive-behavioral therapy for patients following a heart attack to reduce depression; conducting a clinical trial of a stress management program for people who have completed cancer treatment and are now returning to work; or implementing a depression screening process for patients who attend a diabetes clinic.

Clinical licensure also will allow you professional flexibility to establish a clinical practice either within or outside of your job (e.g., as a professor, research scientist). For instance, some clinical health psychology researchers in medical settings devote time at work (such as a day or more per week) to conducting therapy with the same or similar patient populations with whom they conduct research. In fact, by setting up their weekly schedules this way, they can (1) increase their understanding of the challenges that patients face and the gaps in our current strategies to assist them and

(2) develop rapport, trust, and collaboration with the medical teams who care for these patients. Both factors can help you establish a program of meaningful, clinically relevant research.

I Hear I Should Apply Only to Accredited Programs. What Does That Mean?

There is one more factor that will inform your choice of doctoral programs if you have chosen the clinical health psychology route. Like other professions, psychology has a professional association, the APA, which has been the major accreditation body for the profession for over 60 years. Currently, the APA accredits doctoral programs in clinical, counseling, and school psychology, based on the APA Standards of Accreditation in Health Service Psychology.

The accreditation process is voluntary and is designed to make sure that doctoral education meets national standards. Accredited doctoral programs must apply for re-accreditation every three to ten years to maintain their accreditation status. In addition to the APA, the Canadian Psychological Association (CPA) accredits programs at Canadian universities in clinical, counseling, clinical neuropsychology, and school psychology. A third accrediting body is the Psychological Clinical Science Accreditation System (PCSAS). The PCSAS is an independent, non-profit organization that accredits Ph.D. programs that adhere to a clinical science training model. (Recall, this is the model emphasizing the bilateral relationship between conducting research and clinical practice.) Currently, all clinical science programs that have been accredited by the PCSAS also have APA accreditation, although this situation may change in the future.

For prospective students, accreditation by APA, CPA, or PCSAS provides assurance that the program is providing *strong* and *complete* clinical training. In more practical terms, if you are matriculated in an APA, CPA, or PCSAS accredited program, you are allowed to apply to the full range of APA accredited internship opportunities through the Association of Psychology Postdoctoral and Internship Centers (APPIC). Yes, the APA accredits internship sites as well.

Programs that offer clinical training must be upfront about their accreditation status. If it is not clear from their website, ask! If a clinical psychology doctoral program is not accredited yet, it isn't necessarily a "bad" program and might still be an option for you. However, it is important to thoroughly investigate the program. Maybe it is just too new of a program—to be accredited, programs must have graduated at least one doctoral student. However, if a longstanding program is not accredited, use caution when considering whether to apply to the program. The bottom line is that accreditation helps ensure that the program meets the national standards required for many clinical internships, state licensing boards, and future job prospects.

If you do not graduate from an APA accredited program, please be advised that your ability to obtain a license as a clinical (health) psychologist or counseling (health) psychologist will be limited in certain states. You will also have limited access to positions that are designated for candidates who have attended APA accredited programs.

A Preview of What to Expect in Different Types of Programs

In Chapters 5 and 6 we tell you what to expect during your years in a health psychology doctoral program. But it's important to know a little bit here in order to make your decision about which training options are right for you. We present a "typical" course of training for doctoral students in a research-only (Ph.D.) program and clinical (Ph.D. and Psy.D.) programs in Tables 2.1, 2.2, and 2.3.

Coursework

Most Ph.D. programs require 72–90 credit hours; one course is typically 3 credit hours and meets for a total of two to three hours per week, so you will be taking between 24 and 30 courses for your degree. For Psy.D. programs, the credit hour requirement is typically higher, often ranging from 95–120 credit hours. The availability of health psychology courses differs from program to program. Some graduate programs might offer a single health course while others might offer a full array of basic health psychology courses and advanced seminars. A sampling of possible courses includes biopsychosocial mechanisms, health psychology theories of behavior change, psychophysiology, psychoneuroimmunology, and health disparities. In addition to health psychology courses, students can expect to take the usual complement of courses found in graduate programs in psychology that address research methods and statistics, developmental psychology, social psychology, biological bases of behavior, cognition, affect, and ethics. Students in clinical health psychology programs also will be required to take courses that address psychopathology, assessment techniques, and intervention techniques. Specialized clinical health courses, such as health assessment and health interventions, also may be available.

Whew, that's a lot of courses! Coursework provides a strong foundation for the research and clinical work you will do in graduate school and thereafter.

Table 2.1 *Sample Course Schedule: Research-Only Health Psychology Ph.D. Students*

FIRST YEAR

Fall semester
Issues in Professional Development and Research
Behavioral Medicine: Overview of Basic Science, Public Health and Clinical Trials
Psychological Statistics, Research Methods and Design
Social Psychology

Spring semester
Biobehavioral Processes and Disease in Health Psychology
Adult Psychopathology
Multiple Regression and Multivariate Statistics

SECOND YEAR

Fall semester
Cognitive Neuroscience
Biobehavioral Processes and Clinical Research Applications in Health Psychology
Advanced Statistics: Structural Equation Modeling or Hierarchical Linear Modeling

Spring semester
Cognition and Emotion
Diversity Issues in Psychology
Master's Thesis Research

Summer
Master's Thesis

THIRD YEAR

Fall semester
Neuroanatomy
Scientific Writing and Grantsmanship
Teaching Requirement (if applicable)

Spring semester
Developmental Psychology
Psychopharmacology
Health Psychology Elective

Summer
Qualifying Examination

FOURTH YEAR

Fall semester
Dissertation Research

Spring semester
Dissertation Research

This sample curriculum for research-only health psychology Ph.D. students was used with permission from Philip McCabe, Chair, University of Miami Department of Psychology. It was adapted from www.psy.miami.edu/_assets/pdf/grad-handbooks/2018_graduate_student_handbook.pdf

Table 2.2 Sample Course Schedule: Clinical Health Psychology Ph.D. Students

FIRST YEAR

Fall semester

Issues in Professional Development and Research
Behavioral Medicine: Overview of Basic Science, Public Health and Clinical Trials
Psychological Statistics, Research Methods and Design
Adult Psychopathology (plus lab)
Introduction to Psychological Evaluation (plus lab)

Summer

Practicum in Clinical Psychology in the Department Clinic

SECOND YEAR

Fall semester

Cognitive Neuroscience
Biobehavioral Processes and Clinical Research Applications in Health Psychology
Advanced Statistics: Structural Equation Modeling or Hierarchical Linear Modeling
Practicum in Clinical Psychology in the Department Clinic

Summer

Practicum in Clinical Psychology in the Department Clinic

THIRD YEAR

Fall semester

Health Psychology Interventions
Scientific Writing and Grantsmanship
Master's Thesis
Practicum in Clinical Psychology in a Medical Setting

Summer

Practicum in Clinical Psychology in a Medical Setting
Qualifying Examination

Spring semester

Biobehavioral Processes and Disease in Health Psychology
Introduction to Evidence-Based Psychological Treatments
Multiple Regression and Multivariate Statistics
Introduction to Psychotherapy Ethics and Professional Issues

Spring semester

Psychological Evaluation in Physical Disorders
Diversity Issues in Psychology
Master's Thesis Research
Practicum in Clinical Psychology in the Department Clinic

Spring semester

Cognition and Emotion
Teaching requirement (if applicable)
Health Psychology Elective
Practicum in Clinical Psychology in a Medical Setting

(Continued)

Table 2.2 (Continued)

FOURTH YEAR

Fall semester	Spring semester
Social Psychology	Developmental Psychology
Health Psychology Elective	Health Psychology Elective
Dissertation Research	Dissertation Research
Practicum in Clinical Psychology in a Medical Setting	Practicum in Clinical Psychology in a Medical Setting

FIFTH YEAR

Fall semester	Spring semester
Dissertation Research	Dissertation Research

SIXTH YEAR

Clinical Internship

This sample curriculum for clinical health psychology Ph.D. students was used with permission from Philip McCabe, Chair, University of Miami Department of Psychology. It was adapted from the 2018 graduate handbook: www.psy.miami.edu/_assets/pdf/grad-handbooks/2018_graduate_student_handbook.pdf

Table 2.3 Sample Course Schedule: Clinical Health Psychology Psy.D. Students

FIRST YEAR

Fall semester
Adult Psychopathology
Developmental: Child & Adolescent
Developmental: Adult & Older Adult
Ethics and Professional Issues
Ethics and Legal Issues
Assessment: Intelligence Testing (plus lab)
Systems of Psychotherapy
Diversity in Assessment & Intervention

Summer
Cognitive/Affective Aspects of Behavior
Health Psychology

SECOND YEAR

Fall semester
Objective Personality Assessment
Systems/Family Therapy
Child & Adolescent Intervention
Clinical Practicum I
Supervision of Clinical Practicum I
Research Design
Theories of Measurement

Summer
Psychopharmacology
Summer Clinical Practicum I
Summer Supervision of Clinical Practicum I

Winter semester
History & Systems of Psychology
Child & Adolescent Psychopathology
Diagnostic Interviewing
Adult Intervention I
Intermediate Statistics (plus lab)
Pre-Practicum

Winter semester
Projective Personality Assessment
Behavioral Assessment
Case Conceptualization
Clinical Practicum II
Supervision of Clinical Practicum II
Biological Bases of Behavior

(Continued)

Table 2.3 (Continued)

THIRD YEAR

Fall semester
Anatomy & Physiology
Clinical Practicum III
Supervision of Clinical Practicum III
Directed Study: Research
Group Theory/Processes
Integrated Report

Summer
Summer Clinical Practicum II
Summer Supervision of Clinical Practicum II

Winter semester
Assessment in Health Psychology
Clinical Practicum IV
Supervision IV
Directed Study: Research
Social Aspects of Behavior

FOURTH YEAR

Fall semester
Clinical Competency Exam
Advanced Professional Development
Chronic Pain/Illness Management

Winter semester
Consultation & Supervision
Interventions with Medical Patients

FIFTH YEAR
Clinical Internship

This sample curriculum for clinical health psychology Psy.D. students was used with permission from John Lewis, Chair, Department of Clinical and School Psychology at Nova Southeastern University College of Psychology. It was adapted from the College of Psychology Psy.D. Program in Clinical Psychology Handbook (https://psychology.nova.edu/graduate/clinical-psychology/forms/forms/psyd-handbook-1819.pdf [psychology.nova.edu].

Research Training

In addition to courses about how to conduct research, hands-on research training is a central feature of all health psychology Ph.D. programs. Programs often expect students to be engaged in research pursuits for a minimum of 15 hours per week throughout graduate training. (This is one of the reasons that strong applicants to Ph.D. programs have research experience; we'll talk about this more in Chapters 3 and 4.)

Typically, to receive a Ph.D. in psychology, students must complete two major research projects successfully: the master's thesis, sometimes called an "independent" research project, often completed by the end of the second year or the beginning of the third year of graduate school; and the dissertation, a larger and more intensive research project than the master's thesis, which is often one of the final requirements to be completed before obtaining your doctoral degree. Health psychology doctoral students work with their advisors to choose health-related topics for these projects. Topic choices depend on student and mentor interests and mentor's access to relevant participant populations and existing datasets. Research topics may focus on a range of issues across the health spectrum, from health risk or health promotion in healthy community samples to illness progression or control in medical patients and their families. Projects also may rely on basic or applied research techniques (or a combination of both) and may involve input from other health disciplines such as immunology, cardiology, neurology, and public health. Table 2.4 provides a sampling of dissertation titles of recent health psychology graduate students. (And yes, dissertation titles tend to be long!)

It is important for you to know that Psy.D. programs place less emphasis on having had training in research when you apply. Although Psy.D. program research requirements can vary, students in those programs will not have the large research demands described here. Many will, however, be required to complete an applied dissertation or capstone project. The research emphasis in Psy.D. programs is to train students to become practitioners who are savvy consumers of research and whose work is informed by science.

Clinical Training

For students in health clinical or counseling programs, including those in Psy.D. programs, clinical training—always with supervision—begins during the students' first or second year. This usually includes a 10- to 15-hour weekly commitment in Ph.D. programs and a 20- to 25-hour weekly commitment in Psy.D. programs. Clinical training can take many forms. Some programs start students in clinical practica, where they are working under supervision in the university's counseling center

Table 2.4 Dissertation Titles of Recent Health Psychology Graduates

- Psychosocial reserve capacity as moderator of the relationship between chronic stress and cardiovascular health: Results from the Multi-Ethnic Study of Atherosclerosis
- Effects of psychological and structural-level factors on sexual risk and STI incidence in high-risk men who have sex with men
- Distress tolerance, anxiety, and survival in people living with HIV
- Sleep duration, postprandial metabolic function, and the role of insulin resistance in nondiabetic individuals
- Cognitive behavioral stress management effects on social well-being, negative affect, and inflammation after surgery for breast cancer
- The trajectory of sedentary behavior from adolescence to emerging adulthood
- Defining abdominal obesity as a risk factor for coronary heart disease in the US Hispanic Community Health Study/Study of Latinos
- Dyadic study of depression on inflammation and diurnal cortisol variation in cancer patients and caregivers
- Effects of telephone-delivered cognitive behavioral stress management intervention on fatigue interference and neuroimmune function in chronic fatigue syndrome
- Examining weight gain in treatment seeking African-American smokers: A biopsychosocial approach
- Brief psychosocial intervention effects on benefit finding among women with breast cancer and the roles of distress and ethnicity
- Are socioeconomic status, school environment, body mass index, and blood pressure related in an ethnically diverse sample of adolescents? A multilevel approach
- Rewriting the past: The influence of written emotional expression on psychosocial outcomes, physical symptoms, medication adherence, CD4 cell count, and viral load in HIV
- The effects of telephone-delivered cognitive behavioral stress management on inflammation and symptoms in myalgic encephalomyelitis/chronic fatigue syndrome: A computational immunology approach
- The relationship among adiponectin isoforms, brain morphology, and cognition
- Psychological predictors of survival and disease recurrence in women with breast cancer following cognitive-behavioral stress management
- The effects of meditation on cardiovascular recovery from acute stress
- Diurnal cortisol profiles of stress and hardiness in sexual minority young adults
- Using multimedia blood donation education materials to enhance individual readiness to donate blood and increase donation behaviors
- Pain modulation in tension-type headache: The offset analgesia effect
- An examination of the direct and indirect effects of feedback type on cortisol levels
- A test of the Perseverative Cognition Hypothesis using hair cortisol in a sample of dementia caregivers and non-caregiver controls
- Ways of thinking about illness representations of cancer
- The under-explored role of tiredness in alcohol use and sexual risk-taking among gay and bisexual men.
- Latino/a adolescents and young adults coping with parental cancer within a cultural context
- Intra- and inter-personal factors predicting distress and end-of-life planning among individuals with advanced cancers
- Relational processes in support related communication among young adults with cancer

Titles provided by Philip McCabe, Chair, University of Miami Department of Psychology, Tracey A. Revenson, Director of Research Training, Health Psychology & Clinical Science, The Graduate Center, City University of New York, and Peggy M. Zoccola, Department of Psychology, Ohio University or the psychology department's training clinic. With assessment and intervention courses and some practicum experience under their belt, students then move on to health-related *externships* outside the university. For clinical health psychology students, externships often take place at medical centers, hospitals, or clinics. Externship placement is typically coordinated by your graduate program and information about existing placements can often be found on the program websites. As we have indicated previously, clinical health psychology training culminates in the completion of a full-time, one-year clinical internship. Some internships are labeled as behavioral medicine ("BMed") internships, which are ideal for health psychology students. We will describe the internship application process in detail in Chapter 8.

"I completed an elective health psychology concentration while working toward a Psy.D., which introduced me to foundational coursework specific to the practice of clinical health psychology, such as anatomy and physiology for non-physicians, psychotherapy for persons living with HIV/AIDS, and interventions for persons with chronic pain and sleep difficulties. There was a course on working with a multidisciplinary team, which allowed me to learn in the classroom, as well as participation in rounds on the psychiatric-consultation and liaison service. The health psychology concentration also offered supervised practicum opportunities in medical settings, so I completed my second practicum at a large medical center. During this practicum, I taught classes in the wellness center, worked with patients in the cardiac rehabilitation program, and participated in consultation/liaison services across many specialty areas in the hospital".

—Carla M. York, Psy.D., A.B.P.P., D.B.S.M. (Board certified in
Clinical Health Psychology, Diplomate, Behavioral Sleep Medicine)
Clinical Health Psychologist, Walter Reed National Military Medical Center

Can I Receive Health Psychology Training After I Receive My Doctoral Degree?

Not all training in health psychology occurs at the graduate level. Research and clinical training in health psychology can also occur after one receives a doctoral degree. For example, postdoctoral training in health psychology might be pursued by an individual who had little or no opportunity for health psychology during graduate school or by the individual who wants to further hone their health psychology competencies and credentials. We describe postdoctoral training in more detail in Chapter 9.

Moving Ahead . . .

We've presented a lot of options here. It is probably worth taking some time to think deeply about what type of career and program appeals to you before moving to the next step: choosing a set of programs that you want to apply to. Think not only about what you want to do on a day-to-day basis that will give you satisfaction but also be aware that there will be unexpected experiences in graduate school that will pull you in unforeseen situations.

References

Morgan, R. D., & Cohen, L. M. (2008). Clinical and counseling psychology: Can differences be gleaned from printed recruiting materials? *Training and Education in Professional Psychology*, 2(3), 156–164. https://doi.org/10.1037/1931–3918.2.3.156

Nicholas, D. R., & Stern, M. (2011). Counseling psychology in clinical health psychology: The impact of specialty perspective. *Professional Psychology: Research and Practice*, 42(4), 331–337. https://doi.org/10.1037/a0024197

Routh, D. K. (2015). Training models in clinical psychology. In R. L. Cautin & S. O. Lilienfeld (Eds.), *The encyclopedia of clinical psychology*. New York, NY: Wiley & Sons. https://doi.org/10.1002/9781118625392.wbecp061

3

PREPARING FOR GRADUATE SCHOOL IN HEALTH PSYCHOLOGY

Introduction

Now that you've decided a graduate degree in health psychology is the next step for you, it's time to determine which graduate programs will meet your health psychology training needs and interests and whether you have the qualifications to be viewed as a competitive applicant by the graduate programs of your choice.

You might be wondering about *who* makes the decision to admit you to a program. The admissions committee is made up of faculty members. In many programs, each application will be read and rated initially by two to three members of the admissions committee and then those that are reviewed favorably will be examined in more depth. Because some programs receive hundreds of applications, cutoff scores for graduate record examinations (GREs) or grade point averages (GPAs) may be used to create a smaller set of applications that are reviewed.

In many departments, graduate students are often involved in the admissions process, providing information about the program to prospective applicants, interviewing applicants, and in some cases, hosting applicants at their homes during interview visits. Students often do not review applications because of ethical guidelines, and graduate programs vary with respect to whether students can vote or simply provide recommendations to faculty.

One early piece of advice: As most university admissions offices now use software for "sorting" the applications, be sure that your application is complete well before the deadline. Many applications aren't reviewed by the admissions committee simply because they are missing essential elements such as GRE scores, letters of recommendation, or the personal statement.

Before You Apply

What are the qualifications for admission? Many factors go into the equation. Nearly all programs' admissions requirements include both quantitative criteria (course grades, standardized test stores) and qualitative criteria (research experience, relevant clinical work or public service, letters of recommendation, and application essays). Although these criteria domains can be considered universal, the importance of each of the qualifications and how a particular admissions committee will balance them may vary by type of graduate program and even by the faculty members reviewing them.

In Chapter 2, we described several types of graduate programs/degrees that are suitable for pursuing a career in health psychology. Doctoral programs, particularly Ph.D. programs that offer financial support, are highly selective and competition for limited spots can be fierce. As such, successful applicants are those with outstanding quantitative criteria (GRE and GPA) as well as robust research skills and experiences.

We want to emphasize that it's important to talk with faculty members or others in the profession about your career goals and get feedback *at all points* of the application process. These individuals can help you decide where to apply for graduate school, whether now is the right time, and provide advice on how to craft your application. If you are still in college, your academic advisor may be the best person to approach—as long as your advisor knows your skills and interests well. If you are working in a lab, you should talk with the faculty member who runs it. You should also contact other faculty in the department with whom you've taken courses (and done well!) to see what advice they have for you. Peer mentors, such as graduate students, are also good to talk with as they recently have been through the process successfully. Many psychology departments have staff or student advisors who can also assist you, but they may not be familiar with health psychology programs. Thus, they may be less helpful for selecting training paths and programs than someone more familiar with health psychology, although they may be able to offer help with writing the personal statement.

If you have already completed your undergraduate education and are working in a research setting, talk with the senior research staff or postdoctoral fellows. This is a good way to learn what it's like to work in the field, get advice on how to be a strong candidate, know which programs are out there, and understand what graduate program characteristics to be looking for.

Later on in the decision process, you also can contact graduate students in the programs you are interested in. Some programs have a student representative designated for just that purpose. Students are often listed on the program's website or the mentor's lab website with their interests and emails. Regardless of whom you reach out to for advice, have specific questions ready and be prepared to talk about your interests and qualifications. Ask for a brief phone conversation and have your questions ready! Don't start with "Tell me about your program". Ask about the types of research and clinical experiences that the program currently offers, whether students teach or TA courses, how well the courses jibe with the research and clinical experiences. (And when you are a graduate student, you will pass it forward and mentor others!)

To help you choose the right program in health psychology, we want to tell you a bit about the criteria that most graduate programs use to evaluate applicants. Not every program uses the same criteria, but the ones included in this book are fairly standard and will help you evaluate whether you are a competitive applicant for graduate school in that department.

What Is Required to Be a Successful Applicant?

To better understand what types of scores, skills, and experience you need to be competitive for graduate programs in health psychology, it's useful to look at the stated criteria of the programs you are interested in. Most programs spell out what they are looking for on their website. But of course, first, you have to figure out which program websites to review!

A good place to start your search is the *Graduate Study in Psychology* (APA, 2018). This American Psychological Association (APA) online database (http://gradstudy. apa.org) is published annually in August (the three-month cost for online access was $19.95 for the August 2019 edition) and is also available in print. It is possible that your psychology department or university library has an online subscription or copy of the book, so check there first. *Graduate Study in Psychology* contains information on approximately 600 graduate programs in the United States and Canada. Although it is an extensive repository, the current guide represents data from two or more years earlier and it may not contain information on new programs. Nonetheless, it is a very useful place to start in building your list. Among the details included are program descriptions, degrees offered, admission requirements, application information, tuition, fees, financial aid, accreditation status, and contact information.

Once you have access to *Graduate Study in Psychology*, begin a search for graduate programs in health psychology. For some graduate programs, the name "health psychology" will be contained within the degree title (e.g., Ph.D. in health psychology). For others, the degree may be broader (e.g., Ph.D. in experimental/general, social, industrial/organizational, and clinical psychology) with an area of emphasis or specialty in health psychology (e.g., Psy.D. in clinical psychology with health psychology or behavioral medicine emphasis). A quick search for health psychology as an "area of emphasis" (any degree type) will lead to a list of results containing more than 50 institutions. From here, you can narrow your search, browse, and even compare programs on specific criteria.

After you identify potential health psychology programs in the *Graduate Study in Psychology*, be sure to follow up on the guide's information at the program websites. Many program websites provide summary information on prior admission cycles, including the number of applicants that applied, acceptance rates, and average GRE scores of applicants and accepted students. We often suggest that you limit your reviewing to one to two program websites per day, as they may start to blur into each other—and remember to record the information into a spreadsheet or notebook!

For each listing in *Graduate Study in Psychology*, you will also find the program's admission requirements and level of importance (low, medium, high) placed on each of nine criteria (GPA, GRE scores, research experience, work experience, clinically related public service, letters of recommendation, interview, statement of goals, and undergraduate psychology preparation). We leave you to examine your specific schools of interest but will discuss the criteria more broadly here.

A recent survey of more than 500 graduate programs in psychology (not only those with emphases in health psychology) conducted by the APA reveals some important trends regarding importance of the various admission criteria (Michalski, Cope, & Fowler, 2016). Consistently rated by all programs as the *most important* criteria are (1) applicant interviews; (2) statement of goals and objectives; and (3) letters of recommendation. Surprisingly, undergraduate preparation in psychology (i.e., coursework in psychology, having a bachelor's degree in psychology) was rated the lowest; however, it was still of medium importance, so don't write it off. There was more variation in importance ratings of the other criteria. For instance, professional schools in psychology, which typically offer Psy.D. degrees, rated clinically related work experience and public service as more important than programs that offer Ph.D. degrees. Among university-based programs (i.e., those within academic departments of psychology, and not in a medical or professional school), research experience, GRE scores, and undergraduate GPA were all rated at very high importance. These three criteria are of special significance to you as many graduate programs in health psychology are found within university-based departments. Table 3.1 provides a list

Table 3.1 *Admissions Criteria for Doctoral Programs in Health Psychology*

Quantitative criteria	Qualitative criteria
GPA (from transcripts)	Coursework (from transcripts)
Standardized Test Scores	Research Experience
GRE General Test Quantitative Reasoning	Other Relevant Experience (work, clinically related public service)
Verbal Reasoning	Statement of Goals and Objectives
Analytical Writing	Letters of Recommendation
GRE Subject Test (Psychology)	Interview

of quantitative and qualitative criteria for admission to graduate programs in health psychology. Each criterion is discussed in greater detail in the next sections.

Quantitative Criteria

Grade Point Average (GPA)

Your undergraduate GPA serves as an index of your academic performance and may help to demonstrate your potential for academic success in graduate school. Many master's degree programs require a minimum GPA of 3.0 or higher and many doctoral programs require even higher minimum GPAs. If your GPA is currently lower than the program minimum of a school you are interested in, it is probably not worth the time or money to apply to that school. Realistically, a low GPA would need to be compensated for by other factors such as stellar standardized test scores or considerable research or clinical experience.

In addition to the cumulative GPA, some admissions committees use other indicators such as psychology GPA, or GPA over the last two years, as evidence of potential performance in a psychology graduate program. Others may look for patterns of performance in your transcripts. For example, perhaps you had a tough time transitioning to college in your first year and your grades reflect it. If you were able to turn things around and maintain higher grades in subsequent years, a relatively lower overall GPA may not have as much of a negative impact on your application. It is worthwhile to explain this briefly in your personal statement or ask one of the faculty who are writing you letters of recommendation to address it. On the other hand, if you have a record of taking rigorous courses, admissions committee members may be less concerned about your overall GPA.

What should you do if your GPA is lower than optimal? You might be able to retake some courses to improve grades. This may be good to do for important courses such as statistics or research design. However, those earlier low grades will still appear on your transcript. In this case, your best bet might be to enroll in a master's program to show you can handle graduate level work and wait a year or two to apply to doctoral programs.

Standardized Test Scores

The GRE General Test

The GRE General Test (www.ets.org/gre) is designed to reflect the types of skills needed to succeed in graduate school: verbal reasoning, quantitative reasoning, and analytical writing. Faculty at graduate programs in health psychology, particularly Ph.D. programs, want to be sure that their incoming students have strong writing and analytical skills, so they take GRE scores quite seriously. So should you. The GRE is taken by prospective graduate school applicants worldwide and year-round. The computer-delivered format of the exam lasts about 3 hours and 45 minutes and is divided into six sections with a ten-minute break between the third and fourth sections. We suggest you start preparing for the GRE at least three to six months before you plan to take it. Take advantage of the free test preparation materials and practice tests provided by the Educational Testing Service (ETS; Princeton, New Jersey), the organization that administers the GRE. You can also purchase additional preparation materials from ETS and other organizations or enroll in GRE preparation courses for more guidance and instructions.

> "Test prep can be expensive. I found the most helpful thing to prepare for the GRE was doing practice problems over and over again. A less expensive way of preparing is to purchase a book or app containing practice problems. But you have to be motivated to do them".
> —Mariah Xu, B.A., Graduate Student, Hunter College

The range of scores for the Verbal and Quantitative Reasoning sections of the GRE is 130–170 (in increments of 1 point). The Analytic Writing score can range from 0–6 (in increments of 0.5 points). As you could have guessed, for all sections, higher scores are better. Average GRE scores for applicants admitted to graduate programs in psychology are typically higher for Ph.D. programs than master's degree programs. In addition to raw scores, your GRE performance will also be ranked with a percentile score relative to other test takers in recent years. For example, if you took the test in the spring of 2018, a score of 160 for Verbal Reasoning would put you at the 86th percentile and a score of 160 for Quantitative Reasoning would put you at the 73rd percentile (Educational Testing Services (ETS), 2019a). A score of 4.5 on Analytic Writing would place you at the 81st percentile. Percentiles help you understand where you rank relative to other test takers.

Because of the large number of applications they receive, many doctoral programs may not consider applicants who have low GRE scores. In other cases, graduate program admissions committees may focus their review on a subset of applicants, such as those who scored above the median. (As you should know from your statistics course, this means GRE scores in the top 50% of all applicants.) While most programs do not report their minimum or "cutoff" GRE scores for applicants, APA-approved programs are required to post data for admitted students on their website. These data include the mean, median, and percentile for the GRE (verbal, quantitative, and writing) and the mean GPA, if those data are considered in the selection process. As a clinical applicant, you should pay close attention to the scores for the schools to which you are applying so that you can see how your scores compare. Students applying to research-only programs can only use the clinical program data as an approximation.

What should you do if your GRE scores are lower than optimal to apply to the programs of your choice? If you earned a noncompetitive GRE score, you should carefully weigh how to best overcome it. It may be possible to improve a GRE score or compensate for it in another way.

Let's first consider retaking the exam. Currently, you can retake the computer-based GRE test once every 21 days. But just because you *can* retake it, doesn't mean you *should*. If you already spent many hours studying and practicing for the GRE exam, it is unlikely that you will be able to make substantial improvements in your score by simply taking it again. Indeed, multiple mediocre scores may hurt chances of admission to competitive programs. Why? Measurement error. (Again, you should know what this is from your statistics course.) If you do nothing to increase your knowledge between administrations, your score is not likely to improve in a meaningful way and may even be lower. However, if you didn't study at all for the GRE the first time you took it but took a GRE course before the second time, your score may meaningfully jump upwards as you have acquired new knowledge. Unless you make a different selection, your previous GRE scores are sent to schools that you have applied to along with your current scores. This used to be the only option, but now there is the option of "Score Select" (see Appendix) in which you may choose any of your scores to send (and only those scores). However, this costs a little bit more.

Let's be real—everyone's time is limited. Whether you are a busy undergraduate student or working a full-time job, you have to consider what is the best use of your time. Should you keep studying and practicing to retake the GRE or should you use your time to pursue other opportunities that may benefit your application in other ways, such as working on a research study, contributing to a manuscript for publication, or preparing a research abstract to present at a local, regional, or national conference? Unless your GRE score is below the mean or median for a particular school of interest, the decision can be a toss-up, and you may benefit from consulting with someone like your faculty advisor regarding the overall balance of strengths and weaknesses in your application.

It may also be possible to compensate for low GRE scores by demonstrating excellence in other related areas of your application. For example, earning grades of A and A+ in advanced undergraduate or masters-level statistics courses or showing evidence that you are able to perform statistical analyses (such as what might be found in a thesis document or first-authored manuscript) may help offset a relatively low Quantitative GRE score. Similarly, well-written manuscripts that you took the lead on and a high Analytical Writing GRE score may lessen the negative impact of a relatively low Verbal GRE score.

The GRE Subject Test

Besides the GRE General Test, some graduate programs in health psychology require the GRE Subject Test in psychology (www.ets.org/gre/subject/about/content/psychology). This exam contains approximately 205 multiple-choice questions and is administered over the course of 2 hours and 50 minutes in a paper-and-pencil format. The range of scores is from 200 to 990 (in increments of 10 points). The mean overall score in psychology was 618 for test takers between July 1, 2015, and June 30, 2018 (Educational Testing Services (ETS), 2019b).

In addition to an overall score, six subscores are calculated for the following content areas: biological, cognitive, social, developmental, clinical, and measurement, methodology, and other. As with the GRE General Test, you also receive percentile ranked scores. The Psychology Subject Test is offered three times a year (April, September, and October), so you must plan ahead to determine if you will need to take the test and study for it. General ways to prepare include completing psychology courses, reviewing class materials, and taking (timed) practice tests. One of the book's authors was told by her advisor to prepare by sitting down and reading a current introductory psychology textbook cover to cover, as most undergraduates (even psychology majors) haven't taken courses in every area of psychology. (Most psychology departments and some professors will have copies available to borrow.) Be sure to check the websites of the programs you are planning to apply to, as many do not require the GRE subject test.

Qualitative Criteria

Coursework

If you have already obtained or are currently pursuing a bachelor's degree in psychology, you should be in good shape in terms of taking the relevant courses in preparation for graduate school in health psychology. Most undergraduate psychology programs require their majors to take courses in statistics, research design or methodology, abnormal psychology, developmental psychology, cognitive psychology, social psychology, and physiological or biological psychology. If your institution offers a course in health psychology, take it! That is one way to demonstrate to admissions committees that you know what the field of health psychology involves. Having completed courses in human anatomy, physiology, or genetics may be an asset to some programs in health psychology. Other programs value courses in social sciences and cultural diversity, as well as courses in other related fields: public health, medical anthropology, and medical sociology. Health psychologists often work with individuals from other fields, so becoming familiar with concepts and terms from related disciplines can show your interdisciplinary nature.

If you have already graduated from college and didn't take foundational classes, you will probably need to for admission to a doctoral program. If you are working in an academic medical setting as a research assistant, you may have access to free seminars and workshops at your institution on topics such as biostatistics, genetics, grant writing, or research ethics. Take advantage of these resources.

We are often asked whether having a master's degree in psychology confers an advantage when applying to doctoral programs. As you know, we addressed this in detail in Chapter 1 so will not repeat it here.

Research Experience

As soon as you think a career in the field of health psychology is right for you, get involved in research. Let's say it again: As soon as you think a career in the field of health psychology is right for you, get involved in research. Research training and experience is a foundational component of your undergraduate education and is a necessity for most doctoral graduate programs. Why? Research experience shows potential advisors that you are curious and have a drive to be an independent learner. The more experience you have before graduate school, the more independent you can be and the more skills you offer.

There are many benefits to assisting in research—especially when you start in your sophomore or junior year. First, involvement in a research project can help you identify or refine your interests. For example, let's say you join a research team that is dedicated to improving adherence to treatment in adolescents with Type I diabetes. Although you were initially unfamiliar with the topic, you become engaged in the subject matter and decide that it is a passion you wish to pursue. Alternatively, because of a personal experience in your family, you decide to join a research team that is studying how families cope with cancer. After a short time, you realize that the topic isn't actually the best match for you. You wanted to learn the best ways to cope—but you really aren't interested in doing research in the area. Learning what fits *and what doesn't fit* are both valuable experiences. It's not wasted time. And regardless of fit, you can still gain valuable research experience and hone your skills.

Second, working in a research lab gives you the opportunity to get to know a faculty member well. This is advantageous because a faculty member who knows you well will be able to write you a stronger letter of recommendation in the future. Moreover, as part of a research project, you have the opportunity to obtain mentorship from faculty and graduate students.

You might also be wondering what kind of research experience you should seek out. If you wish to pursue graduate training in health psychology, we recommend that you get research experience in health psychology or in another health-related field. If those research opportunities aren't available, research in other areas of psychology are valuable as well. Regardless of the topic area, you'll gain in-depth knowledge and obtain first-hand experience in conducting research, which is valuable for graduate training.

Not all research experiences are equal. In some laboratories, your responsibilities may start out at a lower level—coding or entering data, or transcribing interviews. (Note that research experience is not defined as spending most of your time at the copy machine or printing our papers, although that may be a bit of what you do.) As you gain experience and demonstrate your skills, you are likely to be offered more advanced opportunities.

Some students ask us where it is better to work in several different labs or to stay in one lab. Staying in one lab—particularly if it is a health psychology lab—is advantageous for two reasons: It provides you with a deeper research experience, and it allows for a more detailed letter of recommendation. Many lab directors and faculty members start new research assistants with lower-skill tasks, but once you have mastered them you progress to research tasks that require more responsibility or sophisticated skills. Often undergraduate research assistants will advance to the position of project director or lead research assistant by senior year and some even stay for a post-baccalaureate year to become the lab manager.

If you are not getting progressively more advanced research opportunities in one lab, speak with your research supervisor about this. If it is not going to happen, or if your interests have changed (which is the purpose of getting research experience), then you might consider a different lab. One of author Lara Traeger's students was interested in health neuroscience, but the department did not have faculty members with that expertise. The student gained relevant experience by assisting two different projects—a health psychology project and a neuroscience project at the medical school. These experiences made her competitive for a research opportunity in a lab at another university and ultimately graduate school.

There are multiple ways to find research opportunities. If you are currently an undergraduate student, look to faculty members in the psychology department to see if you can volunteer or get course credit as a research assistant. A good start is to talk with a faculty member with whom you took a course (and liked! and did well in the course!) to see if they have space in their lab. Even if a faculty member does not have a slot available now, they might the following semester, so keep checking back. And in some departments, psychology majors can get course credit for this research experience. Ask.

If you have already graduated or are about to, you could look for paid research assistant or coordinator positions. Admissions committees see taking a "gap year" or two to gain research experience as a positive, not a negative. In fact, it's harder and harder to go straight from undergraduate school to doctoral training in health psychology. Experience (of the right kind) is valued!

Where should you look? Research assistant or research coordinator jobs may be found at nearby universities, hospitals, or other health or research institutes. Many such positions last one to two years and are tied to ongoing health-related research funding at hospitals or medical or academic centers. For example, you might be asked to work on a clinical trial with study participants who have a particular medical condition (e.g., pediatric cancer, traumatic brain injury, inflammatory bowel disease) and assist with recruiting and screening participants, collecting data in laboratory or field settings, coding and managing data, and assisting with manuscript and grant submissions. If no paid opportunities are available, consider volunteering. Some faculty members conducting research would be happy to have you help with their project even on a part-time basis.

You might be wondering, "How much research experience do I need?" Our honest answer is *at least* a year of experience prior to applying to Ph.D. programs, and ideally more than one year. You need less research experience for Psy.D. or master's degrees. We recommend at least a year because it can take quite a bit of time to see a research project through from start to finish, to come up with a "do-able" research question, and to develop advanced research skills.

"Do as much research as you can. My research experience prior to graduate school allowed me to identify areas of interest and formulate research questions that I could knowledgably and passionately reference in my application and interviews. Additionally, in the process of reading published research, I noticed several institutions and scholars that frequently published in areas of interest to me and used this information to decide where to apply and who to choose as a mentor".

—Raymond L. Moody, M.A., Doctoral Candidate,
The Graduate Center, City University of New York

If you are still an undergraduate student and have been working in a psychology faculty member's lab for some time, consider completing an independent study or thesis (sometimes referred to as a senior thesis or honors thesis) under the faculty member's guidance. Completing a thesis demonstrates initiative and can lead to greater development of skills that are particularly relevant to graduate training (e.g., designing studies, analyzing, interpreting, and writing up results). Many of our students have worked with us to turn the thesis into a published manuscript—another indication of your potential as a health psychologist! But remember, you can't decide to do a thesis your last year of college; instead, start working in a lab during your sophomore or junior years to gain basic skills, and work with your advisor to design a study, or use some of their existing data (known as a secondary analysis). Advisors won't agree to an undergraduate thesis if it can't be completed by the time of graduation.

As part of your research experience, look for different opportunities to develop scientific writing and analytic skills. For example, you could present research findings at a conference along with other members of the research lab. There are often opportunities to present your work at local or regional conferences, or at national conferences (more about this in Chapter 7). Presenting your research demonstrates you have strong skills in communicating your research findings to others as well as analyzing and interpreting data. It provides a great opportunity to meet and network with health psychologists, including those that you may want to work with in graduate school. We have all met some of our doctoral students at conferences, where they introduced themselves to us at poster sessions or after talks.

Another way to gain research experience is to apply for summer research programs, either at your institution or nationally. Although most summer programs do not focus on health psychology, they emphasize research methods or statistical skills. These experiences will show admissions committees that you have a strong background in these areas and are not afraid to tackle them. For example, each year APA offers Summer Undergraduate Psychology Research Experience (SUPRE) grants to (different) universities to provide paid research assistantships in psychological science to undergraduate students who have little to no research experience. These summer assistantships last for eight weeks and are typically announced by the APA in the early spring on their website (www.apa.org/about/awards/undergraduate-research-opportunity.aspx). Links to additional undergraduate research opportunities and internships can be found in the Appendix.

Clinical Experience

If you are applying to a clinical health psychology program, you may want to have some clinical-like experiences. For ethical reasons, undergraduates and community members cannot gain extensive clinical experience because they have not had the appropriate training. To varying degrees, admissions committees for clinical health psychology programs will evaluate your clinically related public service experiences. The Psy.D. programs may weigh this type of experience more heavily than extensive research experience. For example, these experiences can be paid or volunteer work in a human service agency or a university-based community outreach program. For undergraduates, these experiences are often conducted as a clinical internship or practicum course.

Most clinical experiences available to undergraduates and master's students are not specific to health psychology. They might include serving as a college peer tutor or counselor, answering crisis hotlines, interning at summer camps for those with disability or mental illness, or volunteering at community mental health centers, substance abuse prevention programs, or hospital child-life programs. You can be creative about finding service experiences that are related to health psychology, such as volunteering on an HIV education hotline or support center, serving as a health ambassador to grade schools as part of a health promotion initiative, doing sexual risk reduction counseling, assisting lifestyle groups (e.g., nutrition, physical activity) at a local community center, or volunteering at a hospice.

These experiences can help to illustrate a variety of personal and professional skills that are valuable in graduate school and beyond. Some experiences demonstrate your ability to work as a team or to work with particular populations that are under stress or ill. Working in medical settings, particularly for applicants who are interested in clinical health psychology, is a particularly valuable experience. You can gain face-to-face experience working with patients, families, and clinicians. These kinds of experiences enrich your understanding of your population of interest, and for people who work with seriously medically impaired patients, these experiences help to demonstrate that you have the social maturity, stamina, commitment, and clinical potential for this kind of work.

Other Relevant Experiences and Skills

You may have other work or volunteer experiences that are not directly relevant to your graduate school interests (e.g., food service or retail work; babysitting, participation in sports; other extracurricular activities). When providing information about work and volunteer experience, stay focused on those experiences that are *most relevant* and explain how they relate to the graduate training you seek. For example, do these experiences highlight your academic or personal skills?

> "I think the most important skills people can bring with them to a psychology Ph.D. program are communication skills—both formal and informal. Writing and verbal communication are important in formal contexts like theses and research presentations, but both are also essential for communicating with your advisor, other professors, and collaborators. If this is not your strength yet, I suggest entering graduate school with an open mind and willingness to learn how to improve!"
>
> —Megan Robbins, Ph.D., Assistant Professor of Psychology, University of California, Riverside

Creating a Narrative

When describing your various experiences in your curriculum vitae (described later in this chapter) or your personal statement (described in the next chapter), you will need to find a way to knit them all together. That is, you need to make a coherent narrative, even if your path to health psychology might seem inconsistent or circuitous. For instance, showing experience on a school newspaper could be used to show writing skills, whereas experience on a varsity team can be used to show that you are good at time management given the demands of the sport on your time. Or you may have been a nurse and decided to become more formally trained in offering psychological services and conducting research on psychological outcomes. It also may be helpful to show skills that reflect your ability to communicate easily with others, which are important skills for clinicians and researchers. Think proactively about how your experiences can help position you for graduate school. If you are unsure whether or not to include specific experiences or skills, ask a psychology faculty member or research mentor.

"Responsiveness to feedback is a critical skill. When you are a psychology trainee, you receive feedback constantly on every aspect of your interactions with patients and professionals: your speaking, body language, writing, thinking, beliefs, and countertransference, absolutely everything. Good psychologists learn how to identify the most important feedback and incorporate it into their practice and research. Great psychologists take all feedback and find the kernels of truth in each interaction, letting both good and bad experiences improve their practice and research".
—Elizabeth K. Seng, Ph.D., Assistant Professor of Psychology, Yeshiva University and Research Assistant Professor of Neurology, Albert Einstein College of Medicine

Improving Areas of Concern in Your Application

Take stock of your skills and qualifications and work to identify and improve any areas that are less developed. Go back to Table 3.1 and look at the criteria for admission. How do you stack up at this point? What are your strengths? List them. What are the areas that you could improve on before submitting the application or while it is in process? This is another good time to check in with advisors to help you do this.

It can be uncomfortable to reflect on gaps in your preparedness as it can lead to regret over missed opportunities or poor choices. Don't be discouraged if you don't have outstanding qualifications in each area. Strengths in some areas may be able to offset some gaps in others. In general, you are not advised to apply to programs for which you do not meet the program requirements (e.g., lower GRE scores and GPA than most admitted students). That said, there are rare circumstances in which exceptional qualifications in other areas may make up for weaker credentials.

The issues presented in Table 3.2 may make it more challenging for you clear the admissions hurdle to graduate school. As we've discussed earlier in this

Table 3.2 Factors That Make It Harder to Get Accepted Into a Doctoral Program in Health Psychology

- Low GPA (below 3.0)
- Weak GRE scores (low percentiles)
- Uncertain or unspecified career goals
- No research experience (for Ph.D. programs)
- Weak or generic letters of recommendation

chapter, potential post-baccalaureate ways to boost your application include taking additional courses that strengthen the skills you need for a health psychology Ph.D. program, enrolling in post-baccalaureate programs, enrolling in a master's degree program, obtaining additional research experience. With regards to individual post-baccalaureate courses or full post-baccalaureate programs, taking specific courses after you graduate with your undergraduate degree may improve your application. Taking rigorous methodology course such as a graduate statistics course and doing well in that course may help make up for a low Quantitative Reasoning GRE score or less-than-stellar GPA. This can show admissions committees that your undergraduate record does not reflect your true academic potential.

We've said this before, but it bears repeating. If your test scores and grades are fine, but you don't have substantial research experience, seeking out one to two years of experience as a research assistant or research coordinator on a behavioral medicine project at a medical school (paid or unpaid) is an excellent way to strengthen your application. It's a way to get daily mentorship, access to datasets and funds to travel to conferences, informed letters of recommendation, access to research participants, and potential exposure to medical settings.

If You Are a Career Changer

Don't worry if you found your calling in health psychology long after you've graduated from your undergraduate institution. There are still ways to obtain the qualifications you need to pursue a graduate degree. If your undergraduate degree was not in psychology or if you did not take the course(s) required by your graduate program of choice, you could consider enrolling in the foundational undergraduate or graduate level-courses (e.g., health psychology, statistics, research methods) at your local university. For those who have a fair amount of psychology courses on their undergraduate transcript, or courses that were taken a long time ago, a course or two may be all you need. For others with degrees in different disciplines, you might consider enrolling in a post-baccalaureate or master's-level program in psychology to acquire the fundamental knowledge in psychology and to acquire some research experience in psychology. Although planning ahead and being proactive is crucial to success, it is truly never "too late" to decide to become a health psychologist and to pursue the necessary training to become one.

"Following my undergraduate degree, I became a licensed funeral director and practiced for four years. My job was to guide people through their grief and help them make important decisions during a difficult time of their lives. Though my interest in the business side of funeral directing became less appealing to me over time, I retained that desire to understand people and help guide them to their best possible outcomes. I eventually went back to school to take prerequisite courses for medical school and a career in psychiatry. My curiosity regarding health outcomes led me to a health psychology class, where topics like shared decision making, resilience, and health interventions piqued my interest. I wanted to gain a better understanding of health psychology outside the classroom, so I became a research assistant in a health psychology lab on campus. This not only gave me practical experience, but it allowed me to build relationships with current graduate students and other researchers in the field. During my year as a research assistant, it became clear to me that I wanted to pursue a career in health psychology.

Despite my degree in psychology and experience as a research assistant during college, I found I needed more research experience to be competitive when applying to Ph.D. programs. With the help of my mentor, I became a Clinical Research Coordinator for a health psychologist at a large health system. Those two years provided a very boots-on-the-ground experience, where I was involved in every aspect of developing and implementing studies with a wide variety of clinical populations. Additionally, this position allowed me to network with researchers and helped me to determine which area of health psychology in which I wanted to focus".

—Sara Fleszar, B.S., Doctoral Student, University of California, Merced

"I had a somewhat unusual career path, becoming a health psychologist after completing medical school. Helping cancer patients made me find my calling. I learned how difficult it was for patients to go through treatment and suffer alone, and the desire to help those people live better lives made me decide to study health psychology. I am compassionate for those who are struggling and grateful for what I have today as I grew up in poverty in China. After 20 years, my research still focuses on helping underserved cancer survivors. Almost every day, I talk with junior faculty, postdoctoral fellows, and graduate students both at my home institution and across the country because not everyone has the opportunity to interact with local mentors who work with underserved populations. I also spend lots of time meeting people, learning about their work, collaborating with colleagues, and providing my expertise and service when needed. I spend a considerable amount of time mentoring others to build a pipeline of health disparity researchers. Every day brings new challenges and new opportunities".

—Qian Lu, MD, Ph.D., Associate Professor of Psychology,
University of Texas M.D. Anderson Cancer Center

Preparing to Apply

Preparing and applying for graduate school can be a daunting and arduous process. However, if you start early, engage in candid self-reflection, and stay organized, you can maximize your chances and reduce the stressfulness of the process. At this stage you may be wondering, "How early do I need to know that I want to go to grad school?" or "Am I too late?" Because it can take a few years of preparation to become a successful graduate school applicant, the earlier you get started on this process, the better.

A Timeline for Applying

Table 3.3 provides a sample timeline for graduate school preparation. For example, if you decide to pursue a graduate degree as a college freshman or sophomore,

Table 3.3 *Sample Timeline for Graduate School Preparation*

Time Frame	Task
2–3+ years before you apply (Freshman–early Sophomore year)	• Explore career options online and in-person • Complete fundamental courses in psychology • Complete relevant and rigorous breadth courses (anatomy, biology, math) • Identify research and service opportunities • Complete any necessary pre-requisites for research and service opportunities (coursework, ethics training, library/PsycINFO® training) • Start getting involved in research under the supervision of a faculty member
1–2+ years before you apply (Late Sophomore–Junior year)	• Take advanced courses in psychology, including health psychology if available • Be an active member of a research team under the direction of a faculty member in psychology • See out opportunities to become involved in conference presentations or publications • Consider participating in an honors program or completing a senior thesis/independent study • Get involved with clinical or other relevant service work • Serve as a student affiliate of the Society of Health Psychology
3–6 months before you apply (Summer before Senior year)	• Draft a CV • Prepare for and take GRE(s) • Narrow down list of potential graduate programs • Begin drafting personal statement/career goals • Create a spreadsheet with application details (schools/programs)
0–3 months before you apply (Early Senior year)	• Take or re-take the GRE at least 2 months before first deadline • Request letters of recommendation at least 1 month before first deadline • Contact potential graduate advisors at target schools • Finalize personal statement and resumé/CV • Maintain good grades (you may be asked to submit a final transcript before admittance to graduate school) • See Chapter 4 for more information on the application timeline

Note. This isn't a set timeline for everyone. For example, if you already have graduated from college, you may be taking coursework and/or working as a research coordinator, and your timeline may look quite different.

you will have more time to take complete relevant coursework and pursue training opportunities and experiences at your undergraduate institution. Even as a junior or a senior, with a concerted effort you can make great strides in becoming a successful graduate school applicant by taking relevant coursework and getting involved with a research group. And contrary to what your parents might tell you, taking a year or two off between college and applying to graduate school can be an advantage, *provided that you are doing activities that strengthen your application.*

The CV

A curriculum vitae (CV) is a professional document that succinctly describes your academic and professional achievements and experiences. An academic CV is similar to a resumé but has a particular structure. Your CV will change frequently as it reflects your skills and accomplishments throughout your career. At this point in the process of applying to doctoral programs, the CV is not only a "list" of your achievements to include in applications but also can be a useful tool for considering your readiness to apply. So draft it now, before you start applying to programs.

Although there are a variety of formats for CVs, there are some near-universal sections to include, which we have listed in Table 3.4. For each section of your CV, consider how you may highlight your health psychology interests and experiences. For instance, as part of your educational history, you might highlight any formal education in other relevant health sciences or relevant workshops or continuing education. As part of your research experience, you might highlight research training in which you interacted with individuals, families, or faculty/staff in medical or community health settings, collaborated with faculty or staff in other health

Table 3.4 *What to Include in a CV*

- Contact information (name at top)
- Educational history, including schools attended (starting with college) and degrees earned or expected to earn. You can list GPA here (cumulative/psychology/last two years).
- Honors/awards and student memberships in professional organizations and societies (e.g., Society for Health Psychology, Psi Chi).
- Research experience, including academic or employment experiences that are directly related to what you would do in graduate school. Include names of supervisors, dates of involvement, and a brief description of your responsibilities.
- Conference presentations and publications (in correct APA style for references). For publications, be clear to note what is published, what has been submitted and what is in progress. You don't want to appear as though you are padding your publication list.
- Clinically relevant experiences (often volunteer or practicum course).
- Relevant skills, such as languages read and spoken fluently or research-related computer software you are fluent in.

disciplines, or completed a research assistantship. Finally, when listing your conference presentations and publications, you should definitely include the work that you presented or published in conferences and publications within medicine or other health disciplines, as well as those presented at student research conferences at your college.

A good way to create a good CV is to start early and ask graduate students in your lab (or department) or your advisor or supervisor to provide feedback on drafts and to see their CVs when they applied! Sample CVs and articles on how to write an academic CV can be found in the Appendix.

> "It is tempting to want to include everything possible on one's CV when applying to graduate school. However, some inclusions come across as an attempt to pad a weak CV. In general, students should avoid including non-relevant achievements and activities including high school awards and scholarships, employment outside of their chosen career field, and membership in non-relevant organizations like social clubs (although leadership in these organizations can be included when applying to graduate school). Also avoid lengthy descriptions of duties and skills, which is common in a typical resume, but uncommon in a CV".
>
> —Jennifer Howell, Ph.D., Assistant Professor,
> University of California, Merced

Making a List (and Checking It Twice)

You now know what graduate schools in health psychology are looking for when they evaluate your application. The next step is to make a list—really a spreadsheet—of those programs that might be right for you. We suggest doing this in a very systematic way. (Searching for and applying to graduate schools is definitely a research project unto itself.) First, go to the program's website. Read the mission statement and the requirements for admission. Read about the program's faculty members and then go to their lab or professional websites, which are often linked. Is their work of interest to you? Can you see yourself on any of the projects described? Are they taking new graduate students the year that you will be applying?

Also look on the website for the biographical statements ("bios") of the graduate students who are currently working with that faculty member. You will be learning from your peers as much as the faculty, and in some programs, current graduate students also will be interviewing you for admission. For both faculty and students, ask yourself the questions: Is this work exciting? Do I want to be doing it? For Ph.D. programs, also consider whether there is more than one faculty member with whom you would be interested in working at a particular program. This can allow for more opportunities for training in your area of interest. In addition, since it is not uncommon for faculty members to move to another institution at some point in their career, it would also help ensure that there may be other faculty with whom you could train if your advisor were to relocate.

It can be a time-consuming and challenging process to identify the schools with the right fit for you. For example, for those of you interested in cancer research in health psychology, there is relatively small number of potential mentors who are housed in psychology departments (versus medical schools). As a result, applicants must grapple with how narrow or wide they make their search outside of their specific areas of interest, which then affects how they present themselves in their applications. If you are interested in a relatively narrow topic, you may need to become more flexible. For instance, maybe you start out interested in studying the health impacts of social support in diabetes. But could you also see yourself studying this topic with a mentor who studies obesity instead of diabetes? Or who studies social support among individuals with rheumatoid arthritis? Or studies adherence to treatment among those with Type II diabetes? Working on closely related topics with the same medical population or on the topic you want with a different medical population gives you a strong knowledge base for your own research, and often you can take your dissertation into the specific direction (or with the specific population) that you want.

Carefully review program websites (remember, no more than two per day) and faculty interests and create an electronic or handwritten spreadsheet to note the important information. Because that's a lot of information, it's important to be systematic in your approach to reviewing programs. Table 3.5 provides a list of what information should be taken from the website and included in your spreadsheet. By the way, you will also want to send your spreadsheet to the individuals writing you letters of recommendation (see next chapter). Now armed with your spreadsheet, you can start the application process for those programs.

As you can see, there are a lot of things to think about when making your list. You might wonder, does it make sense to attend a program that is not a health psychology

Table 3.5 Information to Gather for Each Graduate Program You are Interested in Attending

- Name of program, university, and URL
- Application Deadline
- Average GRE scores (Verbal, Quantitative, Analytic) of those admitted
- Is the GRE Psych Test required?
- How many students do they accept each year into this particular program?
- Faculty member(s) you are interested in working with and why
- Tuition costs/possible funding
- For clinical psychology, clinical health psychology, or counseling health psychology programs: Is the program accredited by APA?

program, if the person you want to work with is studying the very thing that they are interested in? Mirroring this, should you attend a program that is strongly focused on health psychology if there are no faculty members you really want to work with?

First, it's important to note that you may not find a program that includes all aspects of training that are ideal to you right now. One of the most important perspectives that we can share with you is that, as a prospective applicant, you will encounter choices to make at every point in your training and in your career—from selecting your list of graduate programs, to accepting a graduate program offer, to selecting and accepting a clinical internship (for clinical students), to deciding whether to complete a postdoctoral fellowship and which one to accept, and beyond. So maintain your stamina and take the long view. While each choice might take you in a different direction, no choice is irrevocable and the choice that you make may open new doors that you may never even have considered.

> "I looked at a broad range of schools when choosing when to apply. In some cases, I was looking geographically to be close to family, but more important than that was my desire to work with the right faculty member. It is important to explore different health psychology programs and seek a faculty member whose research projects interest you the most. I credit much of my success to the willingness to move out of my comfort zone for the right program and faculty fit".
>
> —Sara Fleszar, B.S., Doctoral Student, University of California, Merced

Moving Ahead . . .

You know you want to go to graduate school in health psychology. You know what type of program you want to apply to. You even have some idea of which programs you are interest in attending. The next hurdle: the application process.

References

American Psychological Association (2018). *Graduate study in psychology, 2019 edition*. Washington, DC: American Psychological Association.

Educational Testing Services (ETS) (2019a). *GRE® general test interpretive data*. Retrieved from www.ets.org/s/gre/pdf/gre_guide_table1a.pdf

Educational Testing Services (ETS) (2019b). *2019–2020 Interpreting your GRE® scores*. Retrieved from https://www.ets.org/s/gre/pdf/gre_interpreting_scores.pdf

Michalski, D. S., Cope, C., & Fowler, G. A. (2016). *Graduate study in psychology summary report: Admissions, applications, and acceptances*. Washington, DC: American Psychological Association. Retrieved from www.apa.org/education/grad/survey-data/2017-admissions-applications.aspx

4

APPLYING TO GRADUATE PROGRAMS IN HEALTH PSYCHOLOGY

Introduction

You know you want to go to graduate school and you have a clear idea of where you want to go. The next hurdle: the application process. In this chapter, we break it down into manageable steps.

Step 1: Finalize the List

Making the list and finalizing the list are not the same. Once you have made your list, go to your faculty advisors and peer mentors and ask them to comment on it. Are you missing a program that they think would be perfect for you? If so, check it out and decide whether to add it to your list. Do they think that some programs are overreaches for you? Did they identify any programs on your list which they think wouldn't be a good fit for you? (The same goes for potential mentors.) Talk it over with your mentors to understand their recommendations and concerns. Be prepared to explain why you think that program would be a good fit for you. Also, conduct your own due diligence: If you are planning to apply to Ph.D. programs that emphasize research, take time to review the recent publications of faculty members that interest you so that you have a good understanding of their current areas of research.

We recommend that you apply to multiple programs. The exact number may depend on your individual circumstances, such as interests, resources, how competitive the programs to which you are applying are, and geographic preferences or limitations because of family responsibilities. This is a very different approach than applying to college, where you might have had some "safe" schools and "reach" schools (and you really didn't want to end up in your "safe" school). Applying to graduate school is different: You should want to attend any of the schools you apply to (think good, better, best). That way, if you end up only getting admitted to only one program, it's still a good one. You will be able to get a better idea about your rankings of programs if you visit them for interviews. (We discuss that more a little later.)

How many programs should you apply to? We believe that six to ten doctoral programs is a good range to consider, particularly if you are a good fit with each. If you are applying to masters-level programs or professional Psy.D. programs, you may not need as large of a list, as they typically admit more students and are less competitive.

Applying to graduate school costs not only time but also money. However, it may be possible to obtain waivers of application fees. Many schools will waive or reduce the fee for members of historically underrepresented groups or first-generation graduate students. Check the admission's office website for this information.

Regardless of your number of schools, you must meet all the qualifications for all the schools for which you plan to apply and should be ready to attend any of those schools. Often, the minimum requirements for a doctoral degree in psychology are some set of undergraduate or master's level psychology courses, such as a course in research design or experimental methods and one or more statistics courses. These are the very basic tools you will need to tackle the more advanced material in a doctoral program. Applications may not even be reviewed if you don't have those minimum requirements. Again, check the department's website carefully.

Step 2: Make Sure the Faculty Members
You Want to Train With Are Taking Students

Some graduate programs use a "mentor model". They admit students to work with a specific faculty member. Other programs admit students more broadly to the program. If you are applying to those programs that use a mentor model, it is important that you know in advance whether the faculty member(s) you want to work with are accepting students. This information is usually on the program's website; if it's not, the surest way to find out this information is to contact each faculty member you are interested in working with directly via email as early as the summer before you plan to apply. For many reasons—too many doctoral students in the lab, sabbatical leave, family leaves, more faculty in the program than there are student admissions slots, limited availability of student funding—faculty do not always take new graduate students in a particular year.

When contacting potential future faculty advisors, be polite and succinct. Send an email; don't call. A sample email can be found is in Table 4.1. Introduce yourself in a few sentences, ask if they are accepting students in their lab next year, and attach your CV. With this approach, you will get more than a yes or no answer. Many faculty members don't have the time to have a discussion with you about what career path you want to pursue or time to elaborate upon all of their planned future projects. Some faculty members are happy to answer questions about the program and their own health psychology research. Don't ask questions that are easily answered by reviewing the program's website. This may reveal a lack of effort on your part. In sum, it is in your best interest to reach out to potential mentors. Sometimes showing that initiative and having contact with professor prior to an interview can be the key to getting an acceptance.

Table 4.1 Sample Email to Future Faculty Mentors

Dear Dr. Future Mentor,

I hope this email finds you well. My name is Hopeful Grad-Mentee and I just recently finished my bachelor's degree in Psychology at Great State University. I am planning to apply to Ph.D. programs in health psychology this fall, and your lab and research interests in cultural influences on chronic illness adaptation stood out to me as a good match. Will you be accepting students for the next academic year?

As an undergraduate student at Great State University, I worked under the supervision of Dr. Advisor on a project on cultural differences in emotion regulation processes. My senior thesis focused on how individuals from individualistic versus collectivistic cultures differ in their reported use of emotion-focused coping. Through these experiences, I have become interested in pursuing cultural differences in coping with chronic illness in graduate school and think that I would be a good fit for your lab.

I have attached a copy of my CV for your consideration.

If you have any questions about my research experience or me, please feel free to ask. Thank you for your time.

Sincerely,
Hopeful Grad-Mentee

TIP Be sure to address the faculty member as "Dr." or "Professor" in your email. Believe it or not, we have gotten emails that say, "Hey, Tracey" or "Dear Miss Revenson". Not professional.

TIP Carefully check that you have the correct information when you send your e-mails! Is the name of the institution correct (e.g., Ohio State University versus Ohio University)? Is the font the same so that it is not obvious that you are cutting and pasting names into many emails?

"I know applicants find the admissions process stressful, but it's also stressful from the faculty side as well, as I want to recruit students to work with me who are a strong match in content and working-style. I determine this through the standard admissions process. Some faculty want students who are applying to their lab to reach out to them, but I don't. For example, our program website lists which faculty are planning to admit a student for the next year and includes information about my research projects and my mentoring philosophy. If applicants check the website thoroughly, they shouldn't need to write. Even still, I think it's fine to send an email of introduction, and to clarify whether or not I'm planning to take a student into my lab for the next fall. However, sometimes those emails from students include a series of other questions, such as "Can you tell me the directions you see your research going in the future?"; "What are some of the current projects you have that a new student could become involved with?"; "Can we have a phone call to talk more about those questions or others?" I always decline. I don't want to unfairly advantage applicants who reach out vs. those who do not. Also, I receive so many applications that it's not feasible for me to connect with everyone individually outside of the admissions process. I empathize with the challenges facing applicants in terms of gathering information to find the best-fitting labs. However, I also appreciate when applicants are mindful that faculty focus on admissions during the admissions process but, at other times, we are focused on a host of other professional activities".
—David Pantalone, Ph.D., Associate Professor of Psychology, University of Massachusetts, Boston

Step 3: Write Your Personal Statement

Nearly every graduate program requires some type of written personal statement as part of the application. Depending on the program to which you apply, you may be asked to emphasize slightly different things in your statement. Some schools may request a series of responses to specific prompts, whereas others may ask for one statement without providing much guidance. Most will ask you to touch upon your training or career goals and objectives: Why are you interested in graduate school in health psychology? What are you currently doing or have you done to point you in that direction? What do you hope to learn and focus on in graduate school? Regardless of the specific essay prompt, your response is your opportunity to introduce your professional self.

A general outline for your personal statement can be found in Table 4.2. Your personal statement should include several components, in no particular order. It should contain a narrative of how you arrived at your decision to pursue the graduate degree, what research, clinical and/or volunteer experience you have had that led to that decision, and what you plan to do in graduate school. What you plan to do in graduate school can be a continuation of the research you have been doing prior to graduate school or it can focus on new interests. Be clear about the reason(s) why you have chosen to pursue graduate training in psychology generally, and health psychology more specifically. This could be a result of a class you took, a research experience, or some volunteering you did. Describe your relevant experiences and skills that would serve you well in graduate school. How do these skills, experiences and plans feed into your career goals? Be sure to state the reasons for applying to the specific program or to work with specific faculty members in program.

Table 4.2 *What to Include in a Personal Statement*

- Reason(s) why you have chosen to pursue graduate training in psychology generally and health psychology more specifically
- Career goals
- Goals for your graduate training
- Relevant research, clinical, and volunteer experiences that would serve you well in graduate school
- Skills that you possess that would make you a good researcher, clinician, teacher, departmental citizen
- Reasons for applying to the specific program
- Faculty members you would like to work with and why

"Think about how your interests and prior work fit in with prospective faculty mentors' current research. What do you bring to the table? What new directions or research questions would you like to explore in the scope of the faculty mentors' research? These types of questions may pop up during an interview".

—Emilia Mikrut, B.A., Doctoral Student, St. John's University

Some programs ask you specifically to name a mentor or mentors that you would like to work with during your graduate training, but others do not. Be sure to tailor your statement for each program. You are not insulting any faculty members by not naming them; the Admissions Committee or full faculty committee are looking to read the applications of students most interested in their work.

In the personal statement, express your training interests and explain your goals. This is important because each doctoral program in health psychology may focus on training students for specific types of careers. Do you want to conduct research in a medical setting? Be a faculty member in a psychology department? Open a private practice? Some programs are designed to train future academic researchers while others are designed to train future health service providers. No matter what your current career direction is, you want to illustrate how your academic or professional skills and accomplishments make you well suited for the program and the faculty member(s) with whom you would primarily work.

TIP Don't be fooled by the name "personal statement" and get *too* personal. Some people are drawn to the field of health psychology due to experiences with mental or physical illness in oneself or among family members or friends. As such, they may want to talk about their inspiration and motivation for joining the field by sharing their personal stories. Although some applicants do well in weaving in personal experience into their essays to help show uniqueness and dedication, it can be risky to reveal mental or physical health information about yourself or loved ones. If you want to include such information into your essay, ask a faculty member that you trust to read through and help you disclose the information in a thoughtful way.

We can't say this enough: Demonstrating fit for the program as well as fit with the faculty member(s) with whom you wish to work is of critical importance. You could be an exceptional applicant, but if you and the program appear to be a mismatch you may not be considered at all. For example, you may be interested in designing and testing weight management programs, but not a single faculty member in the program conducts research on behavior change or obesity. The admissions committee would not see this as a good program for your training (and they're probably right). However, do not state false training interests or goals in order to align with a program. This will become apparent soon enough, and even if you were to be accepted, it is likely that you would be unhappy. Follow Polonius' words: "To thine own self, be true".

The personal statement often doubles as a sample of your writing ability. Do not put it off to the last minute! It is likely to take several drafts (with feedback from mentors and peers) to "get it right". Many people find it challenging to write these statements; some have trouble writing positively about themselves, especially if they learned not to "show off". If this is the case, write about yourself in the third person or pretend you are writing about someone else, and then turn it back into the first person. If you hit a wall writing it, try speaking it into your phone or talking to someone else while they type.

No matter what your circumstances, set aside time to go through multiple revisions of your personal statement. We often tell students to start on their essay several months before the application is due to allow for feedback from others and rewriting. For example, for undergraduate students this often means starting the summer before senior year. If you're hoping to get useful feedback do not send it to your best friend who always says you are great no matter what. Send it those who know what to look for and who will honestly evaluate it (and be sure to ask them to). If you are working in a research lab, ask a graduate student, postdoctoral fellow, or faculty member to look at it since they have obviously written successful personal statements of their own. Definitely ask the faculty members who are writing your letters of recommendation to review your statement as they are in a good position to give constructive criticism. And, as we cover in more detail later, they will need to read your personal statement to be able to write a strong letter of support.

If you have taken time off between your undergraduate degree and applying for graduate training, you should still obtain feedback on your statement. You may choose to ask former professors to write you letters of recommendation. If you feel comfortable, show them a draft of your statement and ask for feedback. But don't do this the week before the letter is due. Faculty members are busy creatures and the more time you give them, the better the quality of the feedback. Be careful about going to general career advisors at a university; the personal statement for a psychology program is different from the statement for other academic disciplines. They may help with your writing but may not know what a potential mentor in health psychology is looking for.

Writing your personal statement is a self-reflective process that can be motivating and re-affirming of your plans. This process might also reveal to you that you are not pursuing the best path for you. Yet another reason to start early.

Step 4: Ask for Letters of Recommendation

Whom Should You Ask to Write a Letter of Recommendation?

Perhaps the most critical decision is who should write your letters of recommendation. Many students worry about this. You must be strategic in choosing your letter writers. Don't be fooled into thinking you should ask the most famous psychologist in your department—especially if they don't know you. Ideal letters come from psychology faculty members who know you very well. These are usually faculty who have worked with you on a project (e.g., research, clinical work, or community outreach), supervised you, advised you, or connected with you in courses or clubs. Letters from graduate students in the lab have less authority than faculty and are generally not advisable. Instead, some faculty and graduate student lab supervisors may co-write letters of recommendation. Family and friends are not an option for recommendations. Their letters will be not be considered by admissions committees and providing these could even be considered poor judgment.

Many graduate programs require a minimum of three letters of recommendation for each applicant. The more your letter writer knows about you, the stronger your letter will be. In other words, make sure to take the opportunity to get to know faculty members at your institution well, especially faculty members associated with the research labs in which you worked, before you need letters of recommendation. If you are a student, go to the professor's office hours (even if you are doing well in the course) to chat about your career goals. Be an active participant in the classroom and get involved in psychology department activities such as Psi Chi, the honor society for psychology majors. More face time with recommenders allows them to craft a more personal and effective endorsement of you.

If you are no longer a student, but are working in a research setting such as a full-time research assistant or coordinator, you should still think about which faculty or senior researchers know your work well. This could involve observations of how you interact with research participants and staff, your basic research skills, and your potential for advanced research activities. If you are working in a clinical setting like a hospital or community agency, identify psychologists and other senior staff who know you well and who can comment on your interpersonal skills, clinical abilities, professionalism, work ethic, and the likelihood of your success in graduate school. When possible, for clinical health psychology programs, identify letter writers who can comment on your ability to work with health-relevant populations, including individuals or groups who are affected by, or at risk for, medical illness, as well as your ability to work with multidisciplinary faculty or clinical staff in medical settings.

You do not want letters from professors who don't really know you and can only comment on your grades. (That's what a transcript is for!) We refer to this as the "kiss of death" letter. A letter that says, "Molly was a student in my Health Psychology class. She received an A. She did well on the exams and was always on time for class", not only tells the admissions committee nothing about Molly's critical thinking or ideas, but it also reveals that Molly didn't make meaningful connections with that faculty member inside or outside of the classroom.

A good rule of thumb is that at least two of your letter writers should be from psychology faculty or doctoral-level psychologists in your research setting. You might also consider additional letters from faculty in complementary disciplines (e.g., math, science, biology, and public health) if they know you and your work well. Perhaps you completed an intensive research project on memory and learning in rats in the biology department. The faculty member who oversaw your project and can speak to your experiences and contributions to the project can be a nice complement to letters from psychology faculty members. Or, perhaps you participated in a small sociology seminar with a lot of writing; the faculty member who led that seminar can provide a lot of specific examples about your strengths as a critical thinker and your ability to communicate both in writing and orally. Or, let's say you work as a research coordinator in a medical setting and the primary investigator for the project on which you work is a physician. It is fine for a physician faculty member to write one letter as long as you can help him or her get a good sense of what graduate programs in psychology will look for in an ideal candidate. (Expectations for medical schools are quite different than graduate programs in health psychology.)

If you worked on a research, clinical, or community project you should definitely include that mentor as a letter writer. In other words, a faculty member or a doctoral-level mentor (not a graduate student supervisor) should write a letter if they have observed you on a regular basis and can write in detail with specific examples. But don't ask the head of the project or lab to write a letter if you have had minimal contact with that person. Some of the worst are letters come from the head of the lab saying, "I don't really know this person".

In fact, the absence of the letter from someone you worked closely with can be seen as problematic. If the faculty member with whom you have worked is going away on sabbatical or moving to another university, ask them if they would be willing to draft a letter before they leave so that they only will have to polish it later. If you are several years out of college, it is still possible to get a strong letter from a former supervisor (or instructor). When you reach out to them to see if they might be willing to write you a letter, offer to provide extra information to help jog their memory. For example, you might send along a photo and the paper you wrote for the course. (Author Tracey Revenson regularly writes a few sentences about each term paper when she grades them so that the notes will be available several years later for future letters. No one's memory is that good!)

Understand What You Are Asking Recommenders to Do

Strong letters of recommendation for graduate school are often quite detailed and take considerable time for faculty members to write. This shouldn't deter you from asking someone to write a letter (we all look very busy and probably are very busy), but we want you to know how much time and work it takes. Beyond your academic accomplishments, letter writers need to speak to your specific skills or attributes, such as critical thinking, the ability to work independently, or expertise in specific research techniques (e.g., analysis of heart rate variability data). For many schools, a rating form accompanies the letter of recommendation. Table 4.3 presents an example of such a form.

Table 4.3 Example Recommendation Rating Form

Please rate the applicant's ability on the scales provided below in comparison with graduating seniors.

	Top 1%	Top 5%	Top 10%	Top 25%	Top 50%	Unable to rate
Motivation						
Intelligence						
Oral communication						
Written communication						
Ability to receive feedback or criticism						
Creativity						
Trustworthiness						
Dependability						
Interpersonal skills						
Emotional maturity						
Independence						
Initiative						
Ability to work with individuals from diverse backgrounds						
Capacity to handle stress						

How to Ask for a Letter of Recommendation

Asking a faculty member or other professional for a letter of recommendation can be stressful. You know how busy they are with teaching and research and how many requests they receive at the same time of year. You now know it takes time to craft a strong letter or recommendation. So, the question is not, "Will you write me a letter of recommendation?" but "Will you write me a *strong* letter of recommendation?" If the faculty member says no (because of time, not knowing you well, or no reason given), move on. You don't want a weak letter.

So how should you go about asking the potential letter writer? Let's start with what not to do. Don't ambush the person by swinging by their office unannounced or by putting them on the spot at the beginning of their class period—especially if you don't have a very close working relationship. Instead, either send the potential letter writer a request via email or ask the person if they would be willing to set up a time to talk to you about your plans to apply to graduate school and the possibility of writing you a letter of recommendation (see Table 4.4 for a sample email). If you take the first approach, an email request, prepare a succinct and professional cover letter that outlines your application plans (types of programs, timeline) and why you would like a letter from that particular person. If it's been a while since you've been in touch with the person, remind them of your work

Table 4.4 Sample Email to Potential Recommendation Letter Writers

---

Dear Dr. Esteemed Letter-Writer,

I am writing to ask if you would be willing to write a reference letter for me for graduate school. I am planning to apply to Ph.D. programs in health psychology this fall. The first deadline is December 1.

I was fortunate to be a student in two of your classes: Research Methods (Spring 2018 semester, earned an A-) and Health Psychology (Spring 2019 semester, earned an A). I really learned a lot about the importance of research and especially enjoyed learning about the many exciting discoveries and opportunities in the field of health psychology.

This past year, I have been working closely with Dr. Advisor on a project on cultural differences in emotion regulation processes. Through these experiences I have become interested in pursuing cultural differences in coping with chronic illness in graduate school. I was hoping that you would be able to speak to my potential as a graduate student in your letter.

I have attached a copy of my CV and a draft of my personal statement for your consideration.

Please let me know if you would like any additional information or would like to meet to discuss it further.

Thank you for your consideration.

Sincerely,
Aspiring Graduate Student

---

together (what you did and when). Attach to your email current versions of your application materials, such as your CV and a draft personal statement. If you take the second approach of an in-person meeting, you should still prepare to share the same information with the potential letter writer. Bring along (or email in advance) current versions of your application materials and be ready to talk about career and training goals as well as any strengths and weaknesses in your application materials.

Give your letter writers plenty of time to write and send your letters. Some faculty with large teams of undergraduate students who are applying to multiple graduate programs may submit dozens of letters a year! To make their task easier, you need to provide them with a lot of material. Table 4.5 provides a number of documents you want to provide to your letter writers. Also be sure to indicate for each program how the letter should be sent: Will they be provided with a link to upload the letter? Do they need to attach the letter to an email? Although most programs now ask faculty members to upload their letter of recommendation to a website, some still ask for individual emails or even snail mail. Indicate this clearly in the spreadsheet you send to your recommenders along with the due dates. One important thing to note is that some programs won't allow your letter writers to upload a recommendation letter until the complete application is submitted. So it's really important for you to submit *your* application materials well in advance of the deadline so recommenders have plenty of time to write their letters and submit them before the deadline.

Although each deadline will be listed in your spreadsheet, let your letter writers know when the *earliest* application deadline is. This information will let your letter writers know how much time they have before the first one is due without having to scour your spreadsheet. (Of course, it can be helpful for your letter writers if you list the programs in chronological order of the application due dates.) And know that the first letter takes the most time, as letter writers craft a first draft and revise it several times. Once the basic letter is written, it's easier and quicker for recommenders to tailor it to specific programs.

What is extremely helpful is a cover letter/email for your letter writers—no more than a few paragraphs—that includes all the important details. (Think of it as a cheat sheet.) The cover letter should include a brief description of your career goals and graduate training objectives, your GPA and GRE test scores (if known), and important facts about you that you want your letter writers to highlight or which may not be apparent in your CV or personal statement. For example, you might ask them to emphasize your leadership skills or that you were president of your college's Psi Chi chapter or you served as co-chair of the Annual Undergraduate Research Conference. In addition to the materials suggested in Table 4.5, in your spreadsheet, do not forget to include all program names, website URLs, letter

Table 4.5 *Materials to Provide to Your Letter Writers*

- The names and program descriptions of all the programs you are applying to
- The dates their letters are due
- How the letter should be sent (upload to a link, email, snail mail)
- Your personal statement (even if it is a draft)
- Your (unofficial) transcript
- Your CV
- A paper you wrote for their class (especially if it was more than a semester ago)
- A bulleted list of things that they should emphasize about you

---

deadlines, and the names of the faculty member or members with whom you want to work (if applicable) for each program.

At the same time, be sure to get the complete and accurate contact information of your letter writers at the time you send them your spreadsheet. Most university applications ask you include this information in your application, most often the recommender's name degree, institutional affiliation, address, telephone number, and email address. This appears on the evaluation form the recommender sends back or fills out online. And, please, be sure to spell the recommender's name correctly! You would be surprised how many applicants do not do this, which suggests a "messy" application.

Recommenders are typically asked how long they have known the person they are recommending, so documenting when your relationship with your letter writer began is very helpful ("I was a student in your Health Psychology class in the fall of 2018"). If they are in your lab, remind them of the month and year that you began to work together. Include any information and issues that you would like the letter writer to address. It's acceptable to request your letter writers to highlight specific strengths (e.g., leadership skills, communication ability, the time you found an error in the data that the graduate students didn't) or to address potential weakness in your application (e.g., low freshman GPA, low quantitative GRE). The more information you provide (and the earlier you provide it), the easier it will be to write a detailed letter of support and the stronger that letter of support will be.

Step 5: Assemble Additional Pieces of the Application

In addition to the criteria listed in Chapter 3, graduate programs may also require additional materials to inform their admissions decisions. This may include your CV (detailed in Chapter 3), a writing sample, or other documents (e.g., a health psychology poster you presented at a national conference). The writing sample may be your senior or master's thesis or a class paper of which you were particularly proud and demonstrates your ability to express ideas.

Beyond the required or optional application material requested in the application guidelines, you should pay attention to unspecified factors that admissions committees or potential advisors may consider. For example, timeliness and attention to detail are both critical for success. Do not submit materials that are late or contain errors. It could be the kiss of death to name the wrong school in your statement or misspell a potential advisor's name. (This happens a lot.) It reflects your organizational skills, a critical aspect of doctoral training or health psychology careers. Staying organized, planning ahead, and double-checking your materials can help you avoid such costly mistakes. Potential advisors may also pay attention to your emails as a reflection of your writing quality, professionalism, and personality. When communicating with potential advisors, be sure to that your correspondence is respectful, well-written, and succinct, and be sure that you have done your due diligence to learn about each potential advisor's areas of interest. And be sure to check the email address that you included on your application daily, since faculty members typically have only a few days to set up interviews.

Once you have submitted your application, you are not done. Check that your recommenders have sent their letters by the deadline. Be sure that your GREs were sent to the right schools. Admissions offices compile applicant folders (electronically or on paper) soon after the deadlines and send them to the appropriate departments/programs. If your application is incomplete at that time, it may be rejected without review.

Step 6: Prepare to Interview

It is very good sign if you have made it to the interview stage of the application process. But note that not all health psychology programs conduct interviews with applicants or require that you travel for a face-to-face interview. Here is where Skype may come in. You will know this from the website or emails from members of the prospective program.

Interviews are more common for doctoral programs than in master's programs and for clinical health psychology programs than research-only health psychology programs. Pre-admission interviews are often used for a few reasons: to confirm the fit of your interests and career goals with the program's mission, to confirm the fit between you as the applicant and potential mentors, and to assess your interpersonal skills. Interviewers will pay attention to how prepared you are for the interview. In addition, faculty members may follow-up on specific points made in your statement of goals and objectives. For example, they may ask you to elaborate on your contributions to any clinical and/or research projects that you named in your personal statement.

"When you receive an invitation to interview from a program, do not put the invitation on hold while you wait for invitations from other programs. And once you commit to an interview, be aware that it is very rude to back out at the last minute. If you are invited to an interview but you are pretty certain you would not attend that program if offered a spot, politely decline the invitation so that it can be offered to another student. Graduate programs have limited interview slots so last-minute cancellations or taking a spot when you have low intention of attending the graduate program is unfair to the program and to other prospective applicants who might want that interview slot".

—Kristin Kilbourn, Ph.D., M.P.H., Associate Professor,
University of Colorado Denver

How do you prepare for the interview? First, (re)read the program's website fully. Know the program's focus and mission. Learn about the research being conducted by all the core faculty members in that program, not just the one or two you would like to work with. However, it is essential that you know the work of the faculty members you want to work with in depth; read their personal webpages and their lab page. Read at least one or two of their recent publications. Be prepared to have a discussion about why you are interested in working with them in terms of their research. The worst question you can ask a faculty member who is interviewing you is, "And what do you do?" Unfortunately, this happens more often than you would think!

Also, read about the students in the program—you might meet them during the interview day—formally or informally—and, once accepted to graduate school, you will be learning from your peers as well as the faculty. Recall that in some programs, current graduate students may interview you. Graduate students may ask you about your research interests, career goals, and prior experiences but also may ask you about personal interests and hobbies. They're usually not trying to pry—they simply want to find out more about you as a person and whether you would be a good colleague to have around. Just as they will want to find out more about you, be prepared to ask the graduate students questions. They can be useful sources of information about the mentoring style of your potential advisor(s), coursework, research opportunities, and more generally what it's like to be a graduate student in the department and live in the local area.

"It's easy to forget that an invitation to interview for graduate school means that the program is interested in you, in the same way you are interested in the program. So, take a deep breath and remember that your application and CV have already demonstrated your competence. On the day of the interview, make sure to balance putting your best foot forward by behaving professionally, being collegial, and conveying your genuine interest in the program. But also evaluate whether this program is truly the right fit for you. Listen to what the faculty and current graduate students are saying, watch how they are interacting, and note whether the program's mission statement aligns with your own goals and research agenda. In short: Expect to impress and to be impressed".

—Sugandha Gupta, M.A., Doctoral Student,
The Graduate Center, City University of New York

Come to the interview with your own questions. Many faculty members (and current graduate students) will end an interview by asking, "And what questions do you have?" Having no questions can signal a lack of true interest in the program or someone who does not prepare adequately. Even if you have asked the question of two faculty or graduate students ask it of the third (or more)—not all faculty or graduate students will see things in the same way!

For example, ask about what types of funding the university provides for doctoral student research, what their current clinical practicum offerings are, and how much students collaborate on research. Ask about the possibility of working with multiple mentors or in more than one lab during your graduate training, and, if you are interested, the programs' opportunities to collaborate with scholars in other health disciplines. For clinical health psychology applicants, you also may want to ask about opportunities for clinical training experiences in specific medical settings or what types of externships their current students hold. Some of us faculty have been asked what our mentoring style is and if our students co-author publications. This is fine to ask in a non-accusatory tone, but be prepared for the faculty member interviewing you to ask what you are looking for in a mentor!

It bears repeating: Faculty and graduate student interviewers will expect you to have questions. A student who sits silently or isn't engaged in the interview process (e.g., texting throughout the day) isn't seen in a good light.

TIP

Ten Interview Tips

1. While health psychology doctoral faculty will vary in what they are looking for in a prospective graduate student, generally they are seeking qualities of social and emotional intelligence, intellect, passion for a particular area of research, strong ethics, and the likelihood that you have what it takes to build a career in health psychology. So think about how you project your personal qualities as you respond to each interview question.

2. During the interview process you likely will meet with additional faculty members besides your mentors of interest. With whomever you meet, show your genuine interest in their work and their clinical or research role in the graduate program. Ask questions.

3. Some faculty members will focus their interview with you on providing information about the graduate program, to the extent that you may not have enough time to share much information about yourself. If this happens, just be gracious, take notes, and integrate yourself into the conversation if and when it feels appropriate.

4. You also will meet great faculty members who may not necessarily be great interviewers. It's okay if the interview feels a little awkward. Just be your best self with whomever you meet.

5. The most fulfilling interviews often are the ones that can transcend "question and answer" format to become more natural discussions between faculty and applicant about shared academic interests and passions. This doesn't always happen, but you'll know when it does!

6. As with faculty members, be your best self when you meet with current graduate students in the program. Current students may not have direct control over applicant selections, but they can have some influence. Remember that they are looking for their future lab mates.

7. During interviews, should you ask about funding or not? If the faculty member doesn't bring it up first, instead focus your limited interview time on sharing your interests, passions, and strengths and on learning as much as possible about the program. You can find out more about funding once you receive your acceptance.

8. On-site interviews often involve long days, so hide a snack in your pocket and make sure your shoes are comfortable! Seriously.

9. After the interview, send a thank you note. It can be a lot of work to send thank you emails to everyone, but a brief note of appreciation can go a long way. In addition to thanking the person for taking the time to meet with you (or for hosting or transporting you), make a reference to something in particular you discussed with them. This can help to demonstrate your thoughtfulness and interest in the person or program.

10. Finally, enjoy the interview experience. Yes, this is possible! Imposter syndrome is normal but remember that you were invited because the faculty think you are worth it. Enjoy your conversations and take it all in so that you can come home with a good sense of the program.

What to Expect During the Interview

Some programs hold interviews with "finalists" in person and others by telephone or Skype calls. Some programs bring all finalists in on the same day and others scatter interviews over a period of weeks, depending on faculty members' schedules. Sometimes you will be interviewed by multiple faculty members at one time or be interviewed at the same time another applicant. This is often because of time constraints and does not reflect on your status as an applicant. Try not to become more anxious if you have a group interview. Realize that different faculty members may be looking for different things in potential graduate students. If you are being interviewed at the same time as another applicant, make sure you are verbally "present" but avoid dominating the conversation. Sometimes faculty look at these joint interviews as seeing how potential students will interact in a seminar or a research lab. The key is to be your authentic self.

During on-site interviews, assume that you are being evaluated throughout the entire visit, including during your interactions with administrative staff about travel logistics and with other applicants and current students during social contexts. Admissions committees commonly solicit feedback from everyone who may have interacted with you before, during, and after the visit. Admissions committees are interested in whether you are cordial, mature, and appropriately engaged in both formal interviews as well in the more informal settings, including social gatherings, campus tours, and other casual interactions.

Although it might not feel like it at the time, the interview is also the time for you to determine if a program is a good fit for you and whether you were intellectually stimulated by the conversations with potential mentors. Hopefully you will be accepted to a number of programs and these perceptions will affect your choice of graduate program.

Interviews can be extremely tiring. If you are travelling far, be sure to arrive the day before and be well rested. (Many students offer to have applicants stay at their homes as guests to avoid the costs of a hotel room. If you have a relative or friend who lives near the university, that's even better, as you don't have to be "on" the night before.) Show up on time (or even a few minutes early) at the beginning of the day. You may or may not receive a schedule of the faculty members (and students) you will interview with before that day. Obviously, receiving it a few days before can make you feel more in control, but even if you don't see it until that morning, don't worry. (Remember, we advised earlier that you know the basic research area of every core faculty member in the program.) Dress professionally, but be aware that academic attire is often less formal than business attire. Bring a copy of your CV with you in case a faculty member asks to see it.

> "I once had to go to an interview in sneakers because I forgot my shoes at home. (I was flying out of state.) I pretended I had a minor orthopedic injury, limped throughout the interview process, and it all worked out fine. Now that's thinking on your feet".
> —Lara Traeger, Ph.D., Assistant Professor, Massachusetts General Hospital/Harvard Medical School

Although you will likely interview with the faculty members most interested in working with you, you may also interview with other faculty members and graduate students who are not as familiar with your application and members of the department with whom you are not particularly interested in working. Still be polite and engaged during these meetings, as these individuals may be influential in admissions decisions. The interview process is stressful, but it is also your time to shine and to gain a sense of whether this is a place where you will be intellectually stimulated and happy for several years!

After the interview, you may be exhausted. But try not to let the post-interview fatigue keep you from sending a few follow-up thank you emails. A short note of thanks to those that interviewed you can go a long way in forming a positive impression. And don't forget to show your appreciation to those people who hosted you, shuttled you around campus, or otherwise helped to coordinate your visit.

> "When I was interviewing applicants this year some of them relaxed a bit too much with me. My advice is to treat everyone (faculty, students, and staff) with respect. Graduate students who are part of the admissions process are giving feedback to their advisors".
> —Rebecca Cippollina, B.A., Doctoral Student, Rutgers University

"When I applied to graduate school, I was fortunate enough to have several mentors whom I could go to for support. While I absolutely credit much of my success in the application process to their guidance, I was shocked by how contradictory their advice would be. One would tell me that I should send out introductory emails to all professors I was interested in working with, while another would warn me against this approach as it can come across as pushy or annoying. In reviewing the first version of my statement of purpose, one mentor advised I focus more on my research interests and cut the personal aspects while another suggested I make the essay more personal. All my mentors were very successfully psychologists and clinicians who were well versed on what competitive programs look for in a candidate, but they still often disagreed! The take home point: There seemed to be no one 'right way' to do things in the application process, which was what stressed me the most. You cannot know whether a professor will be turned off by an introductory email, or if they will appreciate hearing some of your personal history while reading your statement of purpose. In the end, I just had to do what felt right to me. I sent brief emails to about half of the professors I was interested in working with and left my personal history in my essay, but I'm sure not everybody liked it! However, some did, and I was accepted to four of 12 programs. Even in making my final decisions, my mentors, peers, and family members, while all incredibly supportive, did not necessarily agree on which program would be the best fit for me, or what variables I should most heavily weigh in deciding. Again, I ended up trusting my gut feeling. The application and interview process is grueling, but you learn a lot about yourself and what matters most to you. And of course, it is all worth it in the end when you make that final decision and begin to take the first, exciting steps of your academic career!"

—Molly Ream, B.A., Doctoral Student, University of Miami

Making the Decision

The process of applying to graduate school can be a long and emotionally taxing process filled with uncertainty. You may have interviewed in late January, but that does not mean the decision will come in early February. In fact, there is no set timeline except for the final day for doctoral programs to make offers of admission and applicants who have received offers to accept or reject them: April 15. You should know that programs make offers to an initial group of applicants and also create a waitlist of a few candidates to whom they will make offers depending on whether those initially offered admission accept or decline (see the section to follow on the waitlist).

By the time you arrive at the point where you are receiving offers of admission (and rejections), you may be exhausted and feel ill equipped to make a decision that feels like everything is riding on it. How should you decide which school to attend if you have multiple offers? What if you have just one offer to consider— should you take it? Maybe you have been waitlisted at your ideal program and aren't excited about any other current prospects? What do you do if you weren't admitted to any graduate programs this cycle?

Let's first acknowledge that there is no "right" answer to any of these questions. You may have a lot of factors shaping your decisions, both with respect to the program itself (assigned advisor, financial aid offer) as well as other considerations (proximity to family, opportunities for your romantic partner). Some factors may be in your control and some may not. Just as we advised you to seek input from those around you to make decisions about which programs to apply, now is also a good time to get more opinions when considering your options in moving forward. Be bold about questions that you have about potential programs and future advisors. In addition to asking questions of future advisors, make sure to reach out to current or former students of the program of interest. They can often provide a lot of insight about what it is like to be a student in the program to which you've been admitted. They often know more about housing opportunities and graduate student benefits than faculty as well.

Along with receiving advice, however, you might also feel pressure from current and future advisors, parents, or other loved ones, who have a stake in your decision. Ultimately, you will need to decide the best course for you at this time. The decision might be to select the strongest academic program available to you. Or it might be to wait a couple years and reapply after you've strengthened your application.

It is perfectly acceptable to visit a program again (or for the first time, if the program does not hold interviews) before accepting an offer. Send an email to your prospective mentor and ask when a good day would be to do this; also ask if you can sit in on a class or two or attend a lab meeting. If needed, ask if a student can host you overnight to cut costs. At this point, programs and potential mentors are wooing you and will want to convince you to come.

"This is so exciting' seemed to be the catch phrase for my application experience—especially to my mentors (established psychologists and physicians who saw my application cycle as a new adventure), to my family (endlessly supportive healthcare professionals thinking about all of the different places I could end up), and to my friends and coworkers (who were either going through a similar application experience or thinking 'Why are you volunteering to go back to school for five more years?!'). To me, the application process was a pressure cooker. My test scores, my transcripts, my essays, each introductory email, and my final list all felt like ingredients in a recipe that I could not control. I was tying up all of my accomplishments and aspirations into one .pdf file and putting it into someone else's hands while sending them an email expressing my strong interest (Read: Please pick me). Much of the application cycle felt like a gamble, but what became most important was who would be my future mentor—that I find a position in a lab that felt like a place where I could learn, grow, and gain the tools to become a health psychologist. In the end, I applied to 12 programs. I was told at the beginning that all you need is one acceptance with one great mentor, and that became my mantra. After two interviews, I figured, 'ok—you've at least got the odds on your side for the first time in this process'. But those odds were tested in the weeks before my acceptance. I became acutely aware of my chances as way less than certain (while also knowing how much I had to offer). I played email-tag with potential mentors I was waiting to hear from and found myself hitting the send/ receive button more times than I'd like to admit. In the end—I got that one acceptance, and it really was all I needed. I would have never guessed that I would be calling New York City my home, but I can proudly say that I have completed my first year of training, already started seeing patients in a community-based behavioral medicine clinic, and am working with a mentor who has inspired and motivated me in ways I could have never imagined. I feel both challenged and supported and am receiving training that was well worth the rollercoaster ride of the application process. Thankfully, my email-induced anxiety has significantly decreased, and I can now see that this whole process really is 'exciting'".

—Sarah Fishman, B.A., Doctoral Student, Yeshiva University

The Etiquette of Accepting (or Rejecting) an Offer of Admission

Let's say that you are in the enviable position of having multiple offers and have made your decision. How should you communicate it to those programs?

Accepting an Offer

You have been accepted into a doctoral program—whether it is your first or last choice, rejoice! If you are definitely accepting the offer, do so as soon as possible, first with an email to the Admissions Chair or Program Director (whoever made the offer) and then when the official letter or email arrives from the university, accept again, per their instructions. For many universities, you must accept the offer through the Admissions office website; some still want a written or signed document. We repeat, *"Do it as soon as possible"*. This is not only to secure your spot and funding package but also because applicants on the waitlist are "on hold" (more on this in a bit). Sometimes you want to wait until you are giving written confirmation of your funding package—we get that. But do not hold off notifying a program until the deadline of April 15.

Rejecting an Offer

Hopefully you are rejecting an offer because you have multiple offers to choose from! Rejecting an offer also should be done in a timely fashion and in a professional manner. As we have said before, health psychology is a small field and you will likely be seeing faculty and students from the other programs at conferences for years to come. Typically, you reject offers once you have accepted an offer. This makes it easy to write the email: "Thank you for your offer of admission. I was very impressed by your program's [detail one or two things here]. It was a difficult choice, but I have decided to accept an offer elsewhere [or give the name of the program]". Often programs want to know to which programs they have "lost" students to, so it's collegial to provide that information. The sooner you inform a program you will not be accepting their offer, the sooner the first person on the waitlist gets the exciting news.

The Waitlist

You may find yourself on a waitlist. Often the program's admissions committee chair will call or email to tell you this, inform you what their timeline is for hearing from accepted students, and ask whether you have other offers. If this program is honestly your top choice, let them know that. Be sure to stay in email contact every few weeks during the months after offers go out and before the April 15 deadline for acceptance. Because some students get multiple offers, they may decline an offer from the program that is your first choice. "Alternates" are crucial to admissions committees so they can admit a full cohort of students. If you haven't heard from a program several weeks after your interview, contact them by email to find out your status. They may have decided not to offer you a place (or put you on their alternates list), but the university's admissions office hasn't sent the notification. It's better to know this as you consider other offers.

There are a number of online "crowd-sourced" resources (wikis) with information on where different programs are in their admissions process. They are not always updated regularly or accurately, so take them with a grain of salt.

Bringing Financial Considerations Into Your Decision

Let's assume you are in the enviable position of having multiple offers from your top choice schools. On what basis do you make your decision? First, it is perfectly fine to re-contact faculty and students with questions or even to visit the program again. This decision is going to take up the next five to six years of your life and start you on a career trajectory, so it is a very important one. Programs understand this.

Second, the financial package the program offers you may be a crucial deciding factor. Programs may offer you one or more of these things: a stipend (salary), which may or may not have work responsibilities attached to it (e.g., a teaching or research fellowship), a waiver of tuition payments (meaning you don't pay tuition), health insurance, and in rare cases, housing. You need to balance this out with the program's training. For example, let's assume that you have been accepted to three programs that are equally attractive in terms of mentors and training model. University #1 offers you a $25,000 stipend a year for five years and a tuition waiver, but the stipend comes attached with the requirement to teach one course a semester in your second through fifth years. University #2 offers you a $25,000 stipend for five years and a tuition waiver, but you need to work 15 hours a week as a research assistant. University #3 offers you a $25,000 stipend for five years with no work requirements for three years but does not provide a tuition waiver; however, it is at a state university with (comparatively) low tuition costs. How do you compare these offers to make a decision? It will depend on your current financial status, the costs of living in each city, and future prospects, among other factors. Talk to students at University #1 and #2 in terms of how they manage their time with their teaching obligations. At University #3, ask about how students cover their tuition costs.

What if the programs you are admitted to are not offering you financial support? Could you afford to support yourself? How would you be able to do it? If you take out loans, how long will it take to pay them back given the salary you might be expected to earn as a health psychologist, especially early in your career? Graduate student debt is a growing concern.

Psychology graduate students and early career professionals surveyed by APA reported being stressed and burdened by their staggering graduate school loan debt, having to delay important life events like marriage, parenthood, and home buying (Doran, Kraha, Marks, Ameen, & El-Ghoroury, 2016). The early career professionals reported an average debt of approximately $100,000, while current graduate students anticipated that their total average debt would be approximately $130,000. Furthermore, debt varied according type of degree and or specialization. The Psy.D. degree was associated with the highest average debt (~$173,00 for graduate students), while a research-focused Ph.D. was associated with the least debt (~$69,000 for graduate students).

These data underscore the need to be informed about all aspects of the program's training before you accept an offer. It is as important to understand the financial and personal costs so as to understand the training opportunities associated with any given graduate program in health psychology. You'll only be able to make a truly informed decision when you have all the relevant facts.

There is no consensus on whether applicants should consider attending a graduate program that doesn't fund them. We know that in these times a five-year funding package of a tuition waiver and stipend is the ideal but is not always offered. If you are not offered funding, it is worth asking for it. We recognize that universities are often short on funds, but a strong training program makes a commitment to its students. If you are accepted to your first-choice program, and to another program that is offering more funding, it may be possible to negotiate with your first choice using the competing program's funding as leverage. Do this gently and understand that financial packages may be set by the university to ensure equality across students and disciplines. At the same time, there may be discretionary funds or summer funding that can be used. In other words, the program may not be able to increase your annual stipend, but they may be able to provide additional funding for one summer (or more). It never hurts to ask (politely), but it helps to have another offer with a higher stipend amount to do this.

Even with a financial package, it is important to recognize that the stipend may not be enough. In addition to loans, there are a number of fellowships and awards, some attached to a research project and some not. For individuals from groups that have been underrepresented in psychology, there may be additional funding opportunities, such as the Ford Fellowship, APA Minority Fellowship, or a diversity fellowship from the graduate program itself. Also, if your future advisor has an R series NIH grant (e.g., R01), you may be able to apply for an NIH diversity supplement to support you and your research.

If you need to work to supplement your income, try to find something that is relevant to the career you hope for and doesn't take time away from your graduate training. For example, some students have worked part-time on research projects outside their university, tutored students in statistics or writing, or took on additional teaching-related responsibilities (e.g., extra grading, facilitating online courses).

Moving Ahead . . .

As you can see, preparing the application for graduate school can be daunting. But, broken down into steps, it is completely manageable and will hopefully bring you the outcome you desire!

Reference

Doran, J. M., Kraha, A., Marks, L. R., Ameen, E. J., & El-Ghoroury, N. H. (2016). Graduate debt in psychology: A quantitative analysis. *Training and Education in Professional Psychology*, 10(1), 3–13. https://doi.org/10.1037/tep0000112

5

WHAT TO EXPECT IN GRADUATE SCHOOL IN HEALTH PSYCHOLOGY

So you have been accepted into a doctoral program in health psychology. Brava! (Or if you are at the stage of thinking about getting a doctoral degree in health psychology, let's imagine that you have been accepted into a program.) All your energy has been placed into getting admitted into a doctoral program—but what do your graduate school years have in store for you?

In this chapter, we discuss what you will encounter in your day-to-day schedule and some of the opportunities and adventures that are in store. Specifically, this chapter will focus on academic and professional issues—coursework, dissertation, teaching, research, service, and clinical activities. Although we will touch on general issues about the culture of academia, many more general resources exist about this, which you can find in the Appendix. Instead, we continue our long view of career planning—what you can do during your doctoral training to ensure a productive and satisfying career as a health psychologist.

What Is Expected of You as a Doctoral Student?

Doctoral study that prepares you for your career as a health psychologist is very different from what is expected of you in college. In your undergraduate years, a great deal of emphasis is placed on coursework and grades. In graduate school, grades are determined by class papers, presentations, class projects, and contributions to class discussions. However, recall that much of the "work" in graduate school involves learning the skills that you will need to conduct research and, if you are in a clinical health psychology program, to treat individuals. Graduate school allows you to practice research and clinical skills as a novice under faculty supervision. Although you still need a good GPA, these experiential pieces—research and clinical experiences—are what really count for getting a postdoc fellowship or job at the end of your graduate training. A faculty member once told Lara, "If you're getting A+s in all your courses but not publishing, you're doing it wrong". That's a little harsh but not completely unrealistic.

In graduate school you are surrounded by a community of mentors, peers, and colleagues who are interested, motivated, and invested in the same thing as you—health psychology. Even as a first-year student, you are expected to operate on a professional level, thinking of yourself as a junior colleague. Faculty members expect you to be present and dedicated. This means being on time to class, lab meetings, and clinical appointments, completing assignments on time, attending departmental colloquia (research talks), workshops, and events (even if they are not required), and reading the literature in your research area, not just the assigned readings for class. You will need to make efficient use of resources and time to fulfill your course requirements and complete your research and program milestones.

"When I started graduate school, I was anxious about what to expect and how I would be received as the only student in my year coming right out of college. I quickly learned that being a graduate student is fundamentally different than being an undergraduate: Achievement was not based on ability to memorize and reproduce information provided in class, but to demonstrate an ability to critically analyze how the information impacts the field at large and your own research.

"I remember feeling overstimulated the first few weeks of classes because of the sheer amount of course reading and because I had just moved to a new city. It felt like there were so many moving parts to keep track of: reading, papers, stats lab, TAing, research—and subways! I was lucky to have the mentorship of my advisor, the advice of several advanced students and the companionship of my cohort. By the end of the year, the program had become my home. What got me through was the confidence in knowing that, even if the work seemed tough, it was my passion. Finding a program that fits your research interests is fundamental in being able to push through the hard parts. I also highly recommend taking breaks to prevent burnout—join a book club, start meditating, volunteer at a local soup kitchen, or take off a weekend to visit with an old friend! You will be more productive if you prioritize your own mental health".
—Sugandha Gupta, M.A., Doctoral Student,
The Graduate Center, City University of New York

Typical Curriculum

The heading for this section is a misnomer. There is no universal curriculum. Instead, curricular requirements for health psychology training can vary widely from program to program. Most doctoral programs in health psychology have required and elective coursework for the first year or two, leading into greater time spent conducting research and, for those pursuing clinical or counseling degrees, clinical practice responsibilities. Coursework during the first two years typically includes courses in the theoretical foundations of health psychology (and the field of psychology more broadly), research design, statistics, and ethics. Recall that in Chapter 2, we presented sample curricula for a research-only health psychology Ph.D., a clinical health psychology Ph.D. and a clinical health psychology Psy.D. program (Tables 2.1, 2.2. and 2.3, respectively).

If you are in a clinical health psychology program, especially one that is accredited by the APA, it is likely that you will also take required courses in psychopathology, intervention techniques, assessment, history of psychology, and psychometrics, as well as courses in other broad areas of psychology, such as social, developmental, cognitive, and biological psychology. If you are in an experimental health psychology or social health psychology program, it is likely that you will take foundational courses in these broad areas as well as more advanced statistics courses (e.g., biostatistics, hierarchical liner modeling) and specialized seminars that may focus on specific areas of research (e.g., psychoneuroimmunology) or methodological techniques (e.g., ecological momentary assessment, meta-analysis). Some Psy.D. programs emphasize the importance of research for doctoral students, but more from the perspective of being an expert consumer of research rather than a producer of research. As such, you can expect that the breadth and depth of required coursework on research methods and statistics will be more limited in a Psy.D. program compared to a Ph.D. program.

Doctoral study differs from an undergraduate or master's program in several fundamental ways. First, courses are a smaller part of your training after the second year; you are spending most of your time conducting research and/or engaging in clinical practica. Second, most doctoral level courses are small seminars of ten or fewer students where you will be engaged in in a discussion of the assigned readings, led by a faculty member, a student peer, or even yourself. The exception is statistics, which is often taught to a larger number of students from different areas of interest (e.g., health, clinical, and social students together). Third, you will take many of your classes with your cohort (the same group of students who entered graduate school with you) and sometimes with more advanced students in your program. Fourth, multiple-choice exams will be given rarely. Instead, you will be writing theoretical and research papers in order to receive grades. You will also be giving oral presentations in your classes, sometimes leading the discussion of assigned readings and other times giving a brief presentation on your paper topic. This makes sense, as oral and written communication are two of the key skills you will develop in doctoral training. Both are important for your success as a health psychologist.

Academic Milestones

In this book we often refer to *academic milestones*. These are the steps in a program that you must complete before receiving your doctoral degree. Milestones differ among programs, but some common milestones are listed in Table 5.1 Almost all doctoral programs describe these milestones and program requirements in a student handbook, which may be given to you when you start graduate school. You also can find them on the program's website. Keep the handbook close throughout graduate school, refer to it often, and keep an eye out for changes, as it describes all the milestones and requirements that you must reach to receive your doctoral degree, when you are expected to reach them, and what constitutes satisfactory (or unsatisfactory) progress toward the degree.

Master's Thesis or Independent Research Project

This milestone occurs relatively early in your doctoral training, usually in the first or second year. Some programs award an M.A. or M.S. degree after the completion of this milestone (along with the completion of required coursework); other programs require doctoral students to complete a master's-level independent research project *"en route"* to the doctoral degree. In either case, the student conducts a piece of original health psychology research that is typically smaller in scope than a dissertation. There are many options for this milestone. You might design and complete a small-scale study, which is sometimes a proof-of-concept study to test out new ideas or methods. You might conduct secondary analysis of data that already has been collected by your mentor or of a large data set that is available for public use. Or, you may conduct a qualitative study to generate hypotheses for your dissertation or conduct a follow-up to one of your mentor's previous studies.

Table 5.1 *Academic Milestones*

- Completion of required coursework
- A first- or second year independent research project or masters' degree project
- Clinical practica and externships for clinical and counseling psychology students
- Comprehensive/Qualifying examination(s) or paper(s)
- Dissertation proposal
- The Dissertation (written document plus an oral defense of that document)

The key here is that this milestone is "mentored" research—you are not thrown into the deep end of the pool without any support! The aim of the master's-level project is for students to learn how to conduct a project from start to finish (e.g., proposal of research question, analysis of data, presentation of results), learning skills as they go along.

Qualifying/Comprehensive Examinations and Papers

The qualifying examination (sometimes called a comprehensive examination) is typically administered after a student completes the master's thesis or master's-level project and core required coursework, but before the dissertation is proposed. Universities typically require a qualifying or comprehensive examination or paper before a student can be admitted to doctoral candidacy. To clarify: Even though you may be accepted into or enrolled in a doctoral program, being admitted to doctoral candidacy occurs after you complete sufficient requirements and you are considered ready to begin your doctoral research.

Qualifying examinations vary by program. Your qualifying exam may be an actual written examination with questions covering specific topics in health psychology and more general areas of psychological science, a systematic review paper of a particular topic in health psychology, a grant proposal (that hopefully would be used for your dissertation), or sometimes, in the case of some clinical programs, a case conceptualization and analysis. When the review paper or grant proposal options are used, they can serve as the background for the dissertation. For example, to fulfill your qualifying examination requirements you might opt to review the literature examining caregiver stress. This review could serve as the background for a dissertation designed to evaluate a randomized controlled trial to decrease stress in cancer caregivers.

The Dissertation

Although milestones vary across programs, a major and universal milestone for the doctoral degree is the dissertation. All Ph.D. and Psy.D. programs require some form of dissertation, which is almost always an original piece of research, though in some Psy.D. programs it may be a case study or theoretical review. Original research is research that you have designed, conducted, and analyzed independently (that is, it is not in collaboration with mentors or peers). There are many books written on how to "survive" the dissertation, but we prefer the term "engage with" the dissertation. Because you are an advanced student when you draft your dissertation proposal, you actually know what you are doing. And, the topic should be your topic, something you are interested in and hopefully passionate about.

Studying phenomena from a biopsychosocial perspective is often complex and recruiting medical patients can be difficult. Often students come in with an ambitious program of research for their dissertation and the dissertation supervisor's responsibility is to help students shape those ideas into a meaningful *and feasible* project that can be finished in one to two years. This again, underlies the importance of finding mentors with access to health populations or having the methodological or statistical expertise required for the study. If you are interested in psychoneuro-immunology, this may mean working with someone who has a lab equipped for cortisol or cytokine studies or has collaborators with that expertise. Or, if you are interested in ethnic or sexual health disparities, it will be important to work with someone with access to ethnic minority or sexual minority populations.

Beyond the Grades: Research, Teaching, Citizenship, and Clinical Practice

Most of your doctoral education focuses on learning and refining your knowledge and skills in research, teaching, what we call citizenship, and clinical practice, if you are in a clinical health psychology program. These are often thought of as a four-legged stool—all are necessary for the stool to be able to stand.

Research

Realistically speaking, to be competitive for most health psychology careers, you need to develop strong research credentials. This is essential if you are aiming for a position within a research-focused academic setting, medical school, or research or policy institute, and even for teaching-heavy psychology faculty positions in four-year colleges. Although the teaching identity seems like it would be the primary goal of a professor or academic, the reality is that academic jobs are rarely awarded solely on a candidate's teaching ability, and tenure is generally not achieved simply through excellent teaching. Even in liberal arts colleges, new assistant professors are expected to establish and maintain a solid research program. Thus, research is central to the lives of academic faculty in arts and sciences departments and in medical schools.

Our advice is to "hit the ground running" and start working on research the first day of graduate school. Hopefully, you have been matched with a research mentor upon admission to the program or soon after. Even before you start classes, you can start corresponding with your mentor about what research projects you will work on with them.

Health psychology research is defined broadly, reflecting the biopsychosocial model described in Chapter 1. Health psychology research can range from the study of biobehavioral processes (What is the effect of daily stress on cortisol or inflammation?) to more clinical research (How does optimism lead to greater adaptation to illness among women with breast cancer?) to policy-based research (How does participation in an afterschool program change at-home health behaviors, such as diet, as well as body mass index, a measure of obesity?). Health psychology research can involve interviewing a small number of people with a particular medical illness, conducting a large internet survey of health attitudes, carrying out a laboratory experiment with undergraduate participants to examine how social stress affects biomarkers (such as cortisol) the following day, or writing a systematic review or meta-analysis of published research that has been conducted on a particular question (Does pain affect depression?).

What kind of research you start out doing depends on the research experience you bring to graduate school with you as well as your faculty advisor's current research priorities and resources (e.g., existing datasets, ongoing projects, number of students and postdoctoral fellows in your faculty advisor's research laboratory). Some first-year students may find themselves acquiring basic skills and conducting research tasks that are similar to those they performed before graduate school, such as coding data. Other first year students are assigned to run experimental studies or conduct a literature search for a systematic review. As you move through graduate school, you generally move up the ladder in your lab, garnering more and more responsibility as a more senior student member of the lab.

If you have come to graduate school with substantial research experience (a point we have been hammering on and on about in the previous chapters) you may start off with much more responsibility. We have known first year students who were asked to co-author a chapter or conduct a secondary analysis of data and write a manuscript the day after they arrived. Hopefully your mentor already knows what skills you bring to the lab and what skills you need to develop the first year and assigns you appropriate research tasks that will help you grow intellectually.

Many health psychology doctoral programs use an apprenticeship model in which you are assigned to a single mentor and a single lab for your entire training. Others adopt a multiple mentor model where you can work with more than one faculty member during your training. Sometimes this is dictated by funding (e.g., you are being paid by a professor's grant to work on a particular study), but often it is part of the academic culture of your program. (This was one of the questions we suggested you ask faculty and students when considering different programs.) Overall, we believe that working with more than one person often provides stronger training, as you gain different areas of expertise and learn to approach research in different ways. As a graduate student in health psychology, you may even find yourself with mentors or collaborators outside of psychology. This provides useful training in navigating the complexities of interdisciplinary, multidisciplinary, and transdisciplinary collaborations common in health psychology research and practice.

"I often tell graduate students, as well as those looking to apply to graduate school, that having multiple mentors makes you a better scholar. Not only does this ensure that you will get exposed to more ideas and have more opportunities for feedback, but the different positions that faculty come from (the theories they work with, the intellectual investments each has) require that a graduate student work between ideas that may, in fact, challenge one another. This requires that a graduate student becomes more than a passive recipient of knowledge. Instead, you become someone who has to think through ideas from multiple and sometimes contradictory perspectives. For students working in departments that do not allow or encourage multiple mentors, I encourage students to find and connect with scholars in the field to gain new perspectives".
—Sara McClelland, Ph.D., Associate Professor of Psychology & Women's Studies, University of Michigan

What kind of research tasks will you actually do? This varies across labs, across mentors, and across your years in graduate school. In the course of your doctoral training you likely will be involved in research that is wholly designed by your mentor as well as research that you will do in support of your own ideas. Moreover, these can overlap, as many doctoral student research projects grow out of and expand their mentor's research or theoretical approach. At the same time, students may conduct independent research that is quite different from that of their mentor. Again, we need to emphasize that "one size does not fit all" and research expectations can vary by program or even across faculty members within the same program.

"My mentor had a 1-on-1 approach to graduate training. We didn't have large lab meetings. Instead, he worked with each student individually in weekly meetings. I still collaborated with other graduate students and helped mentor undergraduates, so I wasn't isolated, but the structure of the lab allowed me to pursue projects and opportunities I was really interested in from early on. That style of mentorship—scaffolding and a lot of autonomy—gave me a real sense of ownership over my work and productivity and was really motivating".
—Jenny Cundiff, Ph.D., Assistant Professor, University of Alabama

In some cases, the research you conduct may depend on the funding source. Are you being paid as a departmental research assistant and assigned to work with a professor? Are you paid as a research assistant on an NIH grant? Do you have your own source of funding such as a Ford Foundation fellowship or an NIH predoctoral dissertation grant? The source of funding may dictate what your responsibilities are and to whom. For example, if you are funded as a research assistant on a grant, you have

"As my mentor's first graduate student, there was a learning curve for both of us. My first tasks included designing and implementing a study of cardiovascular stress reactivity and recovery to an evaluated speech task stressor. It was amazing to watch participants' heart rate and blood pressure begin to climb on the monitors even though they were not moving a muscle. This effect showed me how powerful thoughts were in altering the body's response".
—Misty Hawkins, Ph.D., Assistant Professor, Oklahoma State University

to work on the grant as written (e.g., assisting with patient scheduling and interviewing). If you have your own funding, you may be able spend most of your time collaborating with your mentor on a joint study or even carry out your own studies.

Core Research Skills

No matter how independent your research, all research experiences serve to develop a core set of skills (see Table 5.2). This is especially true of the early years. First, you gain skills in *framing research questions* and supporting those questions with the research literature. Second, you learn to *critically evaluate a research literature*—going beyond simple summaries of the state of the field to point out connections, contradictions, and implications of multiple studies. Third, you strengthen your *methodological skills* as you design studies. The topics of internal, external, and measurement validity that are the focus of your first-year methods course(s) come to life as you conduct research. Fourth, you enhance your *statistical skills*. Many advanced students report that they really understood advanced quantitative methods only when they had to use them in their own research (and not just for a homework assignment). Fifth, you further develop both *written and oral communication skills*. For example, research is often presented in pieces or preliminary forms at conferences, where you may give a talk or present your work in a poster.

Table 5.2 Core Research Skills Gained Through Graduate School

---

1. Framing research questions
2. Critically evaluating a research literature
3. Strengthening methodological (research design) skills
4. Expanding statistical expertise
5. Building upon written and oral communication skills
6. Developing leadership skills
7. Learning to work as part of a team
8. Developing multidisciplinary or interdisciplinary perspectives
9. Enhancing clinical skills
10. Linking your research to social issues and translating research into policy recommendations

---

If you have been involved in a research project, you may take some role in writing it up as a manuscript for publication. You may be asked to start by writing a methods section or the literature review and move on to writing the results or discussion. On large, multi-part projects, students often "bite off" a piece to focus on a secondary research question, conduct the analyses, and write a manuscript. You have heard the adage: Publish or perish. Simply put, conference presentations and publications are the coin of the realm health psychologists at any career stage. Moreover, graduate students are expected to publish their findings in peer-reviewed scientific journals earlier and earlier in their careers.

We often tell doctoral students that they are going to do more re-writing than writing. In graduate school, you will revise a paper more than once, especially if the paper might lead to your dissertation research or may turn into a published manuscript. As a doctoral student, you will produce multiple drafts of your thesis and dissertation before you "orally defend" your intellectual ideas for a small committee of faculty.

Sixth, you develop *leadership skills*. As you gain experience, you are tasked with more leadership responsibilities. For example, you may be in charge of a group of undergraduates running an experiment or coding data, and it will be your responsibility to make sure that the work is done on time and is error-free. You may be asked by your mentor to take charge of a project's ethics review, drafting research protocols and institutional review board (IRB) applications. You may take leadership of the project's budget, or you may be asked to train research assistants.

Seventh, in the process of doing research you are *learning to work as part of a team*. This means sometimes taking the lead on an initiative and sometimes giving it to someone else. You learn how to meet deadlines and carry your weight on a group project. Eighth, the nature of health psychology research requires the *development and appreciation of multidisciplinary or interdisciplinary perspectives*. It is important to learn how to work with researchers in other fields who may have a different "lens" on the same research question or use a different language for concepts or a different set of methods. For example, you may be participating in a randomized clinical trial of smoking cessation among low-income adults with early-stage lung cancer that involves not only health psychologists but also a health educator, medical doctor, sociologist and anthropologist. Or, if you and your mentor study biobehavioral stress processes, you might collaborate with the social psychology faculty member down the hall who studies forgiveness, to conduct a study on the mechanisms linking forgiveness and health. Or, you and your mentor may partner with a local inpatient hospice to study end-of-life psychosocial care needs and to develop and test a psychosocial care intervention for the patients and their families.

Ninth, the research training that you receive is relevant to clinical training and *enhancing your clinical skills*. For instance, you may be serving as a therapist on a clinical behavioral intervention trial. Even for those who do not envision conducting research as part of their career, reading research and conducting research studies teaches you how to use scientific knowledge and research findings in clinical practice. Many clinical health psychology interventions, especially those reimbursed by health insurance, are "evidence-based", so it is important to be able to review and critically evaluate a research literature.

Tenth, engaging in research provides many skills in other arenas important to becoming a health psychologist. For example, research helps students to think critically about clinical and social issues. As some health psychologists go into policy arenas, and others are called upon to present evidence for government policies, it is important to understand how research findings can support laws and regulations.

> "Throughout my graduate career, I have worked on multiple studies that use unique, theoretically guided methods to promote healthy behaviors in minority children. I was particularly interested in the social-cognitive predictors of healthy weight behaviors in ethnically diverse middle school age girls. My lab responsibilities include overseeing and managing active research studies, data collection, data analysis, and manuscript preparation. I also have had the opportunity to conduct health education presentations throughout the Miami community and implement cognitive-behavioral weight management interventions for overweight/obese children and their families".
> —Mary Kate Clennan, M.S., Doctoral Student, University of Miami

Teaching

As many doctoral students envision careers as faculty members, either in an arts and sciences faculty or in a medical or public health setting, teaching experience is a good thing to acquire during doctoral training. If you think you want to go on to an academic position, it is important that you teach an undergraduate course before you start applying for jobs. This can be done while a graduate student or after, during a postdoctoral fellowship (more on this in Chapter 9). Opportunities vary. Some doctoral programs require all graduate students to teach one class to fulfill their doctoral requirements; in other programs, students may not be required to teach at all.

In many universities, doctoral students are required to be a teaching assistant (TA) as part of their financial package. In our experience, the responsibilities of being a TA can vary widely depending on the type of course, the number of students in the course, and the professor's style. Teaching assistant responsibilities range from simple grading tasks and proctoring examinations to delivering lectures or even acting as a co-instructor. TAs may be expected to attend lectures, hold office hours, answer emails from students, and/or lead weekly discussion sections. We have known graduate students who were assigned to be a TA for large (100+ students) lecture classes, where they mostly graded exams, and others who were assigned to small classes where they were expected to supervise the class lab session once a week on their own, meet with students to plan class research projects, and grade multiple papers over the course of the semester. Sometimes TAs are assigned to split their time between one to two classes per term and to help grade and create teaching materials, but they are not required to attend class or interact much with the students. For example, when author Peggy Zoccola was a graduate student and the TA for the graduate-level statistics course, she attended all classes, held office hours, graded exams and assignments, co-led lab sections for three hours per week to teach students SPSS (a computer software package), introduced and reviewed lab assignments, and conducted review sessions for exams.

If you are assigned to be a teaching assistant, we strongly suggest that as soon as you have been assigned to a class that you ask the professor if you can teach one class during the semester and—this is really important—to have her or him watch your lecture and provide feedback. This not only strengthens your teaching skills and adds to your teaching experiences, but it also gives you a head start on a repository of lectures you will have when you move to your first job.

Teaching on any topic in psychology provides valuable experience for almost all careers in health psychology. You learn how to communicate your ideas and findings from research studies clearly and how to condense a lot of information into digestible chunks. Many health psychology students choose to teach a health psychology or behavioral medicine course if one is available in their department. This can show prospective employers that they really know the material. At the same time, courses in research methods, statistics, or introductory psychology are staples in most psychology departments and therefore likely to be useful to you if you end up applying for academic positions. Teaching research design or statistics has added value: It can help enhance your own understanding of the topic because you have to explain it to others.

> "During my first week of graduate school I had to suddenly lecture to an undergraduate statistics class of 170 students when the professor couldn't be there; it was overwhelming and exhilarating. Teaching courses while in graduate school helps you develop public speaking skills (which are important for research presentations), forces you to master time management skills (so you can balance competing responsibilities), and gives you the opportunity to become proficient in narrating the story of your field. It is also immediately gratifying: Every time I walk out of class I feel like I have made a (little) difference because I imparted knowledge that could be relevant to students' professional, educational, or personal lives".
>
> —Sugandha Gupta, M.A., Doctoral Student,
> The Graduate Center, City University of New York

It is worth noting that if you have been assigned to teach, and not TA, an undergraduate class you should not be sent into the classroom "cold". Most universities offer workshops to help with basic skills, such as developing syllabi, choosing textbooks, and developing exams. This training might be within the psychology department, or at the school or university level. Check out whether your university has an administrative office dedicated to "teaching and learning" that can offer support for students who are teaching.

It is worthwhile to take a credit-bearing course in teaching if your university offers one. For example, there is a 3-credit *Teaching of Psychology* course at the Graduate Center of the City University of New York, where author Tracey Revenson teaches, which includes assignments such as drafting a syllabus for a course they are likely to teach in the next year. Students present mini-lectures that are videotaped and critiqued, and draft a statement of their teaching philosophy, which is often a part of job applications down the line. Ohio University, where author Peggy Zoccola teaches, sets up formal mentoring for first-time graduate student instructors, who take a teaching seminar and enroll in a teaching practicum with supervision by a faculty member during their first class. Similarly, at the University of Miami, where author Patrice Saab teaches, graduate student instructors complete a teaching workshop conducted by a highly experienced psychology undergraduate instructor. In addition, each student is assigned a faculty supervisor who advises on textbook selection, class format, lectures, testing, syllabus requirements, and how to handle student issues. The faculty supervisor observes the student's teaching and provides feedback to the graduate student on strengths and areas for improvement. The feedback from these courses and similar mentoring programs lead doctoral students to feel much more prepared and confident about their abilities. Many resources on teaching also can be found through the American Psychological Association's Graduate Student Teaching Association (2019).

Not all graduate students will have the opportunity to do much formal teaching, especially those funded by grants. However, consider other ways in which you may gain critical informal teaching experience for future job applications. For instance, you may have the opportunity to mentor undergraduate students, working with them on an independent study project or honors thesis, advising on career decisions, or running a research team. If you are now in the process of applying to graduate programs it may seem hard for you to imagine mentoring students like you in the next year or two, but it is likely you will.

There are definitely pros and cons to teaching in graduate school. Doctoral students often love teaching undergraduate courses because it may validate their career choice and takes away the "student" role for at least a few hours a week. Preparing slides for lectures and lecturing once or twice a week also are beneficial for preparing you to give conference talks—something you need to do as a health psychology scholar. You quickly lose nervousness and become an expert on how to present information clearly and succinctly. At the same time, teaching takes considerable time each week. Preparing lectures and exams takes time away from research and clinical activities, so be sure to balance your teaching with your other demands. For example, at the University of Miami, Patrice Saab advises third year clinical health psychology graduate students to limit their enrollment to only one graduate course during the semester they are teaching. This helps them balance the demands of preparing and teaching their own course, completing their clinical health practica, and meeting their research demands.

Some graduate program funding packages require students to do quite a bit of teaching. If you find yourself with such a funding package, keep in mind that while it might seem attractive to have a large repertoire of courses under your belt by the time you graduate, teaching a new course for the first time takes a lot of work. If you will be teaching multiple times over your graduate career, try to teach the same course or otherwise limit the number of new preparations that you have while you are a graduate student.

Clinical Experience

If you are enrolled in a clinical psychology or clinical health psychology doctoral program, then a good part of your training involves learning assessment and intervention (therapy) skills. You often start with courses in psychopathology and the foundations of psychotherapy, along with classes on intervention techniques such as cognitive-behavioral therapy, family therapy, or mindfulness training. Your program also may offer classes that focus on health psychology interventions, including evidence-based psychological interventions in medical settings, and assessment in healthy and medical populations.

The most important source of hands-on clinical training will be your clinical practica and externships, which start at either the end of your first year or the beginning of your second. Typically, you will work at only one clinical site at a time, for approximately ten to 15 hours per week, over the course of your second through fourth years of graduate school. (Recall that Psy.D. programs have higher clinical demands than research-focused doctoral programs.)

For each placement, you will be assigned clinical supervisors (usually not your research mentors) who meet with you weekly to discuss your cases and provide guidance. Your clinical supervisors may review recordings of your clinical sessions to provide feedback. Through these practica experiences, you will accrue sufficient face-to-face clinical hours and supervision hours to be a candidate for a clinical internship, the last step of your doctoral training (see Chapter 8).

Clinical health psychology graduate programs vary with respect to clinical health practice opportunities. You may start conducting your first assessments and psychotherapy at a university student health center, university counseling center, or a university-based clinic that treats members of the local community. University-based sites may not offer specific health psychology opportunities, but they are great environments to begin developing and strengthening your core psychotherapeutic skills. Health psychology issues are common in university settings, and you likely will meet clients or patients who are experiencing psychological distress related to a chronic illness or those who are trying to change health behaviors to reduce risk. You also may be able to start or co-lead a therapy group focused on a health psychology theme, such as reducing insomnia in patients with chronic medical issues, teaching non-pharmacologic pain management strategies to adults with chronic pain, or teaching relaxation and coping skills to women who are trying to conceive.

After completion of your first clinical practicum, you may begin placements outside of your university called *externships* or *traineeships*. The process for choosing or being assigned an externship varies. In some regions, your graduate program may have established relationships with specific medical settings, and your assignment may be relatively straightforward. In cities such as New York and Boston, which have a sizeable number of psychology graduate programs and many medical settings, you may be required to participate in an application and interview process that is similar to the "match system" for internships (see Chapter 8).

Luckily, many externships are relevant to clinical health psychology. Examples include clinics at Veterans Affairs Medical Centers, academic or community medical centers, and private hospitals. You may work in a psychology clinic within a medical center or down the hall from a specific medical unit (such as a pain management center), or you may work alongside other clinicians as part of a team (such as a multidisciplinary weight management clinic that includes psychologists, physicians, nurses, social workers, and nutritionists).

You may be wondering what to do if your graduate program is located in an area with limited health psychology externship opportunities. Your graduate program can work with you to identify sites that closely align with your training goals. However, you may need to think outside of the box and work with your clinical advisors to develop new relationships with a local health setting. This can be a time intensive process but is critical for your career growth. While a graduate student, author Patrice Saab spent one summer at a hospital out of town where she worked in the cardiac care unit and the following summer at a sleep lab, to obtain experience that was unavailable at her university.

Whether you have many or few choices, you may be wondering whether to select externship experiences that align closely with your own research interests or to select experiences that may be outside of your niche. We strongly encourage you to do both if possible, to strike a balance between depth and breadth. At the next phase of your career, those who are considering hiring you will want to see that you have foundational clinical experience with populations of interest and that your research is grounded in a good clinical understanding of the population. At the same time, exposure to other medical populations will help you develop a clinical skill set that is solid and broadly applicable. For Lara Traeger's research and clinical training in graduate school, she primarily worked with adults facing cancer; however, her additional training in pain management and other health psychology concerns helped her, later in her career, to serve as a clinical supervisor and to incorporate her interests into a study of chronic cancer pain.

> "One of my favorite things about my clinical placement in the Department of Psychiatry and Behavioral Sciences at Memorial Sloan Kettering Cancer Center was that I was doing clinical work with patients and caregivers at various stages of the illness trajectory; these were populations I had been researching for some time prior to—and during—graduate school. The way I connected to this particular clinical work was unlike anything I had experienced. Not only was I able to draw on my scientific knowledge about adjustment to illness, but also my clinical training gave me insight into constructs that I then incorporated into my research program. As a result of these experiences, the value of my training in a health psychology and clinical science doctoral program became crystal clear".
>
> —Aliza A. Panjwani, M.A., Doctoral Candidate,
> The Graduate Center, City University of New York

Citizenship and Leadership

Broadly defined, citizenship involves leadership, giving back to your program, and being part of research and professional teams. The APA describes a "culture of service"; that is, a commitment to service in the psychological sciences and in the profession. In academia, this means serving on committees, reviewing for journals and grants, or serving on an ethics board. This is seen as "service" because it is not a required job element or milestone for getting a doctoral degree.

Having citizenship and leadership experience as a student is a plus for almost every type of job in health psychology. Some students participate in their program governance, such as serving as a student representative on department committees. You can also be a student member of many state and national organizations, which we will talk about in more detail in Chapter 7.

How much citizenship experience one should accumulate in graduate school is debatable, in terms of the four-legged stool we described earlier in this chapter. If you choose an academic career, citizenship and leadership are highly valued, particularly in smaller departments where fewer people are available to do the important administrative work. When it comes to applying for internships and postdoctoral fellowships (see Chapters 7–9), we believe that it is more important to have stronger clinical and research experience. For example, it is more important that a student gave an oral presentation at the national meeting of the Society for Behavioral Medicine (SBM) rather than served as a student representative for SBM. However, all citizenship experiences are valuable for things like networking, exposure, learning, and building life-long collegial relationships. On a personal note, as Program Chair for the Society for Health Psychology, Patrice Saab mentored her colleague Tracey Revenson, who had been appointed as the next Program Chair; 25 years later, we are co-authoring a book.

Taking Initiative

Doctoral training seems very formulaic—requirements, milestones, achievements. However, creativity counts. You must take charge of your own education and career path, and always advocate for yourself. Ask for resources and opportunities when you needed them. Do the work to learn skills, but also do the work because you are passionate about it. Don't simply stick with the status quo in your program or give up on ideas you want to pursue because they won't happen "easily".

Taking initiative is important with your mentors, especially if you have a more "hands off" mentor. Do you see something interesting in a data set that isn't the mentor's focus? Ask if you can develop the idea. Perhaps there is another faculty member (not your primary mentor) whose work is interesting and dovetails with ideas you have had. Take the initiative and ask them to have coffee and see if they would be interesting in collaborating with you. Of course you would not do this behind your primary mentor's back, but most faculty know that students will have multiple mentors over the course of their doctoral study.

You aren't in graduate school to become a "mini-me" of your mentor. One goal of your training is for you to become an independent scholar with your own research voice and identity. One incident in author Tracey Revenson's career became a principle of mentoring for her: At one conference, she was introduced to a famous scholar who turned to her mentor and said, "Oh, so Tracey's your student", and her mentor quickly responded, "Oh, no, Tracey is her own student".

As you move into your second and third years of doctoral study you will begin thinking more seriously about what you want to do with your degree and how to get there. Yes, there are a lot of required courses and for clinical students, practicum experiences. But you still have latitude to shape your training. If you are interested in policy, take an elective in public health. Find externships that look like the kind of sites you imagine yourself working in. Create or find summer experiences that get you closer to your "ideal" job.

Sometimes taking initiative means making the hard decision to stop your involvement with a certain project or clinical site, which is taking time away from other experiences that will be more useful for getting you to the career you want. You only have so much time to devote to everything and deciding between different opportunities can be difficult. As a clinical health psychology student, you may decide you want a more clinically focused career, and so you shift your time to taking on more clients or add a day at a different site. If you start to look toward an academic career, you may decide to complete only the required clinical training and increase your involvement in research to produce publications that will make you a more competitive job candidate. Check in with yourself and your mentors often to sort through your priorities and commitments. And at the end of every year, look back to the previous year and the previous CV and see how far you have come.

Moving Ahead . . .

This chapter focused on the academic nuts and bolts of a doctoral program. You may be wondering how to thrive in graduate school, not just make it through. In the next chapter we discuss resources you can draw on during your training.

Reference

American Psychological Association. (2019). *Graduate Student Teaching Association*. http://teachpsych. org/gsta/index.php

6

MANAGING THE STRESSES AND CHALLENGES OF GRADUATE SCHOOL IN HEALTH PSYCHOLOGY

Choosing the "right" doctoral program often means that you will be leaving the comfort of your existing social support system (friends, family, current college or job, community) and starting out in a new place with new people. It takes time to figure out the culture of your new program, but you will not be doing it alone. You will find fast friends and colleagues in the other first year students. Also, do not be afraid to ask questions—information often can relieve anxiety.

What to Expect the First Semester and First Year of Graduate School

You just arrived at your graduate program, but you might as well have landed on Mars. In the span of one week you've uprooted your whole life and you are now living in a new home in a new city. You spend most of your waking hours with new people (some of whom may become life-long friends and colleagues), who are very bright and seemed to have it all figured out (spoiler: they don't). You are given a list of courses, a new desk in a lab, and a lot of deadlines. How are you supposed to acclimate to the new setting and juggle all your new responsibilities? How do you handle all of this?

We often hear that one of the most daunting things about starting a doctoral program is adjusting to the graduate courses. We hear "The classes are not like my undergraduate classes" (so true!) and "How am I supposed to keep up with all the reading?" It takes time to acclimate to a new academic culture. With fewer students in the room, there are more expectations for insight and ideas and as a first-year student once said "the crushing expectation of brilliance every week". Although it is certainly not a realistic expectation to offer clever critiques and profound wisdom to your classmates on a weekly basis, you are expected to be more "present" in the room and to go deeply into the material, especially theory. One way to do this is to start the week's readings early, taking notes right on the text that you can review before class. For every empirical study, you want to understand what the authors' aim was in conducting the study (What gap does it fill in the literature?) and to what extent they were able to answer their research questions. It's unlikely that you will be asked details about an article (how many people were in the sample?). Instead, focus your attention on whether anything stood out to you, such as innovative methods or surprising findings (e.g., all the patients had early stage cancer and high levels of education). Consider the most important questions: Do the findings fit with theory and other studies in the area? What questions are left unanswered and need to be addressed? When it comes to statistics courses, many doctoral students do homework assignments together (if permitted)—not to get it done faster but to make sure that they understand the problems.

When you start clinical work, you may also feel unsure. Just as it can be daunting to adjust to graduate courses, it's natural to feel stressed about meeting your first clinical patients or clients for the first time. You might wonder, "How should I respond if the patient asks me how old I am or how much experience I have?" Or you might worry, "How in the world will I be able to help this patient?" These concerns are natural. From the start, by offering a supportive, trustworthy, and encouraging space for patients, you're already helping to build the necessary therapist-patient bonds that are critical to any treatment that you may provide. Also remember that you are not in this alone; you will have regular supervision meetings to discuss your clinical cases. Be honest with your supervisors about your clinical sessions, including any roadblocks you may be facing. Take your supervisor's feedback earnestly and apply it in your next sessions. And finally, keep in mind that being a "good" clinician is a life-long learning process—rather than a milestone to be achieved.

What is unique for health psychology students is the impact of working with people who are facing serious medical problems and, in some cases, mortality. Although some people outside of health psychology might find it depressing to work with people in these circumstances, many in health psychology feel that it is inspiring work. So, whether you are a clinical health student or an experimental/social/developmental health student, exposure to patients facing daily symptoms, disability, or mortality may help inspire some of you and remind you why you decided to go to graduate school in the first place. However, if you are finding it very stressful to work with health psychology populations, talk with your advisor or mentor at the earliest possible moment. They may be able to help you refine your interests or address your discomfort. Cynthia Belar (2008) provides a checklist that students can use to assess their readiness to provide services to patients with physical health problems that can be used to guide these discussions.

Despite the milestones, courses, and examinations, many students wonder: What should we hope to accomplish professionally, in research, clinically, and psychosocially in our first year? Different programs have different expectations; in some, you are expected to present a poster at a conference during your first year. But think about it—how can you present research if you haven't done it yet? Be sure to give yourself time to do the necessary work; you will rack up the credentials soon enough. In all honesty, it will take time—perhaps the whole year—for acquaintances to turn into friendships, lab mates to become colleagues, and advisors to become mentors. Be open to experiences. If your program needs students to help with the admissions interview day, volunteer. If most of your lab goes to a particular conference, go with them, even if you aren't presenting your research (yet). You will learn the culture of the lab soon enough.

A lot of students tell us they feel like "imposters". They don't fully understand the theories or statistics or how to work with patients (and it may feel like they never will). They start to doubt whether they belong in a doctoral program at all. There is actually a name for this phenomenon: imposter syndrome. And it's more common than you probably realize. Our simple advice: You wouldn't need graduate school if you knew everything when you walked in. These are the years to learn, to soak it in, and not become an immediate expert in everything. In fact, when writing yearly evaluations, faculty look for progress and not simply knowledge or stagnation. Trust us—You will be a very different person at the end of your doctoral training.

Any student who has been offered admission to graduate school has earned that position. Repeat that to yourself frequently. And you are as knowledgeable as others perceive you to be. Getting stuck in the "imposter syndrome" mindset can really hinder your learning experience and your productivity as a graduate student. Identifying the self-doubt early on and learning coping strategies out of that mindset is crucial during their first year. If you still feel this at the end of the first year, discuss it with your mentor during the end-of-year evaluation and devise strategies to go beyond it.

What I Wish I had Known . . .

Each year, students in CUNY's Health Psychology and Clinical Science doctoral program are asked what advice they would give to entering students. Their sage advice can be found in Table 6.1.

Table 6.1 *Advice to First Year Students From More Advanced Students*

- Be open-minded and flexible to all that the program has to offer. Students have to learn to balance all their responsibilities but still maintain an understanding of all the opportunities and learning experiences they will encounter.
- Being a part of the community is an important and special component to being a doctoral student and adds to the unique experience of a program.
- Don't be afraid to ask for help with strategies for navigating the demands of coursework. Fellow students and the faculty can be highly supportive.
- It is important for each cohort of students to be a team. I did not know or believe this my first year. Although each cohort is unique, it is important to create this network so you can rely on with the people around you.
- One essential thing for incoming students is that self-care is important, though it is easy to let that slide and difficult to master. Recharging before the start of the semester(s) is one way to do so.
- Find your own path! While you take classes together the first and even second years, you are all different. Do what *you* want to do; don't always go along with the pack.
- Your time training as Ph.D. students is precious: Use it pursuing what you love in the most supportive environment you can find.
- Appreciate the five years ahead of you because the opportunities are vast, the people are great, and the time will really fly by. So, be sure to buckle in and really enjoy all aspects of the ride.

Developing and Maintaining Relationships With Mentors

Lifespan psychologist Daniel Levinson wrote,

> The mentor relationship is one of the most complex, and developmentally impor-
> tant, a [person] can have in early adulthood. . . . No word currently in use is
> adequate to convey the nature of the relationship we have in mind here. . . .
> Mentoring is defined not in terms of roles but in terms of the character of the
> relationship and the function it serves.
>
> (1978, p. 98)

Your professional career will be filled with mentors, and it is likely that one day you will be a mentor.

Advisor vs. Mentor

Note that there is a difference between an advisor and a mentor, although sometimes they will be the same person. An *academic advisor* provides consultation on curriculum planning and academic matters. You should meet with this person as soon
as the fall semester begins (if not before) to plan your first-year curriculum and

research responsibilities. If the meeting is not set up formally for all first-year students or your advisor does not contact you, email your advisor as soon as possible to meet. An advisor's role is important: Advising ensures that you meet the requirements for graduation.

Modern definitions describe a mentor as a trusted friend, counselor, or teacher, usually a more experienced person.

> Mentoring is an intense, personal, and nonsexual relationship with a high level of commitment. Mentoring is also reciprocal but asymmetrical, which means that mentor and mentee can both benefit from the mentoring, but the primary purpose of the relationship is growth and development of the mentee.
>
> (Sambunjak & Marušić, 2009, p. 2592)

Mentors take a personal interest in their students, seeking to teach and challenge them. Mentors are an ally at times and provide tough love at other times. Mentors help graduate students develop a strong professional identity and competence in their work. Mentors act as role models for successful performance in the field, modeling productivity, competence, and professionalism. Supportive and positive mentoring relationships between graduate students and their advisors are related to less anxiety and depression (Levecque, Anseel, De Beuckelaer, Van der Heyden, & Gisle, 2017).

A good mentor nurtures students' professional development by providing them with support and guidance to pursue their own interests, grow, and develop into successful independent professionals. That support and guidance is often more structured during the first year or two of graduate school, as students get their sea legs. You don't want a mentoring relationship where there is constant "hand-holding"

"I had a wonderful mentor in graduate school, Chris Dunkel-Schetter, who continues to be a friend and guide. . . . I encourage my students to set and achieve their own goals in a timeframe that they determine, to always do their best, to ask for and accept help when needed, and to find the right balance between work and whatever else is important in their life. Each student needs slightly different things from a mentor, so it's important to recognize and be responsive to a student's individual style and needs. And no one is an automaton, so a mentor should help students determine reasonable, achievable goals that don't deprive them of the ability to take care of their health, their emotional state, and to have some fun, too".
—Marci Lobel, Ph.D., Professor of Psychology, Stony Brook University

(the mentor too closely supervises the mentee, which doesn't allow them to develop their own expertise or skills) or one that is completely detached (the mentor lets the mentee work without any supervision or guidance or hands over the mentoring to a more advanced doctoral student or postdoctoral fellow). Rather, a balanced approach in which the mentee is taught specific skills and then given increasing latitude to practice them is desired.

What to Expect From Your Mentor

We advise that you set up a time to discuss expectations at the beginning of your mentorship relationship. For first year students, this means by the first week of the term. Table 6.2 provides talking points developed by faculty and students at Ohio University to help guide the process. Some doctoral programs are even using mentor-mentee agreement forms as a way to clarify expectations and goals.

Table 6.2 *Talking Points for Meetings With Advisors and Mentors*

How to Succeed in Graduate School
- What are your expectations of me as a Ph.D. student? How do you anticipate these expectations changing throughout my time here? (Also see "Expectations" section.)
- What do you see as your role as in furthering my professional success?
- In what ways do you expect me to help in and contribute to your lab?
- How often will you assess me or give me feedback about how I am doing in the program?
- From your experience with past advisees, what specific activities/behaviors have prevented them from succeeding the program? What should I do to avoid these issues, and how have you helped your advisees overcome these issues in the past?
- Do you have specific career goals in mind for your students? How open are you to discussing different career paths with me (e.g., academic vs. non-academic, research-focused vs. teaching-focused)?

Expectations
- What conferences should I attend? How many should I attend per year as I progress through the program?
- When do you expect me to propose my thesis/dissertation? When do you expect me to take comprehensive exams?
- How much research do you expect me to do? For instance, how many projects/studies should I be involved in at a time?
- How many hours per week do you expect students to work? What are your expectations regarding physical presence in the office/departments?
- Do you expect students to stay in town and work during breaks (e.g., summer)? How available should students be during breaks?
- How much time do you expect students to spend on research vs. teaching/TA responsibilities? Do you have suggestions for how to balance these responsibilities?

Early in the relationship, establish specific time-based guidelines for when you (the mentee) can expect feedback on written materials. For each specific piece of work, set a specific schedule with your mentor for the delivery of the work and when you will receive feedback on something you have written. Neither mentor nor mentee should be expected to drop everything, nor should either be in a position of waiting for weeks without a reasonable expectation of a response. From the start, you should plan work together and establish regular and responsive communication patterns. Some people work late at night, others want protected time. It is also important to be available for as-needed communication, in person by phone,

The Research Process
- How do your advisees earn authorship, particularly first authorship, on a publication? What are the criteria for being 1st author, 2nd author, and so forth?
- What are your expectations regarding data analysis? Do you and your advisees typically analyze data together, or do your advisees typically analyze datasets on their own and bring the results to you?
- In what condition do you expect first drafts of my work to be when you receive them? For instance, do you prefer to see an outline of a manuscript draft before I begin writing? Do you prefer for me to send you different parts of a draft piece-by-piece, or for me to send you a complete version from the beginning?
- On research-related work (e.g., manuscripts, conference presentations, study materials), do you typically provide written feedback, verbal feedback, or a combination?

Collaboration
- To what extent would you be comfortable with my collaborating with other faculty members inside and outside of the department?
- To what extent would you be comfortable with my taking on collaborative projects without you being personally involved with them (e.g., projects with other faculty, projects with other students)? Do you want me to discuss any collaborative projects with you first (e.g., do I need you to approve/sign off before I start a new project)?
- Do you have any specific recommendations regarding who would be a good mentor for certain area(s) of my professional development (e.g., teaching, research, and ultimate career goals)?

Communication
- Do you have a preferred method of communication (e.g., email, phone, text)? What types of issues would you like for us to handle in person vs. via email/phone/text?
- How quickly should I expect to hear back from you about basic questions/issues? How quickly should I expect to receive feedback from you on study materials, drafts of conference presentations or manuscripts, etc.? If I don't hear back from you, do you want to be reminded? If so, how (e.g., in person, over email)?
- Do you tend to keep regular hours at work (e.g., 8–9 until 5), or more sporadic hours? When you are in the office, do you have an open-door policy—that is, do you mind if I drop in unexpectedly? Do you have non-work periods (e.g., would you prefer not to hear from me on weekends)?

Source: The information in this table is printed with permission from Kimberly Rios, Matthew Wilkinson, and Gaura Rader.

Table 6.3 *Expectations About Mentoring Relationships*

What your mentor expects from you:
- Listen to and respond to feedback from your mentor in a timely manner.
- Be proactive with respect to suggesting research, assuming responsibilities, etc.
- Have the confidence to ask questions and, when appropriate, provide your views about your work and about your mentor's expectations for you. (We recognize that because of the inherent power difference, it is up to the mentor to provide an environment that fosters honest communication.)
- Engage in regular discussions about your progress toward degree completion. Most doctoral programs have formal student evaluations annually, but we suggest that you check in with your advisor and/or mentor once or twice a semester to monitor strengths and weaknesses or to voice your desires (e.g., to take a course in another department or to be given more responsibility in the lab).
- Communicate with your mentor *ahead of time* when you will not be available to perform expected research responsibilities in a timely manner. Sh—t happens. If you experience a family or health issue, it's important to talk with your mentor (and expect confidentiality from them) about how this might affect your work and the functioning of the lab.

What to expect from your mentor:
- Your mentor should establish communication patterns that are transparent and respectful.
- Your mentor should be clear about expectations for productivity on research projects, providing timelines for completing research tasks, writing, and program milestones.
- You mentor should be clear about the expectations for the content and quality of work, especially for first year students that are new to the lab.
- Your mentor should set clear goals, in advance, for the completion of major program milestones (e.g., a comprehensive paper) and research projects in your lab.

---

or email. This becomes even more crucial, for example, as no-extension deadlines approach (e.g., for grant proposal submissions).

There are no hard and fast rules (see Table 6.3). Your mentor should respond to your inquiries in a timely fashion, as would be expected for any professional communication. The same goes for requests made of you by your mentor. As a rule of thumb, you should expect to receive feedback on written material, such as a comprehensive paper or research proposal, within a few weeks. Emails should typically receive a response within 24 hours, often much sooner, during the workweek (i.e., not on weekends or holidays), and not when your mentor is on vacation!

What Your Mentor Expects From You

Mentoring is a social relationship so there are also expectations for health psychology students. Many things are obvious: Be on time to classes and meetings, complete work on the agreed-upon time frame, and respect the fact that your mentor is likely overworked with teaching, research, travel, journal editorships, and administrative responsibilities of which you may be unaware. Be a colleague and take initiative. For example, if you see an article in a professional journal or newsletter that is relevant to your mentor's or your joint work, send it. Especially when it comes to research, this is much appreciated.

Professionalism in Mentor-Mentee Relationships

Although there may be variability in the individual styles, all mentor-mentee relationships should be professional, collegial, and nonsexual in nature. Graduate school has enough stress. A good mentor views the mentee as a junior colleague or colleague-in-development and establishes a relationship that is appropriate to these roles. This is in contrast with employment relationships that are very hierarchical in nature (boss-underling) or have more diffuse boundaries (friendship or parent-child). The primary content of mentor-mentee interactions will be focused on topics that are relevant to the students' research, teaching, or academic progress. Types of activities that would not be appropriate in this context would not be appropriate in any professional context (e.g., use of illicit drugs, drinking alcohol together excessively, sexual and romantic involvement, or commenting on a mentee's appearance in excessive detail). As a mentee, you are not your mentor's personal assistant; activities like watching children, dusting shelves, or running errands are not appropriate activities for you (and, yes, this has happened).

But a good mentor relationship? Nothing matches it. Many remain mentors for life, staying in touch with students long after they graduate. (In fact, one of the authors of this book, Patrice Saab, was a mentor of another, Lara Traeger.) The mentoring relationship takes time to develop. Some suggest that students should initiate a mentoring relationship; others suggest that faculty move from an advisor to a mentor role with the students in their lab or classes. In either case, research shows that students who feel mentored in graduate school do better (Mollica & Nemeth, 2014).

Sometimes your mentor is not available. A likely reason for this is when she or he is on sabbatical or other faculty leave, which is a "natural" part of an academic's life (see example in Table 6.4). Author Tracey Revenson describes the sabbatical to her students in Table 5.5. Discuss with your mentor how much communication there will be and if it is advisable to have another faculty member supervise your work and co-mentor you during this time period. In other cases, you mentor may become ill or face severe family problems. As a student, you may have more responsibility during this time, or you might feel neglected. Again, first talk with your mentor about how to handle the situation or, if your mentor is not available, talk with your Training Director. Do not let this go on long—alternate arrangements can be made.

As mentoring is a personal relationship, there may be obstacles or conflicts to overcome. It is possible that you may not "click" with your mentor or with the way

Table 6.4 *Tracey A. Revenson's Letter to Students About Sabbatical*

Dear [Student]:

The ancient Jewish tradition of the sabbatical decrees that every seventh year the fields are to be left untilled. Maimonides stated that "By releasing the land it will become invigorated; by lying fallow and not being worked it will regain its strength".

The translation of this Torah portion for academics is a blessing and a privilege. I think of the sabbatical as a year when regular responsibilities [crops] are passed over in favor of allowing the brain [soil] to become rich again with nutrients and for the professor to have the time to think and develop new ideas about her scholarship. And with that restoration, the professor is more productive (and less cranky) when she returns.

I will be on sabbatical from August 2017 through August 2018 and released from all administrative and teaching duties. That means I will not be in the office and won't be answering emails as quickly as I often do. I have a number of projects I plan to complete: to co-author a new book aimed at undergraduates, *Becoming a Health Psychologist*, edit the new edition of the *Handbook of Health Psychology*, and write a number of articles. I won't exactly be relaxing, but I will be on my own schedule for work and won't be setting a wake-up alarm!

I wish you all a productive time while I am away. Please come talk to me about planning how you will continue to progress through graduate school during my sabbatical.

Tracey

---

the lab is run. Or perhaps there is a falling out between you and mentor. If this is the case, you need to handle the change professionally, first talking with your current mentor and then with the director of your program, and then with potential new faculty mentors. Do not just walk away from your current mentor/lab—you need to complete your responsibilities with one research mentor before moving to another. Don't burn your bridges. As we said before, health psychology is a relatively small community.

Students can change mentors, successfully, in the middle of graduate school. Reasons for this may go beyond a lack of personal or professional fit between mentor and mentee. If your research interests change over time, you may decide to work with someone whose work better fits those new interests. Sometimes a new faculty member is hired who more closely fits your interests. Or perhaps your mentor will be relocating to a different institution. You may or may not be asked to move as well; this will depend on your year in graduate school, funding, and other constraints. If that happens, your program director of department chair will help you find a new mentor, and there is no reason you should lose any time toward degree.

We repeat our recommendation to work with more than one faculty member during your graduate training. Although not everyone you work with will be a true mentor, each scholar has a unique perspective that will add to your knowledge base. The University of Michigan has a wonderful guide, "How to get the mentoring you want" (Rackham Graduate School, 2018a) that should be required reading for all first year students.

> "Mentorship is such an important component of graduate school and, I would argue, throughout one's career. Graduate school mentors need not always be faculty within one's program. I benefited from having mentors through professional organizations with which I was affiliated. These 'professional homes' can be an outstanding source of mentorship".
> —Travis Lovejoy, Ph.D., M.P.H., Associate Professor,
> Oregon Health & Science University

Peer Support

An important research topic in health psychology is the relation between social support and health. Support comes in many forms—emotional, instrumental, and informational—and the best outcomes derive from a fit between the support one needs and the support one receives (Revenson & Lepore, 2012). Your peers—other students in your program, lab, or department as well as those in other academic departments—can provide all three types. A piece of advice that everyone needs at some point: Don't look at your peers as competitors but as colleagues. Also know that after first year you will all take different paths to your careers, with different timelines—it doesn't matter who finishes first.

> "Graduate school is an interesting experience in that everyone is expected to complete the same coursework and milestones but also expected to begin developing their own unique scholarly identity. One disadvantage of having a close cohort is the tendency to feel like you need to be doing the same thing your peers are doing and the resulting comparisons that are made between yourself and other students in the cohort, which has the potential to contribute to the inevitable impostor syndrome most people experience. Overall, I have found there to more advantages than disadvantages to having a close cohort, including having the support of people who understand the stress and process of graduate school and the opportunities to collaborate in graduate school and most certainly beyond graduate school".
> —Raymond L. Moody, M.A., Doctoral Candidate,
> The Graduate Center, City University of New York

Evaluations and Self-Assessment in Graduate School

Evaluation is ever-present in health psychology careers—health psychologists receive critical reviews of grant proposals and manuscripts submitted to peer-review journals, teaching evaluations, and clinical evaluations (supervision). The evaluation process is also central to your life as a graduate student, as faculty meet at least annually (or more often) to formally evaluate student progress. Evaluations cover academic (coursework and other milestones), research, clinical, and professional development domains, as well as graduate student program responsibilities (e.g., TA performance and teaching evaluations). Clearly, doing well in all domains is important.

Doing well in coursework shows that you have mastered the basics in theory, research design, statistics, and the competencies required of health psychologists. Indicators of progress include course grades, involvement in class discussions, assessments of writing quality, and timeliness in completing assignments. Research progress is assessed in a variety of ways, including the quality of contributions to the lab's ongoing research projects, progress in developing a master's thesis or dissertation proposal, the degree of success in writing and defending a thesis or dissertation, and whether you have been presenting at professional conferences, submitting and publishing research papers, and applying for grants and awards. Whew that is a lot! But that is part of the four-legged stool we described earlier.

Evaluating research progress is most helpful when students are asked to conduct a self-assessment before they are evaluated. A self-assessment asks you to consider how you have met the program's expectations for your performance. It is also a good idea (even if not required) to outline and discuss your research goals with your research advisor at the beginning of each term and to evaluate your progress in meeting those goals at the end of the term.

Use these meetings as an opportunity not for self-criticism and apologies but to reflect on your accomplishments and goals that did not get accomplished (and why). This will help you understand what can be done differently and what support you need from your advisor to accomplish those goals. For example, if your find it helpful for your mentor to provide more concrete deadlines, you can start with that and move toward making your own deadlines (which is really what you need to do as an independent scholar.) Or, you might ask your mentor to assist more with professional development opportunities. This does not mean that they should find grant opportunities for you or tell you what to present at conferences but to help you use resources to enhance you career. The take-home point is that you should be able to have an open discussion with your mentor about the best ways to move you forward at the particular point in your graduate career. Newer students may require more structure, but advanced students need to be more independent as they have learned basic skills.

Clinical activities are evaluated by practicum and externship supervisors. You can expect that your clinical supervisor will give you ongoing verbal feedback over the course of your work together. At least once a year (and usually at the end of each term) you will sit down with your supervisor for a formal clinical evaluation. The supervisor will complete the evaluation form provided by your graduate program. Typically, you will be evaluated on your professional conduct and ethics and how you use the supervision process, your assessment skills, and your facilitative and clinical therapy skills. In each domain, the supervisor will determine whether your performance is unsatisfactory, needs some improvement, meets expectations, or exceeds expectations. During this evaluation, your supervisor will discuss your strengths as well as the areas you need to work on. Your supervisor will then submit your evaluation to your Director of Clinical Training (the head of your department's clinical program). The Director of Clinical Training and your department's clinical faculty members will discuss your clinical evaluation and make a final determination about your clinical progress.

As you can see, multiple sources of information are considered when evaluating students. For example, at the University of Miami where Patrice Saab teaches, clinical health psychology students are discussed at the end of each semester during three separate faculty evaluation meetings: a clinical faculty meeting, a health faculty meeting, and a general faculty meeting. The information is synthesized and students are sent written evaluations that provide specific information on how they are doing in the program.

The written evaluation you receive is not like a traditional report card—it is about progress and not a grade. Evaluations show whether a student has reached expected competencies (as determined by APA and by your program) for the doctoral degree. They are designed so that one can look at evaluations over time and see change and progress throughout the training period.

The amount of feedback that students receive varies quite a bit from program to program. For instance, APA-accredited programs require detailed feedback on competencies, augmented by written feedback. However, in many research-focused programs, feedback is provided more broadly in the areas of academics (coursework, comprehensive exams, and thesis/dissertation), research, and assistantship responsibilities. Of course, specific feedback and more detailed feedback always can be requested from or given at the discretion of individual faculty members.

Although no one wants to receive a poor evaluation, it is not uncommon to receive feedback that points out areas for improvement. For new graduate students, who are used to receiving high marks for their undergraduate work, this may be a new and uncomfortable experience. Some of author Tracey Revenson's students are horrified when they don't get perfect "scores" on every competency at the end of first year. But how could they, for example, have mastered multivariate statistical skills or writing a theoretical manuscript when they haven't done it yet?

Students that experience notable difficulties in one or more domains should expect to receive a written evaluation that includes a behavior-focused problem statement and a remediation plan. The remediation plan is tailored to the specific competencies that need work and will identify what you need to accomplish to resolve the concerns, and by what date. If you get a bad evaluation, don't panic. Discuss the evaluation with your mentor, your program director, and/or your Director of Clinical Training to determine what specific steps you can take to achieve mastery in particular skill areas. Even if the evaluation doesn't include a timeline to demonstrate those skills, make one! Plan for frequent "check-ins" with your advisor and with the faculty overseeing the remediation plan to provide updates and receive feedback on your progress.

Perhaps you feel, however, that you have been treated unfairly in the evaluation. After discussion with your mentor, you should go to your program training director, the graduate chair, or the "top" person in the department. This person may tend to "agree" with your mentor, as they do not have day-to-day contact with you, but you have put yourself on that person's radar. Again, check in with them during the next semester to see if the situation eases.

If problems are more serious, all universities have an ombudsperson to go to. Your program or university's graduate student handbook should lay out the procedures for student grievances. If you feel discriminated against by a faculty member for any reason, your lab supervisor, or other students, go to your program director, the graduate chair, or the university ombudsperson. Universities are required to have strong policies in place for these types of situations, as well as against retaliation, which are taken seriously.

Health Disparities and Students' Lived Experience

As health psychologists, we often study health disparities concerning gender, ethnic minority status, sexual minority status, physical ability, religion, and social class differences; we also learn cultural competence by working with a diverse set of clients. And the psychology workforce is becoming more diverse, with women, students from historically underrepresented groups, international students, LGBTQ+ students, students with disabilities, students with children, and students who are the first in their family to go to graduate school constituting the majority of graduate students in the U.S. (Rackham Graduate School, 2018b).

Most health psychology programs are committed to promoting diversity and attracting graduate students from diverse backgrounds. Formal and informal discussions between faculty and students can draw attention to the way health psychologists can incorporate a greater understanding of diversity into our curricula, research, clinical roles, and professional development. A good health psychology program will periodically assess the extent to which students and faculty feel that the program is promoting its diversity goals.

Despite these efforts, existing policies and practices may still lead to challenges for underrepresented students. They may feel isolated from other students because they have not had the same life experiences. Some faculty may hold stereotyped expectations about their abilities or performance and withhold important career development opportunities. As a result, a student can feel disadvantaged or mistreated because of identification with an underrepresented group. Raising concerns about mistreatment can feel fraught, but you need to trust your instincts when something doesn't feel right. Universities have rules, processes, and policies in place for addressing concerns. With that said, you may feel comfortable seeking out advice and mentorship from someone you trust— if not your current mentors and colleagues, then a social group within the institution that supports the values and rights of a particular group. Moreover, all institutions have an ombudsperson or administrative group that is tasked to support minority students or students who feel that have been mistreated. Go to them immediately to find a resolution. We agree that this shouldn't be fully on your shoulders, but bringing issues to light—with your peers supporting you—can bring about real change.

"Find your champion. We all need someone to go to bat for us and life becomes easier when we have a mentor we can trust. This person may not be your supervisor or even in your program but is someone who will help. Look around to find that person. Especially if you are from an underrepresented group, you may want to find someone in your field like you. Reach out to them. I welcome any such contact and enjoying being a mentor to those who need it at my university or nationally. There are graduate student organizations and organizations for different groups. Reach out and get involved and you will soon find likeminded individuals and people who will be willing to be your champion".

—Regan Gurung, Ph.D., Professor of Psychological Science,
Oregon State University

> "First, try to avoid buying into questions about *how you got there* and instead focus on *what you can do* with the opportunity. Second, build allies and expand your networks which is important for success in grad school, findings jobs, and general life satisfaction. I also think it is important to acknowledge that we are at the beginning of a renaissance when it comes to recognizing the value of diversity. Most people are well intentioned, and it is to your benefit to embrace that intention".
>
> —John M. Ruiz, Ph.D., Associate Professor of Psychology, University of Arizona

Maintaining Work-Family Balance in Graduate School

Doctoral study takes a large chunk of your day and doesn't always stop for weekends. There will be all-nighters cramming for a statistics exam or submitting a grant proposal or finishing a conference abstract before the online website closes at 11:59 pm. (And yes, this continues well into your career.) You may be juggling your own classwork, teaching, and multiple research projects in any given week.

You have papers to write and exams to grade, but life continues to happen during graduate school: new relationships, marriages, break-ups, children, illnesses, and taking care of family members. All students need to have access to affordable childcare so their lives are not put on hold if they choose to have families while in graduate school. This can be captured by the subtitle of an article in the Yale Alumni Magazine (Labi, 2006), "Do changing diapers and helping with homework leave time for world-class scholarship?" We will keep our advice on this subject brief because this is a larger issue of graduate study, and not unique to those in health psychology. There are many sources written by and for graduate students that provide suggestions for coping and how to keep your sense of humor (see Appendix).

Perceptions count. In a study of department chairs' responsibility for diversity in science departments conducted by Sara McClelland, getting married and having children were discussed explicitly as *choices* made by women, and it was this *choice* that may have slowed down their careers as faculty members (e.g., not getting tenure; McClelland & Holland, 2015). Framing this as a choice signals a distinct way of blaming women as responsible for their own underrepresentation in science departments. One could argue there *are* choices to be made. This is brought home in an article by medical journalist Lisa Belkin, in which she describes her agonizing choice to give a talk at a conference while her son is in surgery:

> I began this column in the surgical waiting room of Mount Sinai Hospital. I didn't get far. There are some places, some situations where real work is simply

impossible. . . . I know, I know, in theory this might have been a good time to call an editor and say my column simply wouldn't run this week. After all, isn't that what I preach? And yet, if the lines were clear, we wouldn't fail to see them so often. [Working] while your son is in surgery, okay that one is straightforward. But what about the next day? Does your answer change when I tell you [my son] is 15, not 5? And what are we weighing here anyway—how badly he needs me or how distracted I am by the thought he might? Is one of those a better reason not to work? And by "better" who, exactly am I trying to convince—myself or my boss?

(2006, p. HW1)

Attending to family or personal concerns—your own children, your aging parents, or major life stressors—is part of life and shouldn't stop your career progress. It means more juggling of roles (e.g., add parent to researcher, teacher, and student) and perhaps more planning and lowered expectations for a time. Everyone—students and faculty—needs understanding at these times. If you find yourself with a family or personal issue, talk with your advisor immediately. A first step is to reduce some of your immediate responsibilities in your program or lab. If the problem is likely to persist for some time, a second step is to take a leave of absence. Most programs will provide a year or so of leave with "no questions asked". This means that will be no expectations that courses will be completed or research deadlines met during a stressful time. Again, talk with both your mentor and program director as to the best course of action for you.

"I am a mother, spouse, daughter, sister, friend, and professor, and each of those roles entails great responsibility (and joy!). Sometimes we achieve balance in our roles, but more often we learn to juggle. The most important advice I have: if you want to be involved in a relationship and have a family while in graduate school (or at any time in your working life), choose a real partner—someone who will genuinely share all that is required, from decision-making to the daily nitty gritty. Sharing does not always require a 50–50 split in the division of labor, but it does require a split that is fair and equitable. And it's important to remember that the best-laid plans of mice, women, and men often go awry. Children get sick even when you have a grant due and your partner is at a conference. Don't catastrophize. Ask for help. One downside of academic life is that many of us take jobs in places where we have no friends or family. Create your own family, find people with whom you can have a mutually supportive relationship. Look around your campus childcare center, that's a great place to find likeminded souls willing to help each other".

—Marci Lobel, Ph.D., Professor of Psychology, Stony Brook University

Self-Care Skills

You will be overworked. You will be tired. There may even be times when you think you made the wrong choice and want to drop out. As health psychologists, we all know that (chronic) stress leads to illness, and we know how the mind and body interact. So it is important to take care of your own body and mind during graduate school. One of the most important skills developed during your first year are self-care skills. It is so important to learn what works for you and, more importantly, what *doesn't work* in managing your stress. Does walking the dog calm you down and give you time to think about new ideas without a computer screen in front of you or a yellow highlighter in your hand? Are you forgetting to eat as you rush from class to clinic and back to class? Are you feeling that all the other members of your cohort are handling first year just fine and it is just your problem?

Make sure to give yourself some downtime on the weekend—get active, socialize with others, or relax with a movie. Your eyes can't be focused on the screen 24/7. Join a local (fiction) book club. If you were on a dance team in college, find one at your new university. And take a break over the scheduled vacation breaks. If you work through Christmas and New Year's holidays, you will be exhausted when the spring semester starts. The same goes for the summer; be sure to give yourself a real vacation for a week or two so you are fresh for the new academic year. Even a long weekend without work after you have turned in your papers and grades and abstracts can make a difference.

The first year of graduate school is the perfect time to discover what you need to do to stay mentally and physically healthy. You can definitely rely on other students to help you figure it out. Don't just turn to those in your cohort—often the

---

"There will be times you have to give graduate school your all. Dissertation proposals, comprehensive exams, grant submissions, and internship applications all take a considerable amount of your time and energy. Talk with your friends and family and problem-solve together how you can get the support you need during these particularly demanding time-limited seasons. After these seasons are over, plan at least a few days where you take a complete break from graduate school and re-engage with your family and other social support networks".

—Elizabeth K. Seng, Ph.D., Assistant Professor of Psychology,
Yeshiva University and Research Assistant Professor of
Neurology, Albert Einstein College of Medicine

"Graduate school hits you in waves. There are times when course work, comprehensive examinations, theses and dissertations, clinical practica for those pursuing clinical, or counseling degrees make it feel as if you have little time for anything else. But it is rarely constant and taking opportunities to do things outside of one's graduate program, particularly during less demanding times, is critical for one's sanity. I spent a lot of time gardening and playing city league softball in graduate school".

—Travis Lovejoy, Ph.D., M.P.H., Associate Professor,
Oregon Health & Science University

"When I first started working as a health psychologist, I was balancing clinical work (seeing patients in a hospital setting), research, and administrative work. The best skill I learned was to really make the best of the time I had. So, if I had an hour off between patients, I would try to be productive for at least 45 of those 60 minutes. Breaking tasks into steps like that and moving things forward really helped me with productivity. Also, during the first years, when being an Instructor or Assistant Professor, I had to spend doing a lot of the work myself, but then as time went by and I was able to hire staff and obtain grant funding. A key to success is learning how to delegate! As time went by, I could work primarily on things that only I needed to do, and was able to delegate the work that could be done by others. This allowed for more free time for family and having fun in the evenings and weekends".

—Steven Safren, Ph.D., Professor of Psychology, University of Miami

more advanced students in your program or lab can really help. In one of CUNY's first year intervention classes, students were asked to test out a stress management intervention on themselves over the semester, and many are still doing it. (A perfect example of an n of 1 evidence-based finding!) But if you feel you are sinking more and more into the mud, it's also a good time to seek counseling—most universities have free or sliding scale counseling services.

Staying on Track and Finishing the Doctorate

Many of our doctoral students say that at some point in their graduate training they stop seeing a light at the end of the tunnel, often when writing their dissertation proposal or writing the actual dissertation. Most universities have time limits for completing the degree, and most students complete their degree in five or six years.

But sometimes students have difficulty finishing. This often happens because of perfectionism or because students have difficulty managing multiple demands both within and outside of their doctoral program. News alert: Your dissertation may not be the best thing that you ever write. A tenet we love is, "A good dissertation is a finished dissertation. A great dissertation is a published dissertation. A perfect dissertation is neither".

What can you do to stay on track? Time management skills, starting in the first year, are essential. In the beginning, it is difficult to gauge how long researching a topic, conducting analyses, or writing a manuscript will take. It differs for everyone and sometimes a deadline can be the prime motivator for finishing a grant proposal or a manuscript. Estimate how long a task will take and multiply it by five. Yes, five. That way you don't have to apologize for not getting something done.

Time management means sometimes saying that what you are writing or doing has to be "good enough". Clearly you want a dissertation proposal or research manuscript to be more than good enough. But everything you write will not be a masterpiece because you need to take time for yourself. Many first-year students say that the most important thing they learned was how to read the many articles required for just one week's classes—when to read in depth, when to skim, and what to look for in either case. This will be the same when you start reviewing the extensive research literature for a new project.

Time management also means sometimes saying "no". This is a tough one for all of us. Opportunities arise: You are asked to contribute to the design of another faculty member's study, conduct journal reviews, co-author a book chapter, serve on a student council, join a journal club, or adjunct teach a course. These are all very worthwhile activities for graduate students in health psychology, adding to your knowledge base and tool kit, but there can be too many things going on at one time for you to do well at any of them. Each semester, first think about your obligations (coursework, lab research, presentations, manuscripts, teaching, clinical hours). Add in blocks of "protected time" to do those obligated tasks well and then think about the other opportunities. This may be a time where you already are overloaded and need to say "no", and trust us, that opportunity will come around again.

Moving Ahead . . .

As a graduate student, there will be so many exciting opportunities in front of you. You've identified your desired field of study, you've gained acceptance to a graduate program (not an easy thing to do) and now you have several years ahead of you to immerse yourself in developing and strengthening your skills to focus on your interests and turn your career wishes into reality. It is easy to get bogged down in minutia and deadlines and to feel pulled in many directions. Remind yourself: You have chosen health psychology because you have some interest in optimizing the human ability to protect or improve our health. Continue to find aspects of this work that inspire you and use those as guideposts during your graduate school journey (and beyond).

> "If I can give one piece of advice: Take advantage of the dedicated time you're afforded in graduate school. You'll never have that kind of dedicated time again—to think, to synthesize, to learn new techniques, and to write. Now, as a faculty member, I juggle teaching, mentoring, service, and research demands. Pressure to secure external funding is high. You must find time to read, write, and think. So, absorb as much as you can from your classes. Take workshops on special techniques. Master knowledge of the literature in your area. Hone new skills when you have others supervising you. In the end, you will build on all of this".
>
> —Shelby Langer, Ph.D., Associate Professor,
> College of Nursing and Health Innovation,
> Arizona State University

References

Belar, C. D. (2008). Clinical health psychology: A health care specialty in professional psychology. *Professional Psychology: Research and Practice*, 39(2), 229–233. https://doi.org/10.1037/0735-7028.39.2.229

Belkin, L. (2006). Two jobs, one choice. NY Times, July 16, 2006. New York Edition, Page HW1. Retrieved from www.nytimes.com/2006/07/16/jobs/16wcol.html

Labi, N. (2006). The baby gamble: Do changing diapers and helping with homework leave time for world-class scholarship? *Yale Alumni Magazine*. Retrieved from http://archives.yalealumnimagazine.com/issues/2006_03/tenure.html

Levecque, K., Anseel, F., De Beuckelaer, A., Van der Heyden, J., & Gisle, L. (2017). Work organization and mental health problems in PhD students. *Research Policy*, 46(4), 868–879.

Levinson, D. J., Darrow, C. N., Klein, E. B., Levinson, M. H., & McKee, B. (1978). *The seasons of a man's life*. New York, NY: Knopf.

McClelland, S. I., & Holland, K. J. (2015). You, me, or her: Leaders' perceptions of responsibility for increasing gender diversity in STEM departments. *Psychology of Women Quarterly*, 39(2), 210–225. https://doi.org/10.1177/0361684314537997

Mollica, M., & Nemeth, L. (2014). Outcomes and characteristics of faculty/student mentorship in PhD programs. *American Journal of Educational Research*, 2, 703–708. https://doi.org/10.12691/education-2-9-1

Rackham Graduate School, University of Michigan. (2018a). *How to get the mentoring you want: A guide for students at a diverse university*. Retrieved from www.rackham.umich.edu/downloads/publications/mentoring.pdf

Rackham Graduate School, University of Michigan. (2018b). *How to mentor graduate students: A guide for faculty.* Retrieved from https://rackham.umich.edu/wp-content/uploads/2018/11/Fmentoring.pdf

Revenson, T. A., & Lepore, S. J. (2012). Coping in social context. In A. Baum, T. A. Revenson, & J. E. Singer (Eds.), *Handbook of health psychology* (2nd ed., pp. 193–217). New York, NY: Psychology Press.

Sambunjak, D., & Marušić, A. (2009). Mentoring: What's in a name? *Journal of the American Medical Association, 302*(23), 2591–2592. https://doi.org/10.1001/jama.2009.185

7

PROFESSIONAL DEVELOPMENT

In graduate school, you will begin developing your professional identity as a health psychologist. This process takes time and continues over the course of doctoral training (and beyond). No longer can students wait until they have the doctoral degree in hand to start deciding what career paths they might take. At the same time, we often advise students to keep their options open and to expect that their interests and career goals may change over the years of training. To support your path in developing your professional identity while maintaining some flexibility, we encourage you to develop the strongest base of knowledge and professional skills that you can while in graduate school. Chapters 5 and 6 focused on the nuts and bolts of graduate school; this chapter will help you to think more about the big picture of your professional development as a health psychologist, including ways to increase your engagement in the health psychology community and to stay on track along the path to your doctoral degree.

The Coin of the Realm—Your CV

As you know from Chapter 3, your CV is an academic resumé listing your research and professional experiences, honors and awards, publications, and conference presentations. A well-developed CV is your calling card for career success. We suggest you create your CV during your very first month of doctoral training if you don't have one already. (Many doctoral programs now request that applicants attach a CV to their application.) Update it regularly. You never know when you must have it ready overnight for a grant, a report, or an award!

We have provided multiple resources on how to prepare your academic CV in the Appendix (under Chapter 3). But there are two excellent sources right in your own backyard: First, seek guidance from your advisors and mentors on how to frame and describe your clinical experiences, research, and "outside" work. You can also use this as an opportunity to discuss the strengths and gaps of your current CV and to help you plan which skills and projects to take on during the first year and over the course of graduate training. Second, ask advanced students in your program if you can model your own CV after theirs.

Long-Term Career Planning: Individual Development Plans

Recently there has been a lot of talk in academia and from the APA about Individual Development Plans (IDPs). IDPs are dynamic (ever changing) documents that help graduate students and health psychologists identify and outline career goals and reflect on past achievements. An IDP helps you map out your career pathway and take the first steps along the way. They are often used by more advanced graduate students, but we have used them with first year students as well.

The idea behind IDPs is that you revise them every semester, as your career focus becomes clearer and you become better at assessing how long individual research projects take to complete. The APA has a website to guide you through the IDP process—self-assessment, career exploration, and goal setting—that you can find in the Appendix. If you decide to create an IDP, don't let it overwhelm you in the early years of doctoral training. It's not a report card—you can use it to document your progress and help you map future goals. We provide an example of an IDP for graduate students to use in Table 7.1. We suggest that you start it as early as the second semester of graduate school.

Involvement With Professional Organizations

As we've repeated multiple times, health psychology is a relatively small field; in 2019, 3,237 individuals were members of the Society for Health Psychology (SfHP), including 719 students. At the time of their annual meeting in March 2019, the Society for Behavioral Medicine (SBM) had 2,472 members of which 919 were students. Thus you have a ready-made set of peers and "distance mentors" on the national level.

Table 7.1 Planning Your Career Path

Career Goals
• What are your career goals for the time in graduate school?
• How will you achieve these goals within the next five years?
• What did you do last semester to achieve these goals?
• What are you planning to do this semester to achieve these goals?

Time Use
What percentage of your time have you spent in the semester on the following components of the graduate experience?
Divide these up to equal 100%:
_____ Coursework
_____ Research activities
_____ Attending research-related meetings or seminars
_____ Background reading
_____ Grant writing
_____ Presenting at conferences
_____ Drafting a publication
_____ Teaching
_____ Committees
100%

Research Skills
• What research-related skills have you acquired since you started graduate school?
• What feedback from faculty have you received on your research skills?
• What further skills do you need to acquire to be successful with your research and future career?
• How will you gain exposure to these skills and evaluate your competency?
• What research collaborations have you established since you started graduate school?
• Are these collaborations beneficial to your scholarly or scientific work? If so, how can you continue to build on those successes for the coming year? If they have not been successful, how can you improve on your collaborative research skills?

Presentations
• What presentations (lab meetings, journal clubs, seminars, scientific meetings or professional conferences) are you scheduled to make in the next year?
• If you haven't submitted presentations, why? What would make this answer change in a year?

Fellowships and Grants
• What fellowship or grant proposals did you write or are you currently writing?
• What feedback from faculty have you received on your grant writing skills?
• How will you improve your grantsmanship skills? What resources are available?

Leadership
• What leadership experiences have you had that allowed you to identify objectives, implement plans, and acquire decision-making skills?
• What positions can you pursue this semester to enhance your leadership skills?

Publications
• What papers are you working on with faculty?
• Will these be submitted for publication this year, or do you need to write different papers?
• What types of feedback, formal or informal, have you received on your writing skills? What specific areas of writing do you need to improve?

Source: This is a sample Independent Development Plan (IDP), adapted from APA, www.apa.org/education/grad/individual-development-plan.aspx

We recommend that you get involved with professional organizations early in your graduate career. Be sure to take advantage of opportunities offered by organizations at the local, regional, and national levels. This can involve attending conferences, where you can present your research, participate in pre-conference educational workshops, and attend professional development breakfasts for students. Or, it can simply entail regular reading of professional organization's newsletter. Many organizations' newsletters have professional development "advice" columns written by students. These include the *Health Psychologist* (the newsletter of the SfHP), *Science Agenda* (the newsletter of the Science Directorate of the American Psychological Association [APA]), and *gradPsych*, the APA magazine for students. Links for these publications are provided in the Appendix.

The major professional organizations in health psychology provide a home for student members to share their unique concerns, to network and present their work at annual research conferences, and to participate in the development of policies and activities to facilitate students' professional development. You don't need to be elected for most student committees—you just volunteer. In the Appendix, you will find descriptions of the major professional associations in health psychology/behavioral medicine, along with website URLs.

> "Professional service is a central role and responsibility for all psychologists. Students often find life-long professional homes during this important time of professional identity development. Professional societies can often nurture peer support and foster life-long professional relationships as well as offer tangible, instrumental support through contacts with senior leaders in the field who model shared values and professional aspirations and who willingly share advice and counsel".
>
> —Robert Kerns, Ph.D., Professor of Psychiatry,
> Neurology and Psychology, Yale School of Medicine

What professional organizations should you becoming involved with and which conferences should you attend? Three prominent examples are the Society for Health Psychology (SfHP; Division 38 of the APA), the SBM, and the American Psychosomatic Society (APS). SBM brings together health fields with a focus on advancing our understanding of human behavior, health, and illness. APS focuses on research that integrates biological, psychological, behavioral, and social factors that influence health and disease.

There are many smaller, focused professional organizations devoted specifically to research, practice, advocacy, education, and networking in a particular aspect of health psychology, behavioral medicine, or related interdisciplinary fields. Examples include the American Psychosocial Oncology Society (APOS), the Society of Research on Nicotine and Tobacco (SRNT), and the American Pain Society. These societies focus on cancer, nicotine and tobacco use, and pain, respectively, and include some degree of attention to psychosocial and behavioral factors within these larger topic areas. The Social, Personality, and Health Network (SPHN) is an organization comprised of many social psychologists who do work in the context of health. SPHN hosts a preconference each year at the annual meeting of Society for Social and Personality Psychology.

> "There are many great professional organizations for social-health psychologists, including the American Psychosomatic Society and Association for Behavioral Medicine. My favorite one is the Social, Personality, and Health Network (affiliated with the Society for Social and Personality Psychology) because they really emphasize the 'social' part of health psychology".
> —Megan Robbins, Ph.D., Assistant Professor of Psychology, University of California, Riverside

Some organizations in psychology, such as APA and the Association for Psychological Science cast a broad net across the field of psychology and have individual sections or divisions devoted to health psychology and other specific interests. The APA also is affiliated with regional associations, such as the Eastern Psychological Association. Each regional psychological association holds an annual meeting, which can be an excellent opportunity for graduate students in health psychology to present their work, network with other students, and engage in professional development.

An important organization for students is APAGS: the American Psychological Association of Graduate Students (American Psychological Association, 2019). Students are automatically made a part of APAGS if they join any APA Division as a student member (recall that Division 38 of APA is also known as the Society for Health Psychology). Membership in APAGS can be helpful for travel or research grants, general FAQs about graduate school, mentor/mentee relationships, networking, and professional development.

All organizations, big or small, allow you to meet individuals who are conducting research and have interests similar to yours, while also helping you to understand the broader landscape of research being conducted in your area of interest and/or related areas of interest. We suggest that you explore meaningful opportunities for student involvement in a particular organization of interest to you. And always talk with your mentor! They may be involved in certain organizations and can make introductions and "bring you in".

What does participating in these activities add to your already busy life as a doctoral student in health psychology? First, you get an insider's view of the cutting-edge developments in the field. You meet leaders in the field, who sometimes end up serving as "long-distance" mentors over the course of your career. More importantly, you develop a network of peers who are not in your program—a network that often lasts through your career. Being a part of these organizations gives you a leg up as you learn more about health psychology nationally and find your place in it.

> "I have been a member of the Society of Behavioral Medicine (SBM) since I was a graduate student. It's a wonderful interdisciplinary organization. It has grown over time, but I would still describe it as not too big and not too small. The organization is very supportive of students, so consider it as an outlet for your research during graduate school and beyond. A more general piece of advice is to find an organization that makes sense given your interests and career objectives. Shop around but settle on one or two. (Cost is a consideration.) Make one to two new contacts at each conference and your network will grow. Do good work and make a point to present that work. It will speak for itself. And get involved. Join a Special Interest Group (SIG) where you can network with a dozen or so individuals who are conducting the same type of research".
>
> —Shelby Langer, Ph.D., Associate Professor,
> College of Nursing and Health Innovation,
> Arizona State University

Attending and Presenting Your Research at Professional Conferences

A wide variety of local, regional, national, and international health psychology and behavioral medical conferences occur every year. Conferences commonly offer opportunities for you to attend scientific sessions focused on the presentation of original research, tutorial workshops focused on a research method, roundtable discussions of a topic or issue, and social events designed to promote networking and collaboration. Many health psychology graduate students start out presenting their work at smaller meetings either at their university or within their local region and work their way up to larger conferences. A good strategy is to start by presenting your work as a research poster at a few conferences and move on to an oral or podium presentation (talk) at the next conference.

To present your work at most conferences, you need to submit a structured abstract that describes the aims, methods, results and conclusions of a study that you conducted. The abstract will be peer-reviewed and then accepted or rejected by the conference's scientific program committee. An abstract may be rejected for numerous reasons, such as not conforming to the scientific scope of the organization or not being "ready" (for example, data have not been collected yet). Some organizations have designated sessions for "work in progress" to allow researchers to get feedback on their protocol before collecting the data. However, the general rule is that you will have collected and analyzed your data *before* writing and submitting a conference abstract.

There are two major formats for research presentations at conferences: posters and oral presentations. Both provide experience for communicating your research and answering questions—essential components for your career development. See and be seen!

Posters are just that—the findings of your study printed on paper or fabric—which are tacked onto on a bulletin board. A poster fully describes your research findings, including Research Aims, Methods, Results, and Conclusions in a truncated and pictorial fashion. Poster sessions typically last one to two hours, during which other conference attendees come by, view your poster, ask questions, and engage you in a discussion about your study. It's a great opportunity to interact with scholars who share your interests without being "on stage" as part of an oral presentation. Some conferences place posters on the same topic near each other so you can have a conversation with your "poster neighbor" during lulls in viewing. Christopher France, a former President of the SfHP and former editor of the journal *Annals of Behavioral Medicine* has confessed that he prefers posters over oral presentations because posters allow him to meet others doing similar research; we're sure he isn't the only one! And some of us have met future graduate students at poster sessions; it's a less stressful way to talk to people you might want to work with in graduate school.

Conferences often give awards (sometimes in the form of travel funds) for the best student posters. Additionally, some conferences include programming that enhance opportunities for poster presenters, for example organizing posters belonging to the same overall topic in the same neighboring poster areas. The European Health Psychology Society, for example, clusters five to six posters on the same theme together and has the authors give a three- to four-minute presentation before everyone is free to view them.

Oral presentations, also known as talks or podium presentations, typically involve a ten- to 15-minute talk about a research project, accompanied by visuals (slides). The talk is usually followed by a few minutes of questions from the audience, which is good training for learning to think on your feet. We provide some resources for presenting a good talk in the Appendix.

During a conference, oral presentations on the same topic may be placed together in one of two ways. *Symposia* are developed and coordinated by a scholar who comes up with an overarching idea and invites several colleagues to present their work together; a symposium often ends with a discussant who draws together the talks and suggests future directions for the area. *Paper sessions* organize individual talks submitted from various researchers into a session about a specific topic or in some cases, by disease (e.g., heart disease) or method (qualitative studies). In contrast to symposia, the conference program committee creates paper sessions by combining individual papers on a "similar" theme. Be sure to check the Guidelines for Submission of Abstracts for each conference to see what type of sessions they provide. For example, APA does not have paper sessions but SBM does.

A newer format for oral presentation of data, and one that is good for students, is the "DataBlitz" (Chamberlin, 2017). In this type of session, researchers have two to three minutes (and just a few slides) to provide an appetizer-size portion of their research. Although most students have looked at us in horror when we suggest it, it is fast and fun! These blitzes are sometimes done in advance of full talk or poster session as a way to advertise upcoming presentations.

A large part of conferences involves networking with others doing similar work in your area. Whether you are presenting your research or simply attending a conference, there are many ways to make connections. For example, you might go up to the podium to ask a question after a talk and introduce yourself to the speaker. You can even ask those whose work they admire if they will have a postdoctoral fellowship open in the next year or two!

Many conferences have mentor-mentee events, for example, having a meal with a few students and a scholar, or a one-on-one consultation with an expert about your current research. Sign up for them early! They are valuable ways to get "face time" with someone you admire and may want to work with in the future. This is not a time to be shy—scholars remember those students over time, especially if they come up to us a year later to say hello and "continue the conversation".

Many conferences also have student-only happy hours and or student-led events that are useful for meeting others or becoming involved in leadership roles. Most organizations also have a student council or student interest group whether the leaders of tomorrow are born. (Sometimes they are combined with early career professionals, those who have just completed their degrees.) One example is the Emerging Leaders Initiative of the American Psychosomatic Society, which offers special events at conferences, networking with other students, and the potential to dip one's toes into the behind-the-scenes of conference planning.

"I first met Dr. Regan Gurung when I was part of the organizing committee for a pedagogy conference in our department where he was the keynote speaker. He delivered a wonderful talk on how to engage students in active learning in undergraduate classrooms. After his talk, I introduced myself and we spoke about the various challenges of teaching in large classrooms and even exchanged ideas on increasing participation! Several months later, he asked me to contribute to chapters to a teaching manual he was writing and later we collaborated (long-distance) on an article examining how health psychology is taught nationally. He has now become someone I can reach out to for professional and career-related advice outside of the mentors in my program. Thinking about how this chain of events started because I took the initiative to say, 'Hi Dr. Gurung, so nice to meet you. I really appreciated your talk.' has motivated me to approach professors and researchers at conference even if I feel intimidated! Think about it—the worst they can say is, 'Sorry, I don't have to time to chat right now.' Would that really be so bad?"

—Aliza A. Panjwani, M.A., Doctoral Candidate, The Graduate Center, City University of New York

Another way to get noticed, especially for advanced students, is to coordinate and submit a symposium with a talk given by you and similar talks by others. How do you find the people to have on your panel? Start with research you have read in your area of interest and reach out to authors who have published on the topic recently. Send an email to let them know that you are interesting in putting together a symposium on your topic for an upcoming conference, and ask if they would be interested in contributing (or know someone else who may if they cannot). Presenting research together at a conference is a good way to "introduce" your work to others. Many times, panelists have coffee after the formal session has ended. Some organizations allow students to chair panels and others do not; in the latter case, have your mentor co-chair it with you. In other words, make the most of your time at conferences!

Although traveling to out of town conferences can be expensive, many graduate programs and departments have student travel funds for presenting work at these conferences. Also note that some organizations waive or reduce registration fees for those students who volunteer a few hours of their time during the conference, so be sure to check. You can (and should) take advantage of travel funds even in your first year.

Peer Reviewing for Conferences and Journals

Another way to develop professional skills and to contribute to the field of health psychology, especially for advanced students, is to serve as a peer reviewer for conference abstracts or manuscripts that are submitted to journals in health psychology, behavioral medicine, or related fields. For conferences, you can contact the Program Chair (often published on the organization's website within a year prior to the conference date) and volunteer to review abstracts. Be sure to inform them of your area of expertise and send along a CV.

The best way to start becoming a peer reviewer for journals in your area is to ask your mentor if you can learn how to review journal articles with them. Most researchers are frequently asked to review manuscripts for scientific journals and they often love the help and second opinion! A first step is to work one-on-one with your mentor on a manuscript they have agreed to review—making notes and discussing them, getting feedback, and even drafting the review. Nowadays, most journals ask a reviewer if she or he wrote the review with another person when the review is submitted, so you will receive credit for co-writing a review. A list of what are known as "*ad hoc* reviewers" usually is published in the first or last issue of a journal each year. Once you have reviewed several manuscripts this way, you can then ask the journal's editor if you can become a more regular reviewer, especially if it is a journal whose topic is your area of expertise. Some journals even have mentoring programs for student reviewers. Reviewing manuscripts is good experience because you get to see both strengths and weaknesses in manuscript preparation, which makes your own writing better and helps you become more proficient when publishing your own work. For a primer on how to review empirical manuscripts, see Lovejoy, Revenson, and France (2011) and other "how-to" guides in the Appendix.

Obtaining Research Grants as a Student

As you become more advanced in your research skills, you may want to apply for funds to conduct your own research. What, you say, write a grant proposal in graduate school? The answer is yes. First, some of your classes may have this as an assignment, which is good practice with low risk. You learn from faculty members' feedback and, over time, you get better at writing grants. Second, many research funding opportunities at the graduate student level will require you to involve your mentor in all key steps of your proposed work, so you will not be out there on your own. Third, you can't get funds without applying for them. And you never know how many others will apply, or what research questions will be of interest. So, go for it! And even if you are not awarded the grant, you can still add it to your CV as "grant submitted (not funded)". It shows moxie.

Some research funding opportunities can be found within your university and some are connected to professional organizations, government agencies, or private foundations. As we described at the beginning of this section, applying for funding can be a critical step in your career, helping you to hone your grant writing skills and collect preliminary data in preparation for your dissertation or for larger scale grant applications in the future. It is always a good idea to have your advisor (and other faculty members) provide feedback on the content of your proposal before you submit it. Most universities also have grants offices that can help with assembling all the components of the grant, drafting a budget, obtaining institutional approval, and finally submitting the grant proposal.

> "Receiving a grant allowed me to collect some additional biological data I would not have been able to collect otherwise, and that's valuable in terms of the questions I could answer in my research. However, I think the biggest influence on my career came from the application process (writing about my research in a different way, asking for money for my research from strangers, putting together a budget, etc.) and the increased confidence I had in myself and the project after receiving the award".
> —Jenny Cundiff, Ph.D., Assistant Professor, University of Alabama

Within Your University

Your department and your university may offer dissertation grants or other types of funds for pilot studies or to launch graduate student studies. Research grants from your university (referred to as "internal" grants) often require short research proposals (two to five pages) and award a few hundred or a few thousand dollars. This can be used for research assistants, supplies, transcribing interviews, or participant incentives. On occasion, they may even award a stipend or travel funds.

Outside the University

There are many sources of funds available to health psychology students outside of the university. Some are for specific research projects and others are to conduct research within someone's lab or as part of a larger program of research. The SfHP as well as other divisions of APA and the APA itself offer research and/or dissertation grants.

"Receiving a student grant from SfHP not only provided the necessary funding for my dissertation research, it gave me confidence to pursue the ideas I was passionate about".
—Matthew R. Cribbet, Ph.D., Assistant Professor, University of Alabama

Private Foundation Grants

Here is a boon for health psychology students. Private foundations that focus on a specific disease (e.g., the Arthritis Foundation, the American Cancer Society) sometimes offer small research grants and/or dissertation grants. Although psychosocial research may be only a small percentage of the grants awarded by a foundation in any year, most of these foundations love psychosocial projects that improve quality of life for those with the disease. You will easily find out information on how to apply on the foundation's website, but don't be afraid to contact the person who heads the research section and talk with them about your proposed project. They will often provide "insider" information as to what is important to the foundation and how to fit your project within the organization's mission.

Federal Grants

The National Institutes of Health offer predoctoral National Student Research Awards (NRSAs). (Predoctoral means *before* you obtain your doctoral degree.) These are also known as Ruth Kirschstein Fellowships, named after a woman who, after doing important laboratory work on the polio vaccine, made history as the first woman to direct an NIH institute, the National Institute of General Medical Sciences (NIGMS), and who later served as deputy director and acting director of the NIH. NRSAs (also known as "F" series or fellowship grants) support training with your mentor(s) in health research. The goal is to help prepare you for a career as an independent investigator after graduate school while conducting a mentored research project in graduate school, most often your dissertation.

NRSA/Kirschstein fellowships are ideal for health psychology doctoral students as the focus of the NIH is about health! The fellowships provide two to three years of funding, including a stipend (salary) and a research allowance. Although many students wait to apply for NRSAs until their fourth year when they have strong research skills and a clear dissertation idea, talented second and third year students also can apply. In fact, you might have to apply more than once, revising a proposal with reviewers' feedback. The one downside of being awarded an NRSA is that completing the project can extend the time before degree completion for a year. This can be a painful reality for some but on balance, it is a major achievement on your CV.

"As a fourth-year student I applied for and received a two-year R36 grant which funded my dissertation. I'll confess that I didn't score highly enough on the first submission, and had only three weeks for the next submission date, so I decided to go for it and forego sleep—but in the end I was awarded the grant. My advice? First, take advantage of coursework and working groups to develop and organize your ideas for your grants. I was fortunate to have two grants funded in graduate school and the research questions for both were developed as part of course assignments and then fleshed out in meetings with faculty and other students. Second, seek lots of guidance and feedback—early and throughout the process—from people who are familiar with the grant for which you are applying. That includes previous recipients of the grant and program officers".

—Raymond L. Moody, M.A., Doctoral Candidate,
The Graduate Center, City University of New York

NRSAs are real NIH grant proposals (with all the forms and signatures), which leads us two important pieces of advice: (1) *You can't submit a successful grant proposal alone* and (2) *You can't write a proposal the week before it is due.* To the first point, although the proposal must be your own work, student grants benefit from mentors' feedback. Those of us who have reviewed these proposals at NIH can see the difference between those written with vs. without faculty input. (And you can guess which gets funded.)

So, why is mentor feedback important? First, your mentors have likely written successful grant proposals and know what a grant review committee is looking for. Second, faculty mentors can help you clarify your ideas, theoretical models, and—very importantly—your writing. Sheldon Cohen, an award-winning health psychologist famous for his studies of psychosocial factors in immune processes (sometimes referred to as the common cold studies) wrote an editorial that author Tracey Revenson read as a graduate student and has carried with her for years: "many a proposal with mediocre ideas gets funded because it is superbly written, and more than a few with really good ideas get rejected because they are poorly written" (Cohen, 1988).

Third, faculty offer the emotional support you need to get the proposal submitted correctly and on time. In fact, as we mentioned earlier in the chapter, many grants for students or early career professionals, like the NRSA, require the identification of a mentor and a formalized mentoring plan.

To our second point regarding starting early, grant proposals take a long time to write and revise (and revise again). Along with the body of the proposal (your research study's background, specific aims, and methods), there are a large number of forms (sometimes called face sheets) that must be completed about all kinds of things, ranging from the institutions' computing facilities and libraries to a complete budget and justification for every line item on that budget. Moreover, your proposal must be read and approved by a university official who "signs off" on the grant and submits it to the agency. Telling you this isn't meant to scare you off from doing a proposal—just to remind you to leave a lot of time and inform university officials of your intention well before the grant deadline. But it is definitely worth it—those reading your folders for postdocs and jobs are impressed that you have submitted grant proposals.

Some NIH institutes offer supplemental grants to faculty investigators with R series research awards (Research Supplement to Promote Diversity in Health-Related Research) that can be used to support studies conducted by students from underserved populations. They provide a stipend and research allowance. In these supplemental grants, a subproject is "attached" to a mentor's current grant-funded project, adding on a study or expanding an existing study. There is also a relatively new grant initiative from the National Cancer Institute for late stage graduate students who have demonstrated potential and interest in pursuing careers as independent cancer researchers: the F99/K00 Predoctoral to Postdoctoral Transition Fellowship (DHHS, 2019). Geared toward training independent cancer researchers, this mechanism provides up to two years of support (e.g., your fourth and fifth years) during doctoral training and up to four years of postdoctoral support after you receive your degree—all in one grant proposal. Talk about getting your career off to a fast start!

The National Science Foundation's Graduate Research Fellowship Program (National Science Foundation, 2019) is available to students early in their graduate training. Individuals can apply as an undergraduate senior (once they are accepted

"Most graduate-level fellowships are looking to find budding scientists rather than funding a specific project. As such, graduate students applying to programs like NSF Graduate Research Fellowship Program (GRFP) should make sure they are putting their best foot forward not only in their project design but also in their personal statements, CVs, and reference letters (choose your letter-writers wisely). For the NSF GRFP specifically, the 'broader impacts' section may seem obvious to health psychologists, but it is worth spending a lot of time to think through and write—the broader impact is often where students report receiving their worst scores".

—Jennifer Howell, Ph.D., Assistant Professor of Psychology, University of California, Merced to a doctoral program) or post-baccalaureate candidate the fall *before beginning graduate school.* You can also apply as a graduate student, but only once and only in your first or second year of graduate school. The NSF GRFP is very competitive, but health psychology students whose research is in the social, developmental, or physiological areas could certainly be recipients.

Networking on Social Media

More and more, students are benefitting from having a research presence on social media, which is especially important in the months between conferences. However, as communication channels proliferate, the lines between public and private information can blur. Personal websites, blogs, email signature lines, voicemail messages, Twitter, Facebook, and media interviews afford numerous avenues for personal expression and increasingly call for discretion and good judgment in how they are used.

Many departments, programs, and labs have Facebook, Twitter, and Instagram accounts. There are also academic social networking websites, such as ResearchGate or Academia.edu, which give researchers the option to upload their own articles, conference papers, and posters to an online repository. In a way, the social media is a form of marketing yourself, but it also allows for much quicker sharing of research. Many graduate students also have individual webpages through the main websites of their department, lab, or advisor.

If you choose to create a webpage or social media account, make sure to keep it up to date and professional. Not only will potential future employers view it, but also prospective graduate students or lab members will check it out. Remember that you are a representative of multiple communities: your lab, department, and university. When using social media students should keep in mind that, as representatives of their university, psychology department, training program, and profession (of health psychology), what is communicated on social media reflects on these entities and even can have an impact on the public's perception of psychology and mental health services. And it should go without saying that when using social media, students should act with courtesy and respect toward others. Table 7.2 contains guidelines for social media use developed for the University of Miami Department of Psychology as part of its Graduate Student Handbook.

Using social media has lots of advantages. Professional conferences now identify some people to be "super tweeters" during conferences; these would be people who have a following and will continuously post information to highlight key talks and findings. And scientific journals are also becoming savvy about putting published articles out on social media.

Table 7.2 *Recommended Guidelines for Using Social Media*

Know that:
• Internship and postdoctoral training programs conduct web searches on applicants' names.
• Employers conduct online searches prior to interviews or job offers.
• Prospective clients conduct web-based searches on potential therapist names.
• Clients often approach therapists via networking sites and email.
• Legal authorities review personal websites for evidence of illegal activities.

Be aware that:
• Once you have posted something via social media, it is out of your control. Others may see it, repost it, save it, forward it to others, etc. Retracting content after you have posted it is practically impossible.
• Any content that you host (e.g., comments posted by others on your site) can have the same (negative) effect as content you post.
• Email signature lines and voicemail greetings that might express your individuality or reflect your sense of humor also may not portray you in a professional manner.
• Consider that quotations on personal philosophy, religious beliefs, and political attitudes might cause unanticipated reactions from people with differing backgrounds and viewpoints.

Some responsible social media practices:
• Keep an eye on your social media "presence". Conduct periodic Google searches on yourself to find out what information can be accessed about you on the Internet. For more information see: www.apa.org/gradpsych/2015/11/corner.aspx
• Consider using the highest privacy settings available (i.e., "Friends only") on Facebook, Twitter, and other social networking websites. Monitor these settings periodically to ensure that privacy settings previously selected remain intact.
• Never become a "friend" of a therapy or testing client online, thereby enabling them to access personal information about you.
• Be respectful and thoughtful about what you post on public psychology forums, including those sponsored by professional organizations such as the American Psychological Association (APA).
• Make sure the content you post is in harmony with APA and state ethical and professional guidelines. For more information about "best practices" check these links:
www.apa.org/monitor/2014/02/ce-corner.aspx
www.apa.org/about/social-mediapolicy.aspx

Source: Based on the Social Media Recommendations for the University of Miami Clinical Program developed by Annette M. La Greca, Ph.D. and BreAnne A. Danzi. Available at: www.psy.miami.edu/media/college-of-arts-and- sciences/psychology/documents/2018_Graduate_Student_Handbook.pdf

Moving Ahead . . .

This chapter and the previous one gave you a taste of what graduate school in health psychology holds in store and how to use those years to prepare yourself for the career head. So even though it seems very far in the future we move on to preview what the first years after you receive your Ph.D. look like and the varied career options open to you.

References

American Psychological Association (2019). *About APAGS*. https:// apa.org/apags/about/ index

Chamberlin, J. (2017). The three-minute pitch. *Monitor on Psychology*, 48(11), 54. www.apa. org/monitor/2017/12/three-minute-pitch.aspx

Cohen, S. (1988). Getting your grant funded by NIH. *The Health Psychologist*, 10(2), unpaginated

DHHS (2019). *The NCI Predoctoral to Postdoctoral Fellow Transition Award* (F99/K00). https://grants. nih.gov/grants/guide/rfa-files/RFA-CA-18-001.html

Lovejoy, T. I., Revenson, T. A., & France, C. (2011). Reviewing manuscripts for peer-review journals: A primer for novice and seasoned reviewers. *Annals of Behavioral Medicine*, 42, 1–13. https://doi.org/10.1007/s12160-011-9269-x

National Science Foundation (2019). *The NSF Graduate Research Fellowship Program*. https://nsfgrfp.org

8

THE CLINICAL PREDOCTORAL INTERNSHIP

If you plan to obtain your doctorate in counseling, clinical, or clinical-health psychology, you will be required to complete a year-long clinical internship before you can graduate with your degree. (Note there are a few part-time internships where clinical students can complete this requirement over two years.) If you have decided on a research-only health psychology program, you can skip this chapter, as you do not have to complete a clinical pre-doctoral internship.

The goal of your internship year is to be a capstone for clinical training, even if your internship program has a strong research component. The internship is designed to provide you with a year of full-time in-depth clinical training, and it may very well be one of the most meaningful and exciting steps in your graduate training. During that year, you will develop advanced clinical assessment and intervention competencies in a health services setting that is independent of your graduate program. In addition to completing clinical work with patients or clients, you will participate in weekly supervision and didactic instruction sessions, which may include readings, lectures, case presentations, discussions, and workshops.

Some internship sites integrate research opportunities into the internship year. In some of these cases, you will receive research mentorship from site faculty and staff, and you may serve as a therapist or co-investigator for ongoing research protocols, or you may develop your own research projects. In other cases, internship sites may offer less intensive or structured research opportunities. For example, many sites give interns four hours a week that they can use to become involved with research there, or to work on their dissertation or other projects they brought with them.

Your clinical internship can play a major role in helping you develop as a clinical health psychologist. The internship year is a chance to strengthen your health psychology background by increasing your exposure to medical populations and to health psychology assessment, intervention, and consultation techniques. Although many personal and professional factors can influence your selection of internship sites, the optimal training will allow you to increase your skills with respect to both depth and breadth.

Let's say, for example, that in graduate school you developed an interest in studying health promotion among people with heart disease. With respect to depth, you may find an internship that offers multiple opportunities within a cardiac unit, such as inpatient treatment to address patient depression after a recent heart attack; follow-up treatment to improve health behaviors after hospital discharge; and supportive care services for family members who are coping with caregiver burden. With respect to breadth, the same internship may offer additional opportunities to treat people with a broader range of health concerns such as epilepsy, cancer, sleep disorders, infertility, spinal cord injury, or chronic pain. Taken together, these internship experiences will prepare you for independent practice and might also open the door to new interests and opportunities.

"It's important to think about what your goals are for both clinical work and research during your internship year. Do you want to gain experience working with a new patient population, learn new types of interventions, or work on a multidisciplinary team? As the capstone to your clinical training, it is important to apply to internship sites that will meet your clinical goals. In terms of research, it's important to consider what feels feasible within a year and the types of opportunities a site has available for interns. During the start of your internship year, work on building mentorship that will help explore both of these domains and be open to the types of experiences that are available to you. I was interested in gaining more health psychology experience working within a palliative care clinic; this has helped to inform my goals for a postdoctoral fellowship. Internship year is when you get to really explore what is important to you and where you want your career to go. My internship experience only reified the important role that research plays in informing clinical work and *vice versa*".

—Megan Renna, Ph.D., Postdoctoral Fellow,
The Ohio State Wexner Medical Center

"I broadened and deepened my health psychology experience during my internship year through a diversity of training experiences. During my graduate training, I studied emotional risk factors for nicotine addiction in people with asthma. On internship I was able to expand this work by serving as the interventionist on clinical trials of behavioral smoking cessation interventions for people with cancer or HIV. Not only did these experiences teach me how treat nicotine addiction in new patient populations, they also expanded my understanding of clinical techniques to treat nicotine addiction in general. Internship also allowed me to gain experience in areas that were completely new to me, such as weight management, bariatric surgery, and psycho-oncology. This diversity of training experiences helped me to round out my training as a clinical health psychologist and demonstrated how valuable psychology's presence in medical settings really is".

—Christina Luberto, Ph.D., Clinical Fellow in Psychology,
Massachusetts General Hospital

Preparing for an Internship in Clinical Health Psychology

Clinical internship programs require you to prepare a comprehensive and detailed application package, as we explain later in this chapter. In most cases, you will apply for your internship during the fall semester of your final year "in residence" at your graduate program and will start your internship during the following summer. This means that you will have completed most other doctoral program requirements, including classes and comprehensive examinations, before submitting your internship applications. In fact, many graduate programs require that you have your dissertation proposal accepted before you submit your internship applications. Such a requirement is in place to maximize the likelihood that you will be prepared to defend your dissertation by the time you complete your internship, if not before. You also will have completed most of your clinical hours by the time you submit your internship applications, although you might continue obtaining more clinical experience during your final fall and spring semesters at your graduate program.

Applying for internships is a competitive process. Because of this, carefully consider what health-focused internship programs will prioritize when they review your application. Of course, the specific criteria deemed to be most important for internship applicants will depend on each internship program. In general, internship programs with a health psychology focus will favor applicants who have completed clinical and research training within the health context (such as working with populations that are affected by specific medical conditions or health risk behaviors). Therefore, we strongly encourage you to seek clinical practica in graduate school that allow you to work with patients or clients on goals, such as increasing health promoting behaviors (e.g., medical adherence or physical activity), reducing health risk behaviors (e.g., tobacco use or sedentary lifestyle), coping with medical symptoms (e.g., pain or fatigue), reducing psychological symptoms that are related to a medical condition (e.g., depression or anxiety related to mild cognitive impairment), and/or enhancing quality of life and functioning in the context of a medical condition (e.g., cancer or diabetes). These opportunities will help you establish fundamental skills for adapting evidence-based therapeutic strategies within the health context and for collaborating with individuals from other health disciplines. If these clinical opportunities sound exciting or inspiring to you, then this is yet another sign that health psychology is the right field for you!

"Several experiences in graduate school helped me become a competitive applicant for internship. I became interested in health psychology in my first year, but my program did not have a health track. I was able to take a number of relevant courses, including motivational interviewing and psychosocial oncology, which connected me to researchers and clinicians who suggested health-oriented practicum sites. I ended up working at a primary care clinic, a urology clinic, and a family medicine practice. At each placement, I had the opportunity to provide cognitive-behavioral therapy to patients with co-occurring medical and psychological concerns. My favorite placement was the urology clinic, where I met with men and women who had sexual health problems, often secondary to cancer or spinal cord injury. These individuals were looking for brief, solution-focused therapy, and they helped me learn how to adapt my approach to treating sexual dysfunction to meet their needs. I also found it helpful to serve as a co-therapist with my supervisors. As trainees, we do not have many opportunities to watch our supervisors do therapy. When I saw my supervisors in action and observed their interactions with complex patients, I felt confident that I could employ my therapy skills in medical settings".

—Amelia Stanton, B.A., Psychology Intern,
Massachusetts General Hospital

Clinical internship programs that have a health psychology focus while also including a research component will seek applicants who have solid training and experiences in conducting, presenting, and publishing health psychology research. No matter what type of research experience you obtain as a graduate student, internship program faculty and staff may look for you to be able to discuss the clinical implications of your dissertation research for health populations. For example, how could your graduate research findings on the relationships between social support and immune functioning be applied to advance the well-being of patients in a HIV primary care clinic?

What Clinical-Health Opportunities Do Clinical Internships Offer?

If you want to continue with health psychology training during internship, you'll find that numerous internships offer training opportunities that focus on health conditions or medical populations (see Table 8.1). Relevant internships may be located within Veterans Affairs healthcare systems, academic medical centers, community hospitals and clinics, or other healthcare settings. Within each site, you may find clinical opportunities vary with respect to whether health psychologists are integrated within medical units (such as being part of an obesity treatment team), co-located with medical units (such as having an office in a weight management center), or located in separate clinics (such as serving as a referral source for the weight management center). All of these settings would provide excellent training opportunities, though the skills that they emphasize may differ. For example, if you are located in a separate clinic, you may develop consultation liaison expertise, whereas if you are integrated within a medical unit you may contribute to scheduled patient care visits.

A clinical internship year can involve experiences or "rotations" through multiple clinics or medical units. Rotations might extend for a full year or might be as brief as four months. For example, during your internship year, you might complete a single half-time 12-month rotation in a cancer care clinic and spend the remaining half of each week completing a sequence of three half-time four-month rotations in traumatic brain injury, women's health, and primary-integrative care clinics. Internship sites can vary quite a bit in the amount and type of available rotations. You likely will have input into selecting at least some of your internship rotations, whereas other rotations may be required components at your internship program to ensure training depth and/or breadth. Still other internship programs, particularly those with a larger number of interns, may assign you to rotations based on rank order preferences that you submit prior to starting your internship year.

Table 8.1 Examples of Health Psychology Internship Experiences

Internship experience	Sample activities
Infectious disease clinic	• Provide group or individual psychotherapy to HIV-positive adults • Deliver interventions to enhance adherence to antiretroviral medications
Consultation-liaison	Evaluate patients who are referred for mental health concerns by their primary care or specialty care clinician and provide consultation to the clinician
Reproductive health	• Provide coping skills interventions for adults who are facing stressors related to trying to conceive
Weight center	• Conduct psychosocial assessments of adult candidates for bariatric surgery • Provide coping skills interventions during the year following bariatric surgery
Cancer center	• Assess depression and anxiety in patients with newly diagnosed cancer • Conduct psychotherapy with patients and families affected by cancer
Sleep medicine clinic	Provide assessment and treatment of patients with sleep disorders such as insomnia and sleep apneas
Sexual health program	Assess patient concerns about sexual health due to a medical condition, medical treatment, or other factors Provide education, consultation, intervention, and/or referral for patients and their partners
Intensive care unit	Provide brief coping skills interventions for family caregivers of patients in intensive care
Hospice unit	Provide assessment and treatment of patients and families at the end of life
Transplant center	• Conduct pre-transplant assessment for transplant recipients and living donors • Provide coping interventions post-transplant
Diabetes clinic	• Provide adherence counseling to patients and families affected by diabetes • Conduct healthy lifestyle interventions with adults at risk for developing diabetes
Cardiac rehabilitation unit	Assist patients with making changes to health/lifestyle behaviors, adhering to behavior change goals, and reducing depression symptoms following a cardiac event
Smoking cessation service	Deliver interventions to assist patients with quitting tobacco or remaining quit
Gastrointestinal clinic	Conduct group coping skills interventions for patients with disorders such as Crohn's disease, irritable bowel syndrome or colitis
Pain clinic	Conduct evidence-based behavioral interventions for individuals with chronic pain
Palliative care	Provide psychotherapy to assist patients and their families facing advanced stages of illness to manage complex symptom burden, existential distress, or future end-of-life concerns.

"My internship at the University of Miami/Jackson Memorial Medical Center offered a specialized health/medical track. I spent approximately half the year working as an integrated provider on the renal dialysis unit, as well as in cardiac care services. Perhaps the most rewarding component was the opportunity to participate in aspects of the cardiac transplantation program, including brief cognitive screenings for inpatient candidates, and conducting brief 'bedside' interventions including medication adherence, weight management, and addressing family concerns. I also had the opportunity to observe team meetings where difficult decisions regarding transplantation are made. The second half of my internship year was spent working as a team member on the psychiatric consultation/liaison service. Consults across multiple specialty areas of the hospital in a single day was the standard expectation. The learning curve was steep, but I left my internship feeling prepared for independent practice as a clinical health psychologist. I also completed an elective 'mini-rotation' in pediatric health psychology during the year, with consultation services provided to general pediatrics, pediatric nephrology, and the pediatric burn unit".

—Carla M. York, Psy.D., A.B.P.P., D.B.S.M. (Board certified in Clinical Health Psychology, Diplomate, Behavioral Sleep Medicine)
Clinical Health Psychologist, Walter Reed National Military Medical Center

How Can I Stay Engaged in Research During My Internship Year?

Although the internship year is primarily clinical in nature, it can also be a time to further strengthen you research skills. If you are interested in a clinical health psychology research career, look for internship sites that offer protected research time or that describe specific research opportunities. You should be able to find this information on internship sites' websites. Internship programs vary a lot in how much research they encourage or expect you to do during your internship year (beyond completing your dissertation, if you haven't already done so). The internship programs with the most intensive research focus will go as far as providing you with protected time to become involved in ongoing research, develop your own projects, write research manuscripts, attend conferences, and apply for pilot grants to support new research projects.

Before you apply to a clinical internship with an intensive research focus, find out which faculty might be interested in expanding their work in your direction. Reach out to potential internship faculty you would like to work with before you apply (via email or meet them at national conferences—just as you would have done when you applied to graduate school) and to reference their work in the cover letter of your internship application—as we describe later in this chapter. If your research interests are not a perfect match for faculty mentors at the internship program, be flexible. Many interns also advise that you reach out to current interns to see whether a program's assertions about research involvement (e.g., protected research time, opportunity to work on research projects) come to fruition. Talking to current interns can provide a good preview of what the internship is actually like and whether the site is a good fit for you.

A Brief Snapshot of the Clinical Internship Application Process

The basic steps of applying for a clinical internship are the same whether you apply to sites with a clinical health focus or not. There are many wonderful written resources available on the application process (e.g., Williams-Nickelson, Prinstein, & Keilin, 2018), but it also helps to talk with former students, current interns, and internship directors. We will briefly describe the general steps here, while referring to specific internship factors to consider if you are preparing for a health psychology career.

To describe the internship application timeline, we must first introduce the Association of Psychology Postdoctoral and Internship Centers, or APPIC, an organization that promotes quality training by setting standards for internship training programs. APPIC is comprised of an elected board representing its member training programs. As a clinical health psychology student, you will become quite familiar with APPIC because you will use its online directory to search for internship training programs and then use its online application service to submit your application to internship sites. APPIC also manages the process by which you will be matched with an internship based on rank order preferences from you and the relevant internship sites. For you to be eligible for the APPIC match, your doctoral program must authorize your participation.

To do this, your doctoral program must be (1) accredited by the APA or the Canadian Psychological Association or (2) in the process of gaining accreditation (i.e. has been granted an initial site visit by an accrediting organization), and (3) approved by APPIC. If you are attending a doctoral program outside of the U.S. or Canada and you would like to participate in the APPIC application and match, you will need to consult the APPIC policies and guidelines for demonstrating equivalency of your graduate training. A link to the list of the APPIC Doctoral Program Associates (i.e., doctoral programs that meet certain training criteria outlined by

APPIC and have paid their dues and match fees) who are eligible to participate in the APPIC internship match is provided in the Appendix.

If you attend a doctoral program that does not meet eligibility criteria for the APPIC match, you will still have options to apply for an internship. If you attend a program that is not accredited, you are eligible to participate in the APPIC internship match system if (1) your program is in the middle of the accreditation process and has been awarded a "site visit" to evaluate the program, and (2) your program is an APPIC Doctoral Program Associates.

If your non-accredited program is not eligible to participate in the APPIC internship match system, you might be eligible to participate in the Post Match Vacancy Service (PMVS) after the formal match process is over and only if your program has been granted a time-limited exception. The PMVS allows eligible internship programs to fill remaining internship positions after the initial match process is complete. The worst news is for students from non-accredited programs who do not receive the exception: They are barred from participating in the PMVS. However, you also may apply for internships that are non-accredited and non-APPIC member sites.

We recommend that you refer to the APPIC website for the most up-to-date information on whether your doctoral program may be eligible to participate in the PMVS during the specific year in which you intend to apply for your internship. The guidelines change quickly (the most recent change was only implemented in 2018), and these regulations may change again to completely exclude non-APA accredited programs in the future.

It is important to note that although you may find high quality non-APPIC member internship sites, some state licensing boards require you to have completed an accredited doctoral program and internship in order for you to be eligible for state licensure. So in some cases, if you attend a doctoral program that is not accredited or not eligible for accreditation, your options for internship, and subsequently for licensure, may be more limited. (To find more information about state licensure requirements, refer to http://psybook.asppb.org)

Step 1: Select Your List of Internships

Online registration for the APPIC match typically begins during late summer before your last residential year at your graduate program. You may search the APPIC internship site directory, which allows you to filter by key internship characteristics such as geographic region or type of clinical opportunities. You also may want to search both the APPIC website and individual internship program websites for the terms *health psychology* and *behavioral medicine*.

"In selecting your list of internships, do your homework. Talk to your advisors, search for information about training programs with a substantive focus on clinical health psychology and behavioral medicine, seek consultation from leaders, identify training faculty who share your interests and values and reach out to students and trainees in programs who represent a good match. Internships vary greatly in terms of flexibility and opportunities for tailoring of experiences, allocation of time and expectations for clinical training, scholarly and scientific productivity, other professional activities, quality and quantity of mentoring and supervision, and relative independence".

—Robert Kerns, Ph.D., Professor of Psychiatry, Neurology and Psychology, Yale School of Medicine

Table 8.2 provides some sample questions to consider when looking for internships. These questions will help you to understand the spectrum of health

Table 8.2 *Questions to Consider When Researching Internship Sites for Health Psychology*

1. Does this internship provide inpatient or outpatient experiences?
2. What are the opportunities to work with individuals who have, or at are risk for, medical conditions?
3. Are there opportunities to work with informal caregivers such as patients' family members?
4. What is the general perception in this hospital or clinic setting of psychologists and the role of psychology in patient healthcare?
5. Will I have opportunities to participate in multidisciplinary patient care teams (including physicians, nurses, social workers, nutritionists, etc.)?
6. Will I be integrated into medical units, co-located with medical units, or located in separate clinics?
7. For general behavioral medicine clinics or departments of psychiatry, what are the more common medical conditions and presenting concerns of patients who are referred for care?
8. What are current opportunities for research? What are the health psychology research interests of current internship faculty? Do internship faculty already have working projects or collaborations with medical clinics or clinicians in my research areas of interest?
9. For internship sites that place strong emphasis on research, how closely do my research areas of interest need to align with current faculty mentors?
10. Will there be opportunity to develop a new collaboration with a specialty medical clinic that is in my professional area of interest but not currently represented in the internship?
11. Will there be opportunities for starting groups if interns are interested, especially in the second half of the year (for example pain management techniques for those with chronic pain or coping skills for caregivers)?

psychology training opportunities that are available at each site. Answers to these questions may help you narrow down your own priorities when it comes to making decisions about which internship programs may be right for you. While there is no single source for finding answers to these questions, we suggest that you first review the information provided on internship program websites and then talk with your mentors, former students from your graduate program, current internship faculty, and current or recent interns at internship programs that pique your interest. Some national organizations, including the APA and the Society of Behavioral Medicine, host behavioral medicine internship meet-and-greet events at their annual conferences. These are great opportunities to learn more about internship programs directly from training directors and faculty. You can use the questions in Table 8.2 as a guide when reviewing internship websites, networking with internship faculty and current or recent internship fellows, and visiting internship sites during your interviews. It can get very costly in terms of applying and flying to interviews, so it's good to choose wisely.

Step 2: Prepare and Submit Your Applications

As you narrow your list of internships, you will begin to prepare your application package. This includes your cover letter (that you will tailor to each site), CV, a set of essays (addressing topics such as your autobiography, theoretical orientation, research, and approach to multiculturalism/diversity), a summary of your clinical hours, your transcript, and recommendation letters. Doctoral programs vary in how much they systematically review their students' internship application materials prior to submission. The Director of Clinical Training (DCT) may advise students on how to prepare their internship materials and review each student's application materials; however, both your DCT and graduate mentor should review your materials.

Most internship sites set application deadlines sometime between late September to mid-November. But as you might guess, the application package takes quite a bit of time to put together so you should start drafting your materials in the summer. Be prepared to go through lots of rounds of edits! Your cover letter, CV, and essays are the most important parts of your application that you will write yourself. Your cover letter serves as your introduction to the internship site. If your cover letter makes a good impression, internships are likely to examine the rest of your materials more closely. Good cover letters are tailored to each site and address the following: status in your graduate program, internship and career goals, general clinical and clinical-health experience to date, rotations you wish to complete, experiences you hope to gain, and reasons why you would be a good candidate for the internship site. Use your CV to highlight your clinical experiences, research experiences, presentation and publication record, honors that you have received, and any grant awards that you have obtained. Use your essays to present these experiences in a cohesive narrative that summarizes the clinical and research path that you have taken, while emphasizing your motivation for entering the field of health psychology, your goals for clinical internship training, and your mid- and long-term goals for your health psychology career.

Internship programs with a strong research component will be particularly interested in your research scholarship and will look for your cover letter and essays to articulate your research interests and your goals for establishing an independent (i.e., grant-funded) research career. Also, we recommend that you familiarize yourself with the research activities of the training faculty, and then use your cover letter and essays to identify the faculty member(s) who match your research interests.

The summary of clinical hours that you submit with your application will allow you to highlight the different types of clinical assessment and intervention experiences that you have obtained, along with the diversity of the patient populations that you have served and the number of integrated reports completed. At this point, hopefully you have been tracking your clinical hours since starting your clinical experiences in graduate school, so that you do not rely on memory! While many internship programs require a minimum number of face-to-face clinical hours and supervision hours, the number of hours beyond the minimum likely will not be as relevant as the rest of your application—particularly for internship programs with a strong research component.

Your recommendation letters are the final critical piece of your application. Most sites require three letters of recommendation plus a letter from your DCT indicating that you are eligible to apply for internships. A good rule is to have two letters from clinical supervisors and one letter from your research advisor. Your clinical supervisors will describe your clinical acumen, maturity, interpersonal skills, strengths, and potential areas for development. Your research advisor will describe your progress to date on your dissertation and, for research-focused sites, your research acumen, productivity, and potential for an independent research career. Internship sites prefer to have interns who have made considerable progress on their dissertations so they can focus their energies on the internship experience. Depending on your health psychology interests, it may be important for your recommendation letters to highlight your ability to work with patients and families affected by serious medical illness and to work with clinicians in other disciplines within healthcare settings.

Step 3: Prepare for Internship Interviews

Because most internship sites schedule interviews for select applicants during early December through January, begin preparing for your interviews in November. Your DCT will advise you on the types of questions that internship sites may ask you. At the minimum be prepared to succinctly answer questions about your dissertation, specific assessment or therapy cases you have had, your interest in the internship site, why you are a good fit for the internship, what attracted you to health psychology, and your career goals. More specific to health psychology, your interviewers likely will ask you about your experiences and interests in working in healthcare settings, treating people affected by (or at risk for) medical illness, and collaborating on patient care with other health professionals. Have good case examples that you can talk about at the ready.

Learn in advance about the opportunities at each internship site for working with health populations, so that you can discuss these opportunities during the interview. At internship sites that emphasize a research training component, consider that the internship faculty may seek applicants who plan to develop a career in health psychology research, so be prepared to discuss potential next steps or new directions that your current research activities and interests may take.

If the training faculty members believe that their program would be a good match for you—and that you would be a good match for them—then they will contact you to set up an interview. Note that the relationship goes both ways because an internship program will most want to interview applicants for whom they feel that they can meet their training needs. Interviews typically take place on-site at the internship program and may take a half or whole day during which you and several other applicants will meet with a series of faculty members and current interns. If you have been invited for an interview, rest assured that the faculty is impressed with your accomplishments. So use the interview day to allow your character, your motivations, and your interests to shine! Also, refer back to Table 8.2—these questions can help you take advantage of your internship interviews to learn as much as possible about each site.

Much of the advice that we gave you in Chapter 4 about preparation for, and decorum during, the graduate school interview applies to internship interviews. Take some time to review that information. Keep in mind that while you are being interviewed you are also determining whether the internship will meet your training needs.

"By the time applicants get to the interview, we know that they are accomplished and very likely to be successful behavioral medicine interns. On interview day, everyone's goal should be to work to determine whether or not there is a good match between the program and the applicant. It is helpful when an applicant demonstrates knowledge of our program and can articulate exactly why they are interested in our internship program for their next step of training".

—Tamara Somers, Ph.D., Associate Professor of Psychiatry and Behavioral Sciences, Duke University

Step 4: Participate in the Internship Match Process

After you complete your applications and interviews in mid-winter, you will rank order the internship sites that you are interested in attending and then submit your list to APPIC by a set deadline (usually in early February). At the same time, each internship site will submit its own rank order list of applicants. Once you submit your rank order list, now it's time to sit back (and try to relax!) for the next several weeks. The APPIC will use the rank order lists to match applicants to internship programs and will send you the results of your own match on a specific date known as Match Day (usually in late February). You will be matched with a single internship program. However, for those applicants who do not secure an internship placement, APPIC will conduct a second selection process (known as Phase II) to help match as many applicants as possible with open positions that were unfilled during the first match. The timeline is relatively fast—Phase II begins immediately after the first Match Day results are sent to all applicants. The Phase II process mirrors the first selection process, although interviews may be conducted via telephone or video conference, and the Phase II Match Day is typically at the end of March.

We mentioned that the internship application process is competitive. However, the likelihood that you will match with one of your top ranked choices may not be what you think. In 2019, of the 3,683 applicants who submitted their rank order list to APPIC, 88% matched during the Phase I match. Of those who matched, almost half (49%) matched their top choice, 71% received one of their top two matches, and 85% received one in their top three (Association of Psychology Postdoctoral and Internship Centers, 2019). As the statistics show, a portion of students may not secure an internship position (whether accredited or not accredited). This may be due to any number of reasons that are unique to each student's situation. For students who do not match during Phase I or Phase II and wish to apply again, they may work with their graduate program faculty to carefully plan their next academic year in preparation for applying during the next year.

A Few Tips for the Internship Year

In starting your clinical internship year, you may face some of the same excitement and challenges that you had when starting graduate school—for instance, you may be acclimating to a new city or town, new peers and faculty, and a new work culture. You also will face new experiences, such as doing much more clinical work, along with clinical supervision and didactics, than you are used to—particularly if you went to a research-heavy graduate program. Another key difference is that, unless you remain at your internship site for a postdoctoral fellowship or staff/faculty position, you will be training there for one year only. So how can you hit the ground running and take advantage of this time?

If you find yourself affected by the same old "imposter syndrome" that we described in Chapter 6, wondering whether you are qualified enough for your internship site, rest assured that the internship faculty are looking forward to welcoming you and working with you throughout the year. Your clinical internship is designed to help you strengthen your professional skills and address remaining gaps in your training, so we encourage you to take an honest look at your training needs and to work with your supervisors to meet those needs. For instance, let's say that your first client has a chronic health condition that you have never heard of before. Or you are writing your clinical notes in an electronic health records system for the first time. Or you find yourself as the sole health psychology person on a multidisciplinary patient care team. These can be daunting but fantastic learning opportunities; seek out the supervision or mentorship that you need.

At the same time, consider your strengths and how you will be able to contribute to your new clinical and research community. In fact, as a current graduate student, you may have received the most recent training on a state-of-science clinical intervention or a research technique that your new colleagues may be excited to learn about! Finally, if you are joining an internship with a strong research component, a key way to take advantage of your internship year is to complete as much of your dissertation as possible before you arrive. This will allow you to dive in to new or ongoing projects with research mentors at your internship site. At the same time, if you have developed important relationships with your graduate school mentors, consider ways to stay connected with them during the internship year and beyond—such as getting together for lunch at annual research conferences and setting up a regular check-in call about unfinished or ongoing projects.

The health psychologist's role in medical settings depends on collaboration with physicians, nurses and other allied health professionals in the clinics and units. Multidisciplinary respect for the field of psychology, for the role of health psychologists,

"To quote what a former clinical supervisor once said to me when I was about to begin my first rotation in a cancer center: 'Let the work affect you.' He explained that there is a balance to be found between feeling moved by the struggles of those people we are there to serve and (over) identifying with their sadness, anxieties, and grief, so we do not become so overwhelmed by their distress that we become unable to offer our help. Genuine empathy, found somewhere between clinical detachment and over-identification, is where we can be of most help and where we are most capable of developing as clinicians. On occasion, even the best among us will lose that balance, but by ensuring time for reflection, peer supervision, recreation, self-care, and reaching out for help when needed, we are more likely to reestablish that balance when we lose it. When I interview prospective trainees, I listen for their capacity and interest in finding this balance. Most everything else they will learn through training and supervision".

—Scott D Siegel, Ph.D., M.H.C.D.S., Director of Population Health & Community-Based Research, Value Institute Christiana Care Health System and Research Associate Professor, Psychiatry & Human Health, Sidney Kimmel Medical College, Thomas Jefferson University

and for the type of research we conduct may be something that internship faculty mentors have worked hard to develop over time. During your clinical internship year you will be able to rely on these relationships and serve as ongoing ambassadors for the field of health psychology. Notably, some internship program faculty view the internship as a "pipeline" for identifying strong candidates who could stay on as postdoctoral fellows and junior faculty. This trajectory is particularly relevant for careers in health psychology because the multidisciplinary relationships that you develop during your internship may lay a foundation for future collaborations, mentorship, and productivity. If you are planning for a career in clinical health psychology research, these relationships will help you to develop a rigorous line of research that is highly clinically relevant.

Moving Ahead . . .

We hope that this chapter has provided a view into the exciting health-focused opportunities that await you as part of the clinical internship. Health-focused clinical internships offer unique opportunities in your training trajectory to focus in-depth on honing your clinical skills in the health context. The internship year is a great time to learn about different career paths as you think about your own next steps. As you think ahead about postdoctoral fellowships, academic positions, and other jobs, you can use the internship year to set yourself up to be competitive for your desired career.

References

Association of Psychology Postdoctoral and Internship Centers. (2019). *APPIC Match Statistics.* Retrieved from https://www.appic.org/Internships/Match/Match-Statistics

Williams-Nickelson, C., Prinstein, M. J., & Keilin, W. G. (2018). *Internships in psychology: The APAGS workbook for writing successful applications and finding the right fit* (4th ed.). Washington, DC: American Psychological Association.

9

PLANNING FOR YOUR CAREER
IN HEALTH PSYCHOLOGY
AFTER GRADUATE SCHOOL

Even as you start on the road to becoming a health psychologist, it is important
to know about life after graduate school. There are many paths you can take to
develop your health psychology career. Think about what you want to do once you
receive your degree (although it will likely evolve during graduate training). Try to
imagine yourself taking the different paths described as follows. Planning for your
career and considering the range of options that lie ahead can help you to stay both
focused and inspired along the way.

Postdoctoral Fellowships

After graduate school (and for clinical psychology students, after your clinical
internship), you may choose to complete a postdoctoral fellowship as a next step
in your health psychology career. Pursuing a postdoctoral fellowship is an increasingly common and sometimes necessary next training step after graduate school in
psychology broadly, and health psychology more specifically.

A postdoctoral fellowship or "postdoc" can be a critical way to help you obtain
more mentored professional experience in your area of interest in preparation for

independence as a clinician, faculty member, or researcher. As a result, postdoctoral fellowships are quite varied and can serve different purposes for different people. If you are interested in a postdoc, look for one that best matches your own needs and will help you achieve your goals.

There are many research postdocs available in health psychology and behavioral medicine. A research postdoc may help you to strengthen a specialization that you already have begun to establish. Alternatively, if you have had only minimal health psychology training at this point, you might search for a postdoctoral fellowship that will allow you to gain expertise in health psychology generally, or a particular area that you need in order to move forward in your career. Postdoctoral fellowships typically last one to three years, depending on factors such as your own training needs and the funding that is available at the training site.

Both experimental and clinical health psychology students may seek postdoctoral fellowships. If you are a clinical health psychology student, you may choose a postdoctoral fellowship that focuses on clinical work, research, or a combination of the two. Although clinical licensure requirements vary from state to state, you may need to complete additional supervised clinical hours as part of your postdoctoral fellowship before you are eligible to obtain your clinical license.

One common feature of postdoctoral fellowships is that they offer you additional opportunities to gain more experience and build your CV prior to applying for jobs. For instance, during your postdoctoral year(s), you can finish up and submit manuscripts that you were not able to complete in graduate school or draft a new grant proposal that you will take with you to your first job. If you are interested in eventually applying for competitive tenure-track faculty positions, the postdoc is an important time to establish your program of research, build collaborations that will continue beyond your postdoctoral year(s), and make you a more attractive candidate.

Consider the following scenarios in which a postdoctoral fellowship in health psychology may benefit you:

Scenario A: Strengthening Your Specialization

As a clinical psychology doctoral student, you studied cancer survivorship and completed a clinical internship where you worked with adults affected by cancer. You now obtain a postdoctoral fellowship at a comprehensive cancer center that matches you with a leading clinical investigator and mentor in cancer survivorship. While directing the investigator's current clinical trial, you will be able to hone skills in research leadership and grant development, strengthen your publication record in psycho-oncology, and gain access to a network of oncology researchers, all while further developing your clinical psycho-oncology skills and completing requirements for clinical licensure in an oncology clinic.

Scenario B: Refining Your Area of Interest

After developing your interests in psychoneuroimmunology during experimental psychology graduate training, you obtain a NIH-sponsored postdoctoral fellowship with a medical school-based multidisciplinary research team. As part of your fellowship, you take additional classes in immunology (at no cost to you), while working in a lab that has all the materials you need and has access to existing databases focused on immune markers that interest you. Moreover, you will be part of a team that is examining mechanisms linking stress and health, something you are interested in but never have studied. During the postdoctoral fellowship period, you also will be able to continue developing your own research ideas, with pilot funding available to complete a small research project to serve as preliminary data for a junior investigator grant.

Scenario C: Obtaining New Training to Move Forward in Your Career

With your graduate psychology mentor, you studied a specific behavioral risk factor for smoking relapse and developed a novel experimental paradigm for studying momentary risk. Before entering the job market for a faculty position at a university psychology department, you decide to seek a postdoctoral fellowship in a hospital setting. You obtain a fellowship that will allow you to broaden your research portfolio in smoking cessation and gain experience in smoking cessation curriculum development for medical residents. Notably, your fellowship team conducts research that is more applied than your graduate school experiences. Unexpectedly, through this work you discover a new interest in intervention development, which broadens your thinking about behavioral risk factors for smoking relapse.

Scenario D: Developing a Specialization in Health Psychology

You received a doctoral degree in general clinical psychology. After you gain experience working in a primary care clinic as part of your clinical internship, you decide to pursue postdoctoral training in clinical health psychology and you obtain a postdoc at a university-based hospital. Your fellowship will provide you with opportunities to receive didactic training in clinical health psychology and gain further experience in assessment, consultation, and intervention with a variety of medical patients. You will work as part of a multidisciplinary team providing psychosocial perspectives concerning patient care and program development. This experience will prepare you for a career as an independent clinical health psychologist (and the added bonus is that you will be able to acquire those much needed supervised "post" internship clinical hours required in most states to apply for a psychology license).

Navigating the Landscape of Postdoctoral Fellowships

In all four scenarios described you will end up with new or strengthened skills. So how do you go about finding the perfect postdoctoral fellowship? In comparison to identifying and applying to health psychology graduate programs, finding the right health psychology postdoctoral fellowship can be a murkier process. Postdoctoral fellowships can vary substantially from one institution to another and from one position to another and do not always operate on the traditional academic calendar.

Because health psychologists commonly collaborate with professionals in other disciplines and work in multidisciplinary teams, you will find health psychology fellowships in a broad range of exciting settings. In addition to postdoctoral fellowships with faculty members in academic psychology departments, relevant fellowships in health psychology may be located within other graduate departments (such as nursing or global health), multidisciplinary programs, medical schools, Veterans Affairs healthcare systems, the National Institutes of Health, hospitals and healthcare institutions, or other public or private health-related settings.

"My experience as a postdoc was invaluable to my career from both a professional and personal standpoint. It was a luxury to have time to focus exclusively on developing research and writing skills—a luxury I don't expect to ever have again. The postdoc also offered a unique opportunity to train in other paradigms and world views, such as those from public health. It was also a time to develop and nurture relationships and collaborations with others, including experts in the field and other postdocs that have developed into long-term colleagues and friends. I learned to understand more fully the challenges and opportunities in the field more broadly, rather than the issues limited to my specific area of expertise. I believe that the experience made me much more effective in my current position, particularly in working with people from different disciplines, communicating clearly about my work to a variety of audiences, and thinking critically about the biggest issues in the field".
—Laura Forsythe, Ph.D., M.P.H., Director of Evaluation and Analysis, Patient-Centered Outcomes Research Institute

"Honestly—I was not excited about doing a postdoctoral fellowship and felt I was ready for a tenure-track faculty position when I finished graduate school. However, the confluence of a tight job market and supportive mentorship led me to an amazing postdoctoral fellowship experience, so I highly recommend them. I completed a postdoc in public health, which exposed me to interdisciplinary perspectives and another fabulous mentor, who provided me with opportunities to write manuscripts and advance my career. The resources and time that I had during my postdoc were absolutely critical to my current level of productivity and the strength of my record".

—Lisa Rosenthal, Ph.D., Associate Professor
of Psychology, Pace University

"I had a three-year postdoc before starting my faculty position. It was crucial in several ways. First, it offered me a chance to see university life up close, including faculty governance, advising, and teaching, which look different (and take on new importance) when one is no longer a student! Second, my postdoc offered me the chance to develop an ambitious mixed methods study that I would not have had the time to do if the tenure clock had started. Through this study, I was able to develop relationships with physicians and patients, learn more about the empirical work that was needed (and possible) in the medical setting, and, ultimately, design a multi-year study. This gave me a head start when I did start a faculty position. Finally, the postdoc brought me into conversation with colleagues in different fields from across the university. This offered me the chance to learn how to describe my research and its applications without jargon and with greater clarity. This experience has continued to influence how I think and write, even a decade later. For those that do not have this kind of opportunity in a postdoctoral fellowship, seek out how to build relationships with scholars outside your field when possible. It will make you a better scholar".

—Sara McClelland, Ph.D., Associate Professor of Psychology
& Women's Studies, University of Michigan

If you are interested in a health psychology fellowship, you may find such opportunities through multiple channels. There is no single database for searching postdoctoral fellowships, and the descriptions of postdoctoral fellowship openings that are posted via email listservs or online tend to be brief (e.g., see the positions posted on the postdoc and job posting resource pages of the websites of the Society for Health

Psychology or the Society for Behavioral Medicine). The Association of Psychology Postdoctoral and Internship Centers (APPIC), introduced in Chapter 8, provides a directory of postdoctoral fellowship positions as well as internships. However, this is done as a service for the psychology community: the postdoc listings are not comprehensive, and APPIC does not vet them for program quality or information accuracy. Another resource is the Psychology Job Wiki (2019), which includes post-doc postings toward the bottom of the page but, again, it is neither comprehensive nor checked for accuracy. However, one can get a sense of "timelines" by looking at the previous year's wiki—the length of time between submission date, phone interviews, and offers/rejections.

While some institutions regularly offer postdoctoral fellowships in health psychology on a set academic calendar, other postdoctoral fellowships may become available at variable times throughout the year. (We have chosen not to present a list of postdocs in our Resources section as they become outdated quickly.) This variability is due in part to the fact that some postdocs are funded by institutional grant awards to institutions and faculty, so funding and application deadlines come and go.

Based on the landscape that we have described so far, we encourage you to seek full information about the parameters and expectations of each postdoctoral fellowship that you find. Some are structured with formal class work, whereas others require you to gain teaching experience. Some may expect you to serve as the Project Director for a study, with varying amounts of time or resources to initiate your own pilot research. Others may "leave you alone" to develop your own ideas with minimal mentoring.

Many of these parameters will depend, in part, on the source of funding for the postdoctoral fellowship. If you are interested in a postdoctoral fellowship that focuses on research training, one helpful way of differentiating them is by type of funding source: individual vs. program (training) grants. Individual postdoctoral fellowships may focus on research plans that you develop in collaboration with a mentor or mentorship team in your particular area of health research.

Individual Fellowships

To support the fellowship, you and your postdoctoral mentor may submit a funding application to the NIH. One program that supports postdoctoral research is the National Research Service Award NRSA OR F32 grant, also known as a Ruth Kirschstein fellowship, or a Research Supplement to Promote Diversity in Health-Related Research. Both of these funding opportunities were described in Chapter 7, as you may apply for them as a predoctoral student or for a postdoctoral fellowship. Usually, these applications are to conduct research with a new mentor and in a different institution than where you obtained your graduate degree, so you will work with your postdoctoral mentor on preparing the application. Alternatively, your mentor may support your postdoc on her existing grant funds. As we described earlier, this type of funding may involve striking a balance between being part of a mentor's research project and developing your own line of funded research.

Programmatic Fellowships

Programmatic postdoctoral fellowships (that is, programs with several postdoctoral fellows and even predoctoral fellows) are often supported by a large training grant that is awarded to an institution or department. This type of grant typically focuses on training junior investigators on a particular research topic. NIH grants of this ilk are identified as "T" grants; they are awarded to an institution to support recruitment and training of students or postdoctoral fellows in research areas that are critical to national health. When you search for a postdoc, you may find formal positions that are supported by this type of grant, for research training with a specific health population or issue. The first two authors of this book both participated in postdoctoral grants of this kind; Tracey Revenson was a postdoctoral fellow in an NIH-funded program titled, "Environment, Development, and Health" that was awarded to the University of California, Irvine, and Patrice Saab had a similar experience at the University of Pittsburgh. These types of postdoctoral training grants are very common but, at the same time, are quite competitive.

Choosing and Applying to Postdoctoral Fellowships

Which postdoctoral fellowship may be the right choice for you? A helpful initial exercise at this point in your career will be to review your five- and ten-year career aspirations, and then clarify specific skills or experiences that you want to obtain in a mentored environment in order to achieve these aspirations. Then look for fellowship sites that offer targeted mentorship, training and resources in these areas. You also might look for postdoctoral fellowship opportunities that will allow you to train with specific scholars in your subfield who may offer critical mentorship opportunities. Sometimes, individuals want to train with a senior, well-known scholar who influenced your thinking in graduate school, but you are as likely to be productive with a more junior investigator who is developing a program of research. It's all about the fit with the research area, the skills you will gain, and how you will "get along" with your future mentor.

Table 9.1 provides some sample questions to consider when looking for a postdoctoral fellowship that will help you transition to independence in your health psychology career. As we did for our list of questions about clinical internships, we

Table 9.1 *Questions to Consider When Researching Postdoctoral Fellowships in Health Psychology*

---

1. What are the research, teaching, and/or clinical interests of current faculty who will mentor postdoctoral fellows? (How closely do my areas of interest align with these?)
2. What types of positions have past postdoctoral fellows or research team members taken after finishing the postdoctoral fellowship?
3. What kind of balance will I have among research, teaching, and/or clinical opportunities and responsibilities? What specific tasks will I be responsible for on a weekly basis?
4. What, if any, kind of learning opportunities (seminars, lectures, classes) will I have during the postdoctoral fellowship?
5. What will be my main source of funding and research involvement: institutional funding, a faculty mentor's funded project, a program training grant, or something else? How secure is this line of funding and for how long will the support be provided?
6. How much protected time will I have to develop my own areas of interest and/or prepare grant applications for a career development award or other type of funding?
7. What kinds of opportunities will I have to strengthen specific research skills, such as grant writing, manuscript writing, conference presentation, or research project management/leadership?
8. What is the mentorship style of the PI? Does she or he have a track record of effective and supportive mentorship?
9. What are the characteristics of the PI's lab? Is it a small or large lab? How hands-on is the PI? Are there other postdoctoral fellows or senior researchers with whom I would work?
10. Will there be any opportunity to develop a new collaboration with someone in another health or health-related discipline to support my multidisciplinary area of interest?

---

recommend that you use the questions in Table 9.1 to understand the spectrum of fellowship opportunities while also identifying your own training priorities. Again, we suggest using these questions as a guide when reviewing fellowship postings, networking with potential fellowship mentors, and interviewing for fellowship positions.

Once you have located the postdoctoral fellowship(s) that interest you, your job is to prepare a solid application. (Yes, we know, you thought you were through with applications once you got into graduate school!) This can be done in a few steps.

Step 1: Prepare Application Materials

The materials that are required for applying to a postdoctoral fellowship will vary from position to position, but most will require a research and/or clinical statement, which may or may not be combined with a cover letter, along with a CV. Names of references or reference letters may also be required. Last, representative publications or preprints may also be requested as samples of your writing and research skills.

Just as we encouraged you to start your statements early when applying to graduate school, it is a good idea to start outlining and drafting your application materials, especially your research and/or clinical statement(s), well in advance of application deadlines. To help you in this process, talk to your current mentor and seek examples of application materials from faculty members in your department who have recently been hired or from upper classmates you know who have recently applied to postdoctoral fellowships (hopefully, successfully!). Solicit feedback from all those willing to give it to you, including those who are not familiar with your specific area of research (sometimes we get bogged down in jargon when describing specific theories or methods and smart, non-expert reviewers can help catch this!).

Step 2: Sign Up for Listservs and Review Ads

A lot of postdoctoral opportunities can be found on the listservs of professional organizations such as the Society for Health Psychology or the Society of Behavioral Medicine. You will also find more targeted opportunities on listservs for organizations in your areas of interest, such as the American Psychosocial Oncology Society, the Society for Research on Nicotine and Tobacco, or the Social Personality and Health Network.

Step 3: Network, Network, Network

We can't say this strongly enough: Seek assistance from your current circle of mentors, colleagues, and collaborators in identifying research investigators or the directors of training programs in your field of interest who may have a postdoctoral opportunity to offer. While some are posted on listservs or websites, others are disseminated via "word of mouth". Remember that postdoctoral opportunities don't follow a strict academic calendar, so they may begin at any time during the year.

Step 4: Continue Networking

Attend annual scientific conferences for professional organizations in your area of interest. (We describe some of the major conferences for health psychologists in Chapter 7 and in the Appendix.) Presenting your research at conferences is a fantastic way to continue to expand your network. You will also find postings for postdoctoral fellowships, with potential opportunities to meet the hiring faculty and staff on-site during the conference. In addition, scheduling a one-on-one meeting with a potential mentor at a conference is a great way to foster professional relationships even if your exact fellowship plan or project is not fully developed. This approach can also help you stand out in potential mentors' memories later when you apply to work with them.

Transitioning to Career Independence

In the next sections of this chapter, we will explore the process of entering the job market and give you an insider's view into different health psychology careers. Before we start, let us share two key activities that may help you flourish in several career paths. These activities reflect a spirit of learning, creativity, and collaboration that can help you develop a successful and meaningful career.

Be a Life-Long Learner

As you transition from graduate school and/or any postdoctoral fellowship training, your opportunities to continue learning do not—and should not—end. As we have emphasized many times throughout this book, the work of a health psychologist overlaps with an exciting range of health disciplines. Whether you are conducting research or clinical work (or both) your career will continually challenge you to expand your knowledge. One of our colleagues in tobacco cessation research obtained a master's degree in public health to strengthen her skills in analyzing community-level data and to help her implement interventions that target environmental influences on tobacco use. Another colleague, who studies medical adherence, attended a week-long intensive statistical workshop to learn the latest techniques for analyzing the ecological momentary assessment data that he had collected on pain medication use and daily pain scores. Yet another colleague with clinical and research interests in personalized medicine took a seminar series in genetics and ethical issues at the academic hospital where she serves on faculty. This series helped her to partner with a clinical trials researcher to study the impact of personalized medicine on patient health disparities. As you can see from these examples, being a life-long learner will help you take your health psychology career in exciting new directions.

Network and Collaborate

Your career in health psychology also will thrive on connections with others in health psychology and other health disciplines. Psychological, behavioral, social, cultural, and physiological health processes are critically related to each other. Even if your research interests and work are more basic than applied (for example, perhaps you focus on the physiological mechanisms linking social stress to immune function), it is important for all health psychologists to be able to think and talk about how their research is applicable to specific health conditions, diseases, or general well-being. The more you understand about how your research or clinical work fits into the broader picture of patient illness, health, and wellness, then the more relevant your work will be to the evolving healthcare landscape and health research priorities. In short, the field of health psychology needs to reflect multi-disciplinary efforts in order to survive and be useful.

With that said, as an ambassador for the field of health psychology, your work may depend on your ability to network and collaborate with physicians, immunologists, epidemiologists, nurse researchers, and a multitude of clinicians in medical settings. You may work in settings where these relationships already are established, or you may find that achieving your professional goals may require you to devote significant time over several years to lay the groundwork for collaboration and mutual respect. It may be that your work depends on your ability to develop necessary connections with researchers and resources at other institutions and to learn about the work of other research teams.

You may find that researchers in other areas do not understand what health psychology is or what a health psychologist does, so you will often need to educate them. Make sure to have that elevator speech ready! An additional tip for navigating conversations with potential collaborators outside of your area is to attend presentations of individuals from those fields at your own institution or at conferences. This will give you a sense of the topics studied as well as specific terms and methods used. In addition, you might be inspired to develop a new collaboration with someone after hearing about recent or ongoing projects.

When you are among physicians, show your strengths as the "other" kind of doctor! Your health psychologist role may bring you into contact with physicians who are increasingly interested in behavioral influences on health and illness, among other topics, yet have received only limited research training during medical school. As a health psychologist collaborator, you may play a critical dual role, offering both an integrative perspective on health and a host of skills for developing and conducting research and analyzing the results. One researcher colleague at an academic medical center had expertise in using qualitative research to study patient healthcare experiences. She became the "go-to" collaborator for a group of physicians who were interested in studying physician-patient communication patterns at the end of life. Alternately, if you are working as a clinical health psychology provider, your health psychologist training also will prepare you to collaborate with physicians and other health professionals to advance patient care. For instance, a clinician colleague at a cancer care center collaborated with physician and nursing staff to create a clinic for managing difficult-to-treat symptoms like pain and fatigue, using a multimodal approach that combined pharmacologic and behavioral treatment approaches.

"As a physician, working with health psychologists has contributed tremendously to my professional and personal growth. Caring for patients with blood cancers and those undergoing stem cell transplantation requires close attention to addressing the psychosocial impact of their illness on their lives and families. Working closely with my psychology colleagues to provide patients and families with the necessary resources has improved the care we provide in our transplant clinic. We integrated psychologists and their perspectives in developing and building our transplant survivorship program. Our patients and families constantly comment on the success of the program in addressing their psychological and emotional needs. And I would not be able to do the meaningful research I am currently doing if it wasn't for my close collaborations with psychologists who share common interests. My clinical expertise coupled with the psychological training that my psychology colleagues bring has allowed us to build innovative models of healthcare delivery for patients with cancer and their families, and my psychology colleagues have helped me become a better clinician, capable of recognizing patients' various coping strategies and helping them think about how to strengthen their resilience and ability to deal with the challenges of a life-threatening illness. Psychologists have made immense contributions to my thinking and perspective on illness and medicine".

—Areej El-Jawahri, M.D., Assistant Professor of Medicine, Massachusetts General Hospital

"As a nurse practitioner, I am often the provider spending the most amount of time with the patient. Given the chronicity of symptoms, it is essential to have a health psychologist partner caring for my patients to ensure we are addressing all aspects required to care for the patient, including conventional medicine, cognitive behavioral approaches, and alternative modalities (e.g., acupuncture or tai chi). Setting expectations for care and establishing a therapeutic relationship are key to optimal patient care and having a health psychologist as part of the care team further reinforces treatment goals with positive outcomes".

—Andrea H. Thurler, D.N.P., F.N.P.-B.C. Nurse Practitioner, Director of Ambulatory Gastroenterology Advanced Practice Providers and Nursing, The Center for Neurointestinal Health, Massachusetts General Hospital; Assistant Professor of Nursing, Massachusetts General Hospital Institute of Health Professions

"Health psychologists and social workers are experts regarding the psychological and social determinants of health, and so they help me establish warm, trusting relationships with the people that seek my care. I can't imagine not working in a setting where the services and expertise of health psychologists were not readily available".
—David Ring, M.D., Ph.D., Associate Dean for Comprehensive Care, Dell Medical School/The University of Texas at Austin

Open the doors to collaboration and networking, attending national and international conferences whenever possible. Your relationships with colleagues and collaborators will form a basis for your work in health psychology. Therefore, developing, nurturing, and expanding your professional network will be a key to success.

We also think it is critically important that health psychologists are able to communicate about health psychology to patients, families, and members of our communities. In addition to more formal methods like contacting journalists or writing policy briefs, think about how you might directly get the word out about clinical resources or the latest research findings through social media channels. Once again, make those elevator speeches and sound bites ready for the people who may benefit the most! At the same time, their voices need to be heard and integrated into our ideas for new or ongoing clinical programs and research studies. So part of your work as a health psychologist should involve sharing your ideas and getting feedback from people who are involved in patient, family, and community advisory boards or local organizations.

Here You Go! Entering the Job Market

As we have mentioned repeatedly throughout this book, there are many paths to becoming a health psychologist. You will find health psychology faculty and staff positions in a broad, multidisciplinary range of settings. You may find positions of interest at a university or college psychology department, another graduate department, medical school, hospital, or medical center, other healthcare setting, the National Institutes of Health, and a host of other public and private sector settings.

In a sense, you have been preparing for this point in your career from the first day of graduate school, as you develop your knowledge base in health psychology,

"I could never have imagined my job in graduate school. I lead the Evaluation and Analysis team at the Patient-Centered Outcomes Research Institute (PCORI), a research funder that aims to produce evidence guided by patients and their caregivers to better inform healthcare decisions. My team helps PCORI and its stakeholders assess the institute's progress and make informed decisions about its approach to research funding by evaluating current work. This position allows me to encourage and support research that is meaningful to both patients and clinicians and is useful in real-world contexts. It also allows me to implement my skills in understanding and measuring behavior in unique ways".

—Laura Forsythe, Ph.D., M.P.H., Director of Evaluation and Analysis,
Patient-Centered Outcomes Research Institute

strengthen your research, teaching and/or clinical skills, and begin developing your professional network. For example, during your graduate training you might have approached a symposium speaker at a conference to introduce yourself and discuss some shared professional interests and then maintained contact via email. Then in your last year of graduate school, you may have coordinated your own symposium with other speakers in your area of interest, as a way to continue establishing your professional network. All of these efforts will now be extremely valuable when you enter the job market.

"Finding a great job is a marathon, not a sprint. The means you have to pace yourself. It also means you have to learn to love running and not just finishing the race. If you are excited about your work, excited to talk to people about your scholarship, and look forward to engaging with others about what your future will look like, then all of these things help make the job search more bearable. There are many great kinds of jobs out there that need smart people who know how to think about big issues with a strong sense of research design. In terms of considering a particular institution or position, it is crucial to keep an open mind: You never know what you'll find until you go and meet the faculty, students, staff, and community. Don't disregard any position until you've had a chance to see for yourself. That's the only way to determine if it's a good fit for you".

—Sara McClelland, Ph.D., Associate Professor of Psychology
& Women's Studies, University of Michigan

Job Security

Some health psychology jobs are more "permanent" than others are. For example, many health psychologists want a tenure-track job in an academic department. The tenure track exists in most American and Canadian universities. A tenure-track position indicates that the person hired will be considered for eventual tenure according to the timeline and policies of the institution. Tenure grants professors permanent employment at their university and protects them from being fired without cause. Tenure is closely tied to the concept of academic freedom, as the security of tenure allows professors to research and teach any topic. Usually, tenure is granted within five to seven years of initial appointment. The "tenured and tenure-track faculty" is composed of those individuals holding the ranks of assistant professor, associate professor, and professor. The "non-tenure-track faculty" is composed of those individuals holding the ranks of instructor, lecturer, visiting (assistant/associate/professor), adjunct (assistant, associate/professor), and research or clinical faculty.

Most positions in medical schools and research institutes do not offer the possibility of tenure. Non-tenure track faculty positions do not have the long-term job security enjoyed by tenured faculty. In this case, faculty members are offered contracts for a set period of time that, depending on their success, can be renewed or extended. This is not necessarily a bad thing; it is the way most other professions work. When choosing a non-tenure track position, know from the beginning what is expected of you to have your contract renewed as well as how often you will be evaluated and by whom, so you can focus your work on meeting those goals.

Another way of differentiating job positions is by what are called "hard" vs. "soft" salary sources. For hard money positions, the institution may fund some or all of your salary indefinitely, perhaps through tuition or institutional endowments. Hard money positions may or not put you on the tenure-track. In comparison, for soft money positions, you will need to raise funds for some or all of your own salary from non-permanent sources, such as grant awards from federal agencies (e.g., NIH), private foundations, or clinical activities. At some medical centers, you also may collaborate with key stakeholders such as patients and their families who want to direct their charitable giving to fund a clinical or research project or an endowed professorship that holds particular meaning to them.

For positions that are largely or entirely funded from soft money, the primary responsibility is often to conduct research. These types of positions may be ideal for individuals who prefer focusing on research as they can bring a great deal of independence in your daily life. However, having to rely on grants to secure your salary also can bring a great deal of worry; we know colleagues who have moved from soft money to hard money positions to have salary security. At the same time, hard money positions may include greater teaching and service obligations than soft money positions. And, even though there is greater salary security with a hard money position, there still may be institutional pressure to obtain external funding to support research activities and salaries. The differentiation between hard and soft money salary sources is just one factor to consider when exploring career options. You should also consider what might be your ideal balance of activities is (teaching, research, clinical work, service) and what support and resources are available to carry out such activities.

And something for the future: The NIH Loan Repayment Programs (LRP) are a set of programs established by Congress to recruit and retain highly qualified health professionals into biomedical or biobehavioral research careers. In simple terms, they repay up to $35,000 annually of a researcher's qualified educational debt in return for a commitment to engage in NIH mission-relevant research. So holding a research postdoctoral fellowship or a faculty position will allow you to apply for an LRP.

"My past experience working in an academic medical center was amazing in so many ways. I had many collaborators and opportunities to do almost anything related to health psychology. Collaborating with physicians who were interested in behavioral science aspects of their area of medical specialty was key. My current position is in a psychology department—also amazing, but different in many ways. As a health psychologist, I collaborate more with my own students and postdoctoral fellows than with physicians at the medical school. As an established health psychologist in a department that is also well established, I am able to reach out to other psychologists to collaborate on overlapping ideas, although my day-to-day interactions are more with medical school faculty who study the same thing (HIV). In the academic medical setting I was with colleagues most of the time; in the psychology department, I'm most often in my own lab working with students. Another nice thing about working in a psychology department is that aside from teaching, my schedule is my schedule—so I can be maximally productive at the times when I am able to work but also can be flexible to balance family life".
—Steven Safren, Ph.D., Professor of Psychology, University of Miami

Applying for Tenure Track Jobs

If you are planning to seek a tenure-track faculty position, you will find that the job application process is more structured than the process for applying to most other types of positions. Most college and university departments will begin to post their open positions during the summer and fall, about one year in advance of the position start date (international job advertisements may appear earlier). You will be asked to submit an application package, including a cover letter, CV, and essays that describe your research portfolio and approach to teaching. Faculty search committees will schedule brief phone or video interviews with candidates to determine whom to invite for an in-person interview. After the phone or video interviews, a "short list" of select applicants will be invited to visit the department for a day or more of interviews with current faculty, meetings with students, and lunches or dinners with faculty or students. The centerpiece of the interview is a job talk in which candidates present their current research, including how their work complements current departmental research activities and would involve collaborations with current faculty and research mentorship for students. After the talk, candidates are asked questions about their work, so it's important to be able to think on your feet. Candidates might also be asked to teach a class, or to describe their approach to teaching. As you can see, this is a more intense version of the application process you will have completed to gain admission to graduate school and possibly to match with a clinical internship!

Is This the Right Time for Me to Enter the Job Market?

Whether you first complete a postdoctoral fellowship or not, the decision to enter the job market should involve a self-assessment of your current skills, experiences, and capacities. (Go back to the IDP you started in graduate school, described in Chapter 7.) Consider how these factors match the characteristics and skills that a job search committee is seeking, as well as how the positions you are finding on the job market match your professional goals and personal life goals. For instance, if you are seeking an academic faculty position with a strong research component, you might consider what resources you need to develop your line of health research, and how your research goals mesh with your interests in teaching, supervision, mentorship, and clinical work.

While you do not want to cast too wide of a net when searching for potential positions, we also caution you against being too narrowly focused. For instance, even though you identify as a health psychologist, your training, expertise, and program of research may fit well in a particular social psychology or developmental psychology position. Similarly, health psychologists are sometimes hired in medical schools or other departments (e.g., kinesiology, epidemiology), or even business schools (e.g., behavioral health economics). As a result, do not search only for jobs with the phrase "health psychology" in the title. Also, if a job posting specifies a set of qualifications that you do not have, consider whether these are skills that you could feasibly develop in a reasonable amount of time and how you could address current gaps in your application materials in a constructive way. Ask your mentors and recommendation letter writers for their candid feedback about your concerns. In some cases, it will better to move on to another job opportunity rather than waste everyone's time.

Here are just a few examples of how you might begin to launch your independent health psychology career:

Scenario A: Develop a Pathway From Your Fellowship

You are completing a postdoctoral fellowship at an academic medical center focused on bio-behavioral factors related to chronic pain. To fund your position, you are serving as a project manager on your mentor's behavioral trials in pain management. She and other senior investigators have helped you connect with the chronic pain clinic and an immunology laboratory to conduct your own series of pilot studies. You also have applied for an early career investigator award from the National Institutes of Health, and you are waiting to receive your scoring results. The medical center has a pathway for fellows to transition to faculty positions, which you are seriously considering in order to continue developing the relationships and lines of research that you have started, with the medical center resources that will help you to complete your work.

Scenario B: Enter the Faculty Job Market

You are approaching your final year of graduate school in experimental health psychology. Your career goal is to secure a tenure-track faculty position in a university psychology department. As a first step, you take stock of your accomplishments so far. You received a competitive grant award to fund your research, you proposed your dissertation, you have several first-authored publications in your research area, and you taught two courses and mentored undergraduate students in research. You're on track to complete your dissertation data collection, write-up, and defense by late spring. You know this is important since a university will want you to have completed your Ph.D. before starting a tenure-track position. You've consulted with your mentor who agrees that you are a competitive applicant.

Now you consider what you expect to do in the upcoming months prior to going "on the market" for faculty positions this fall. You'll submit any half-written manuscripts that have a reasonable chance to be accepted or published by the fall or winter and then you'll start preparing your application materials. This includes your research and teaching statements as well as your "polished" job talk. After submitting your application materials, you'll wait to hear about interviews.

Scenario C: Enter a Professional Job Market

In your postdoctoral fellowship at a university psychology department, you are serving as the project manager for a NIH-funded study of a stress management intervention for women with HIV infection. You chose this fellowship as an extension of your graduate training, which focused on health behaviors in the context of chronic illness and health disparities. During your fellowship, serving as the therapist for the stress management intervention has been your most challenging and rewarding activity. You start seeking a clinical position to follow your fellowship. You successfully apply for a job as clinical director of psychology for a large clinic that provides medical and behavioral treatments for weight management and that serves as a primary site for studies of behavioral weight management. You are thrilled to find a position that will allow you to focus on lifestyle behaviors to improve health and to participate in national efforts to establish evidence-based behavioral treatment guidelines.

Seeking Early Career Research Funding

If you are planning to become an independent investigator, then applying for your first research grants will be a large, important, exciting (and sometimes daunting) part of launching your career. Typically, you will begin to apply for research funding during your postdoctoral fellowship or first faculty position, if you have not already submitted applications as a graduate student. The goal of applying for funding at this stage in your career likely will be to secure financial support and mentorship for conducting initial studies and obtaining preliminary data to support larger scale studies and grant applications in the near future. As you begin to develop your own funded research portfolio, you will be able to spend more and more of your time engaging the health psychology research that brings identity and meaning to your career and everyday work experiences.

The grant review committees for many health-related research funding sources will likely include multidisciplinary reviewers (including Ph.D. and M.D. researchers) and, for some (e.g., private foundations), the review committee may involve patient and family stakeholders. This means that you will need to write your proposal to be understood by people outside of your field of interest, while highlighting the significance and potential impact of your work to both researchers and lay people who are affected by the health issues that your research will address. It is crucial for you to obtain feedback from peers on early drafts (including from those who are not familiar with your specific research) and even obtain examples of funded grant applications from mentors or people who do even remotely related research so that you can see how grants are written and "what works".

There are too many research funding opportunities for early career investigators to describe them all here. However, we summarize some of the major ones so that you have a bird's eye view into what may lie ahead in your career as a health psychology researcher. These opportunities may incorporate ongoing mentorship and training into the award budget, or they may provide small but critical amounts of funding (i.e., pilot or proof-of-concept studies) to initiate the first steps of your long-term research goals. In addition, if you are currently affiliated with a university, your institution (such as an Office for Research and Sponsored Programs) may have a database available for exploring grant opportunities.

The NIH offers awards for which you can apply directly in collaboration with your mentors. One series of NIH awards, known as "K" grants, supports training in health research after you have obtained your doctoral degree. These awards provide up to five years of protected time (i.e., time free from teaching and service obligations to focus on research) and financial support for training via mentorship, didactics, and a research project that you specify, to help you transition into your research career. The protected time and support can be critical at this career stage, as you begin to launch your own independent line of research. NIH also offers additional research awards that, while not targeted at early career investigators, might be useful funding mechanisms for early career investigators who collaborate with more senior researchers. For instance, an early career investigator may apply to the NIH for supplemental funding to add a sub-study to a mentor's existing NIH award, (e.g., adding a sub-study of ethnic disparities in smoking cessation outcomes to a larger randomized clinical trial of a community-based smoking cessation intervention).

Other organizations (including the American Psychological Association) provide funding opportunities to support mentored or pilot research opportunities. For example, the Veterans' Association (VA) offer career development awards are similar to K awards (U.S. Department of Veterans Affairs Office of Research & Development, n.d.). Some of these award mechanisms are particularly interested in patient-oriented health research, which can be a great fit for health psychology researchers in collaboration with multidisciplinary mentors or collaborators in medical settings. Some institutions also may provide awardees with unique opportunities for training and networking and may encourage awardees to engage in national or local advocacy efforts and present research findings in community settings. Such opportunities can help early career investigators to engage in meaningful career activities

Depending on where you start your postgraduate career, you may find that your institution offers internal funding sources to launch pilot studies. As we described at the beginning of this section and in Chapter 7, applying for these funding sources can be a critical step in your career, helping you to hone your grant writing skills and collect preliminary data in preparation for larger scale grant applications in the future.

"A pilot grant from the American Cancer Society was my first grant funding. Without a doubt, this grant benefited my career from the time of conception through publication. Prior to submitting that grant, I had a lengthy history of coordinating clinical trials as a research assistant, graduate student, and postdoctoral fellow. There is something experientially different, however, about designing your own trial. Writing that proposal immediately forced me to put into practice everything that I had learned about through reading or by playing a sidekick role for other investigators. It was in writing this grant that I learned how to communicate my science in a manner that balanced brevity with depth and that adequately convinced my reviewers that the question merited attention and that I had the ability to carry out the work. Once funded, every turning point made me question each decision I made, from the measures used, the timeline for follow-up, and my behavioral change model to its interaction with my treatment model. I learned the value of asking different researchers the same questions and getting different responses. This further taught me how to integrate their feedback. Ultimately, although the trial fed into the 'imposter syndrome' we all feel at some point, it strengthened my confidence to do the work that I loved doing. Ultimately, this pilot grant served as the stepping stone for my National Cancer Institute career development award ("K" series) by showing which parts of my approach did and did not work".

—Giselle K. Perez, Ph.D., Assistant Professor, Massachusetts
General Hospital/Harvard Medical School

"The unfortunate truth is that funding is easiest to find in well-funded environments. If you want a soft money career, try to get involved in a lab that has a track record of successful grants. University-level funding, foundation awards, and professional organization awards can be a great starting point for grant writing. However, take a look at percentage of proposals funded before spending a lot of time on applications: many of these small opportunities have lower funding percentiles than grants from the National Institutes of Health! Plan to apply to at least three different organizations in succession, so choose applications that are pretty typical in terms of writing guidelines".

—Elizabeth K. (Betsy) Seng, Ph.D., Assistant Professor of Psychology,
Yeshiva University and Research Assistant Professor of Neurology,
Albert Einstein College of Medicine

If you have accepted a tenure-track faculty position, your college or university may provide you with a one-time sum, known as "start-up funding", which you may use to set up your research laboratory, fund postdoctoral fellows, graduate students or research assistants, and/or launch new research. Every institution is different, but it can be useful to think through what resources you would need to launch your program of research (even before you interview). Talk to recent hires at that institution or similar ones to find out typical start-up packages, costs and restrictions. These can vary widely by type of institution, area of psychology, and even research specialty within an area. For example, someone who conducts health neuroscience research with fMRI and a wet lab for processing biological specimens may need substantially more money than a researcher who primarily uses survey-based methods. Also, don't wait for your start-up funds to run out before you start applying for grants to fund your own research. It is important to start that process early on if you need funding to continue your program of research.

Oh the Places You'll Go! (With Apologies to Dr. Seuss)

The ending of this book is not the ending of your health psychology career—in fact, it's really the beginning. Once you set out on a health psychology career path, you will still find opportunities to shift course. Through your graduate and post-doctoral training and career experiences, you may accumulate flexible skills as a teacher, mentor, researcher, research consumer, advocate, and clinician, or at least some portion of these. You also will establish collaborations and working relation-ships with people in other health disciplines.

These skills and resources will translate across settings as your professional and personal life preferences and needs evolve. For instance, two brilliant colleagues of ours each transitioned from their positions at academic medical centers—one as a psycho-oncology clinician and the other as a clinical researcher in diabetes management—to join the faculty at a liberal arts college. Their undergraduate students are now benefitting from the invaluable health psychology experiences!

It goes without saying that all of us have hit bumps in the road and had to take detours. The key to getting through seems to be perseverance, or what our col-leagues Greg Miller and Edith Chen have written about in a different context: shift and persist coping strategies (Chen & Miller, 2012). The first part is being able to shift perspective and reframe situations in order to handle them. The second is not to give up—to continue to see a future for you as a health psychologist.

So if you don't get into your top choice program or any program on the first try, email the head of the Admissions Committee and ask what would make you a stronger candidate. (And no apologizing!) Use this advice to beef up your skills and apply again the next year. And consider whether you chose programs with the best fit. Often after interviewing at a program, applicants realize it really wasn't the right program for them.

The job market is expanding in health psychology although most of these are not jobs as professors in psychology departments. Thus after graduate school or your clinical internship you may have to shift your vision of what the "ideal" first job would be. We also know that the landscape of health psychology and behavioral medicine will not look the same ten years from now. Will we all be wearing activity trackers and monitoring our health on an hourly basis? Will we go to medical centers to receive care or will it be offered online or offered only in Big Box stores? Will we have learned so much about biomarkers that precision medicine will be a prevention strategy? Given all of these unanswered questions, keep in mind that as a health psychologist, you can be at the forefront of finding the answers and shaping the directions that our healthcare will take!

References

Chen, E., & Miller, G. E. (2012). "Shift-and-persist" strategies: Why low socioeconomic status isn't always bad for health. *Perspectives on Psychological Science, 7*(2), 135–158. https://doi.org/10.1177/1745691612436694

Psychology Job Wiki (2019). *Psychology Job Wiki 2019–2020.* Retrieved from http://psychjobsearch.wikidot.com/

U.S. Department of Veterans Affairs Office of Research & Development (n.d.). *Career Development Program.* Retrieved from https://www.research.va.gov/funding/cdp.cfm

APPENDIX: RESOURCES

Chapter 1 What Is a Health Psychologist?

https://societyforhealthpsychology.org/
- Division 38 of the American Psychological Association (APA), the home of the Society for Health Psychology.

www.sbm.org/
- Society of Behavioral Medicine, which brings together behavioral and biomedical researchers who are interested in human behavior, health, and illness.

www.psychosomatic.org/
- American Psychosomatic Society, which is focused on biological, psychological, behavioral, and social factors in health and disease.

http://sphnetwork.org/
- Social Personality and Health Network, which is focused on social and personality psychology in health contexts.

www.psychwiki.com/wiki/Main_Page
- The Psychology WIKI is a crowd-sourced forum with a large range of information on psychology graduate school, training, the career trajectory, and more.

Chapter 2 Training Options for Health Psychologists

Norcross, J. C., Sayette, M. A., Mayne, T. J., Karg, R. S., & Turkson, M. A. (1998). Selecting a doctoral program in professional psychology: Some comparisons among PhD counseling, PhD clinical, and PsyD clinical psychology programs. *Professional Psychology: Research and Practice*, 29(6), 609–614. http://dx.doi.org/10.1037/0735-7028.29.6.609

*   Although this article was published over two decades ago, it highlights similarities and differences between clinical and counseling psychology programs, including "historical" data on number of applications, credentials of accepted students, research areas, and theoretical orientations.

Norcross, J. C., Castle, P. H., Sayette, M. A., & Mayne, T. J. (2004). The PsyD: Heterogeneity in practitioner training. *Professional Psychology: Research and Practice*, 35(4), 412–419. http://dx.doi.org/10.1037/0735-7028.35.4.412

*   Contains information on admissions, financial assistance, theoretical orientations of Psy.D. programs and differences between Psy.D. and Ph.D. programs.

Raque-Bogdan, T. L., Torrey, C. L., Lewis, B. L., & Borges, N. J. (2013). Counseling health psychology: Assessing health psychology training within counseling psychology doctoral programs. *The Counseling Psychologist*, 41(3), 428–452. https://doi.org/10.1177/0011000012439611

*   Contains information on counseling health psychology program training.

www.div17.org/sections/counseling-health-psychology/

*   Health Psychology Section of Division 17 of the American Psychological Association (Society for Counseling Psychology) focuses on the science and practice of counseling psychology in health-related contexts.

Chapter 3 Preparing for Graduate School in Health Psychology

http://gradstudy.apa.org

*   Requires log-in; $19.95 for three months of access; provides in-depth information on programs, including concentrations, components of application, housing, finances, deadlines and fees, and contacts.
*   Book edition: *Graduate Study in Psychology*, 2019 Edition; American Psychological Association; Softcover—August 2018; ISBN: 978-1-4338-3011-2

www.apa.org/
• Home of the American Psychological Association, posts highlights and news from the field, current research, educational opportunities, grants and funding, and about the history of the field.

www.apa.org/science/about/psa/2017/09/graduate-program.aspx
• APA guidance on choosing a psychology graduate program, considers a variety of personal, work, and external factors driving graduate program decisions.

http://cchptp.org/
• Webpage of the Council of Clinical Health Psychology Training Programs. It includes pages on resources and links for applicants, an overview of the field. The relevant page for potential applicants is a list of programs from across the country that offer degrees in clinical health psychology.

www.apa.org/education/undergrad/research-opportunities.aspx
• Research and undergraduate internship opportunities.

www.ets.org/gre/revised_general/about/scoreselect
• The option to send your best GRE® scores to designed schools.

CV Resources and Examples

www.psychologicalscience.org/members/apssc/undergraduate_update/under
graduate-update-summer-2013/how-to-write-a-strong-cv
• An article written for students that provides tips on preparing an academic CV.

https://careers.uiowa.edu/sites/careers.uiowa.edu/files/SampleUndergraduateCV_0.
pdf
• Provides an example of a CV written by an undergraduate.

www.careerprofiles.info/psychology-resumes.html
• Describes the differences between a resume and a CV and provides examples.

www.psychologytoday.com/us/blog/career-transitions/201110/writing-
effective-cvs-and-resumes
• Provides information both resume- and CV-specific, also touches upon differences between the two.

www.apa.org/gradpsych/2003/09/cv.aspx
* This website provides similar information to others in this appendix but also provides a full list of all the sections that should be included on a CV.

http://ccpweb.wustl.edu/pdfs/MDMCV.pdf
* Clinical Psychology Doctoral Candidate CV, Washington University.

www.weber.edu/wsuimages/psychology/Advising/GradSchool/WritingACV.pdf
* Contains several example CVs at the end, provides various structures and sections of what can be included.

Smith, B. L. (2015). Build a better CV. Simple steps to help graduate students improve their CVs. *gradPsych*, 28. Retrieved from www.apa.org/gradpsych/2015/01/curriculum-vitae.aspx.
* Tips for refining a CV and highlighting what is important.

Bannon, S., & Rowe-Johnson, M. (2013). How to write a strong CV. *APS Observer*. Retrieved from *www.psychologicalscience.org/members/apssc/undergraduate_update/undergraduate-update-summer-2013/how-to-write-a-strong-cv*
* Emphasizes the difference between a CV and a resume and tips on how and when to create one.

Chapter 4 Applying to Graduate Programs in Health Psychology

https://psychology.yale.edu/sites/default/files/files/APPLYING%20TO%20GRADUATE%20SCHOOL%20IN%20PSYCHOLOGY.PDF
* Provides a lot of information about many components of the application process, how to improve your application, decide on a program, and develop your CV.

Norcross, J. C., Ellis, J. L., & Sayette, M. A. (2010). Getting in and getting money: A comparative analysis of admission standards, acceptance rates, and financial assistance across the research—practice continuum in clinical psychology programs. *Training and Education in Professional Psychology*, 4(2), 99—104.
* Compares six types of Ph.D. and Psy.D. programs across the practice-research continuum in the application process and incoming student traits.

www.apa.org/education/grad/application-video-series.aspx
- This is a video series provided by APA which is useful for an introduction to what the application process for a general doctoral degree in psychology will entail (i.e., not specific to health psychology).

American Psychological Association. (2007). *Getting in: A step-by-step plan for gaining admission to graduate school in psychology.* Washington, DC: American Psychological Association.
- This handy book simplifies the process for graduate school applicants and increases their chances of being accepted. Useful timelines, tips, and tools break the tasks into manageable steps and help readers define their goals, select programs and navigate the application process.

http://mitch.web.unc.edu/files/2017/02/MitchGradSchoolAdvice.pdf
- A very useful guide to almost every aspect of the application process. It includes specific information regarding clinical health psychology programs.

https://psychology.unl.edu/psichi/Graduate_School_Application_Kisses_of_Death.pdf; *Kisses of Death in the Graduate School Application Process*
- Article describes results of a survey of graduate school admission committees and highlights several traits and aspects of an unsuccessful graduate school application, otherwise known as the "kiss of death" for an applicant.

Personal Statement Resources

http://psychology.uga.edu/sites/default/files/StatementofPurpose1.pdf
- Research-oriented program personal statement tips: addressing strengths and weaknesses, structure, and presenting your motivations and program fit.

https://psych.iupui.edu/sites/default/files/guidetowritingapersonalstatement_1.pdf
- How to start writing, things to consider before writing, do's and don'ts from psychology faculty, notes from *How to Avoid the Kisses of Death in the Graduate School Application Process*.

www.apa.org/ed/precollege/psn/2016/09/graduate-school-applications.aspx
- FAQs for preparing a personal statement for graduate school.

www.ohio.edu/cas/psychology/careers/grad-school/statement.cfm
- Describes key components of a personal statement and breaks down what to include in each paragraph.

Chapters 5 What to Expect in Graduate School in Health Psychology

Leong, F. T., & Austin, J. T. (2006). *The psychology research handbook: A guide for graduate students and research assistants.* Newbury Park, CA: Sage.
* This is an ideal textbook for graduate students studying advanced research methods in courses such as Research Methods in Psychology, Advanced Methods, Experimental Methods, and Research Design and Methodology.

www.apa.org/education/grad/applying.aspx
* The American Psychological Association's guide to applying to graduate school in any area. The website hosts links to financial support for graduate students and applicants.

http://teachpsych.org/gsta/index.php
* Home of Division 2 of the APA, the Graduate Student Teaching Association.

Chapter 6 Managing the Stresses and Challenges of Graduate School in Health Psychology

Sternberg, R. J. (2016). *Starting your career in academic psychology.* Washington, DC: American Psychological Association.
* This book provides a systematic guide for jump-starting your career in academic psychology, from applying and interviewing for academic positions, to settling in at your new job and to maximizing your success during the pretenure years.

Hoyt, S. K. (1999). Mentoring with class: Connections between social class and developmental relationships in the academy. In A. J. Murrell, F. J. Crosby, & R. J. Ely (Eds.), *Mentoring dilemmas: Developmental relationships within multicultural organizations* (pp. 189–210).

Levecque, K., Anseel, F., De Beuckelaer, A., Van der Heyden, J., & Gisle, L. (2017). Work organization and mental health problems in PhD students. *Research Policy, 46,* 868–879. https://doi.org/10.1016/j.respol.2017.02.00

Belar, C. (2008) Supervisory issues in clinical health psychology. In C. A. Falender & E. P. Shafranske (Eds.), *Casebook for clinical supervision: A competency-based approach* (pp. 197–209). Washington, DC: American Psychological Association.

Rackham Graduate School, University of Michigan. (2018). *How to get the mentoring you want: A guide for graduate students.* Retrieved from www.rackham.umich.edu/downloads/publications/mentoring.pdf

- This guide from the University of Michigan provides a frank look at mentoring for a graduate student, including tips on how to choose a mentor and navigating the mentor relationship.

Chapter 7 Professional Development

General Resources

Prinstein, M. (Ed.). (2003). *The portable mentor: Expert guide to a successful career in psychology* (pp. 163–173), New York, NY: Springer.

Darley, J. M., Zanna, M. P., & Roediger, H. L. (2004). *The compleat academic: A career guide* (2nd ed., revised). Washington, DC: American Psychological Association.

- A book that describes and comments on the challenging but rewarding academic landscape; it is filled with practical and valuable advice to help new academics set the best course for a lasting and vibrant career.

Silvia, P. J. (2018). *How to write a lot: A practical guide to productive academic writing* (2nd ed.). Washington, DC: APA Books.

Note: There are professional development "advice" columns written by students in the *Health Psychologist* (the e-newsletter of the Society for Health Psychology), *Science Agenda* (the e-newsletter of the Science Directorate of APA), and the APA magazine for students (*gradPsych*).

- *Science Agenda:* www.apa.org/science/about/psa
- *GradPSYCH: www.apa.org/gradpsych/*

Individual Development Plans

www.apa.org/education/grad/individual-development-plan.aspx

- Individual career development plan for psychologists; emphasizes self-assessment, personal goal setting, and implementing your plan for success.

Professional Organizations

American Psychological Association (APA): www.apa.org/, www.apa.org/about/students.aspx

- The largest professional association for psychology, which accredits doctoral training programs, coordinates internships, sponsors several dozen scientific journals (including *Health Psychology*) and holds an annual conference.

Association for Psychological Science (APS): www.psychologicalscience.org/, www.psychologicalscience.org/members/apssc)
- An international organization dedicated to advancing scientific psychology through research, teaching, and application of psychological science.

American Psychosocial Oncology Society (https://apos-society.org)
- Brings together professionals working in the psychological, behavioral and social aspects of cancer.

Society of Research on Nicotine and Tobacco (SRNT) (www.srnt.org/)
- A professional associated dedicated to supporting research and knowledge on nicotine and tobacco.

American Pain Society (http://americanpainsociety.org/)
- A community of diverse professionals striving to increase knowledge, prevention, and treatment of pain.

Regional Psychological Associations www.apa.org/about/apa/organizations/regionals.aspx

EPA: www.easternpsychological.org
MPA: https://mpa.wildapricot.org/
NEPA: www.newenglandpsychological.org/nepa.html
RMPA: www.rockymountainpsych.com/
SEPA: www.sepaonline.com/
SWPA: www.swpsych.org/ www.swpsych.org/Membership
WPA: https://westernpsych.org/

Writing Grants

(No author). Who Was Ruth L. Kirschstein, and Why Was the National Research Service Award Program Named After Her? www.nigms.nih.gov/training/pages/ruthkirschstein.aspx and https://grants.nih.gov/grants/about_grants.htm.
- NIH grants overview, everything from getting started to the post-award process.

Crafting effective specific aims. Session 3 in *Grantsmanship 101: Developing and Writing Effective Grant Applications*. Univ of Washington: Harborview Medical Center. https://depts.washington.edu/anesth/research/grantsmanship/session3_WritingEffectiveSpecificAims.pdf

Gerin, W., Kinkade, C. K., & Page, N. L. (2017).*Writing the NIH grant proposal: A step-by-step guide* (3rd ed.). Los Angeles, CA: Sage.

How to Give a Good Presentation

Bourne, P. E. (2007). Ten simple rules for making good oral presentations. *PLoS Comput Biol*, 3(4): e77. https://doi.org/10.1371/journal.pcbi.0030077 http://journals.plos.org/ploscompbiol/article?id=10.1371/journal.pcbi.0030077

Adler, A. (2010). Talking the talk: Tips on giving a successful conference presentation. *Psychological Science Agenda*. Retrieved from *www.apa.org/science/about/psa/2010/04/presentation.aspx*

Cosme, C. (2015). Making your scientific talk memorable. *Psychological Science Agenda*, 29(12). Retrieved from www.apa.org/science/about/psa/2015/12/scientific-talk.aspx

Cohen, L. L., Greco, L., & Martin, S. (2012). Presenting your research. In M. Prinstein (Ed.), *The portable mentor: Expert guide to a successful career in psychology* (pp. 133–143). New York, NY: Springer.

Erren T. C., & Bourne, P. E. (2007) Ten simple rules for a good poster presentation. *PLoS Comput Biol*, 3(5), e102. https://doi.org/10.1371/journal.pcbi.0030102.

Chamberlin, J. (2017). The three-minute pitch. *Monitor on Psychology*, 48(11), 54. Retrieved from www.apa.org/monitor/2017/12/three-minute-pitch.aspx

Peer-Reviewing Articles

Lovejoy, T. I., Revenson, T. A., & France, C. (2011). Reviewing manuscripts for peer-review journals: A primer for novice and seasoned reviewers. *Annals of Behavioral Medicine*, 42, 1–13. https://doi.org/10.1007/s12160-011-9269-x

Stilller-Reeve, M. (2018, October 8). How to write a thorough peer review. Career column, *Nature*. Retrieved from www.nature.com/articles/d41586-018-06991-0

www.scisnack.com/wp-content/uploads/2018/10/A-Peer-Review-Process-Guide.pdf

Carroll, A. E. (2018, November 5). Peer review: The worst way to judge research, except for all the others. *New York Times: The Upshot*. Retrieved from www.nytimes.com/2018/11/05/upshot/peer-review-the-worst-way-to-judge-research-except-for-all-the-others.html

Hagger, M. S. (2013). Editorial: What reviewers want: How to make your article more appealing to peer reviewers. *Health Psychology Review*, 7 (Supplement 1), S1-S7. https://doi.org/10.1080/17437199.2013.782963

Drotar, D., Wu, Y. P., & Rohan, J. M. (2012). How to write an effective journal article review. In M. Prinstein (Ed.), *The portable mentor: Expert guide to a successful career in psychology* (pp. 163–173). New York, NY: Springer.

Determining Authorship Credit

APA Science Student Council (2006). A graduate student's guide to determining authorship credit and authorship order. Retrieved from www.apa.org/science/ leadership/students/authorship-paper.pdf

Gaffey, A. (2015, June). *From the science student council: Determining and negotiating authorship.* Retrieved from www.apa.org/science/about/psa/2015/06/determining-authorship.aspx
* The site provides several authorship negotiation checklists, worksheets, and agreement forms.

Mentoring

Rackham Graduate School, University of Michigan. (2018). *How to get the mentoring you want: A guide for graduate students.* Retrieved from www.rackham.umich.edu/down-loads/publications/mentoring.pdf
* This guide from the University of Michigan provides a frank look at mentoring for a graduate student, including tips on how to choose a mentor and navigating the mentor relationship.

https://medschool.vcu.edu/media/medschool/documents/fmguide.pdf
* Faculty mentoring guide; good background information on mentoring as a practice and trends, how to mentor/find a mentee, and why mentoring is important for individual and mentee development.

Work/Life Balance

Cosme, C. (2016). So you want to have a baby in graduate school: Communication and planning will help you prepare for a new arrival. *Psychological Science Agenda.* Retrieved from www.apa.org/science/about/psa/2016/04/baby-graduate-school.aspx
* An article from the American Psychological Association, which considers pros and cons of having a baby during graduate school.

Boettcher, H., & Cummings, J.R. (2016). The Goldilocks lifestyle: Finding your own work-life balance. *Psychological Science Agenda,* www.apa.org/science/about/psa/2016/01/goldilocks-lifestyle.aspx

- A reflective article on how to weigh your values and priorities in finding work/life balance.

www.insidehighered.com/blogs/gradhacker
- A blog with posts highlighting a variety of topics related to graduate school work/life balance and beyond. Posts are written from graduate students from any field, including psychology.

www.chronicle.com/article/The-Joy-of-Pregnancy-in/236606
- An honest opinion article from a criminal justice professor, who had a baby during graduate school and yearns to change academic culture around students and family planning.

Evans, E., Grant, C., Peskowitz, M. (2008). Mama, PhD: Women write about motherhood and academic life. Rutgers University Press.
- A collection of essays from women in academia who speak to the trials and successes of balancing work, life, and family.

Networking

Palmer, J. C, & Strickland, J. (2017). Academic social networking websites: A guide to managing your online presence. Psychological Science Agenda. Retrieved from www.apa.org/science/about/psa/2017/02/academic-social-networking.aspx
- An article that highlights the use of social media and an online presence as a strength for rising academics.

Palmer, J. C. (2016). Navigating your first academic conference: A guide for first-time conference attendees and presenters. Retrieved from www.apa.org/science/about/psa/2016/10/academic-conference.aspx
- An overview of how to find, submit, present, and navigate your first research conference.

Chapter 8 The Clinical Predoctoral Internship

Williams-Nickelson, C., Prinstein, M. J., & Keilin, W. G. (2018). Internships in psychology: The APAGS workbook for writing successful applications and finding the right fit (4th ed.). Washington, DC: American Psychological Association.
- This hands-on book provides doctoral-level psychology students with resources to successfully navigate the internship application process.

www.appic.org/
- The web site for the Association of Psychology Postdoctoral and Internship Centers is a formal resource for internship applications, deadlines, and programs. This site is directed toward advanced doctoral students who are looking for internships.
- For information about APPIC membership, see: www.appic.org/Match/FAQs/Applicants/Eligibility-and-Participation#q4

www.apa.org/education/grad/internship-toolkit.pdf
- This resource is a "toolkit" for psychologists who are interested in developing an internship program. The toolkit also may be of interest to graduate students who want to learn more about the general structure and goals of internship programs as well as the ways in which internship programs can differ from each other.

https://natmatch.com/psychint/directory/schools.html
- This web page contains a database of all doctoral programs that are eligible to apply during the Match or Post-Match Vacancy Service (PMVS).

http://psybook.asppb.org/
- This web page contains basic licensure information for the U.S. and Canada.

Chapter 9 Planning for Your Career in Health Psychology After Graduate School

https://societyforhealthpsychology.org/councils-committees/student-council/graduate-student-funding-opportunities/
- This web page lists research funding opportunities for graduate students in health psychology, sponsored by the APA Division 38.

www.psychwiki.com/wiki/How_to_find_grants/awards%3F
- This page from the Psychology WIKI outlines grant and award opportunities organized by training and career stage.

http://psychjobsearch.wikidot.com/
- This psych job wiki lists postdoctoral opportunities near the end of the page.

www.nimh.nih.gov/funding/training/funding-opportunities-for-early-career-investigators.shtml
- This web page lists National Institute of Mental Health funding opportunities for new investigators.

www.lrp.nih.gov
- The NIH Loan Repayment Programs are designed to help repay educational debt in return for NIH-relevant research.

www.apadivisions.org/division-31/news-events/blog/early-career/index.aspx
- This blog created by and for members of the APA (Division 31: State, Provincial, and Territorial Affairs) includes helpful topics related to early psychology careers.

www.apa.org/workforce/publications/index.aspx–
- Here you'll find psychology workforce information including data on employment and salaries.

INDEX

For Product Safety Concerns and Information please contact our EU
representative GPSR@taylorandfrancis.com
Taylor & Francis Verlag GmbH, Kaufingerstraße 24, 80331 München, Germany

www.ingramcontent.com/pod-product-compliance
Lightning Source LLC
Chambersburg PA
CBHW050429280326
41932CB00013BA/2042